COOPERATION WITH EVIL

THOMISTIC TOOLS OF ANALYSIS

KEVIN L. FLANNERY, SJ

The Catholic University of America Press CUA *Washington, D.C.*

The paper used in this publication meets the minimum requirements of American National Standards for Information Science — Permanence of Paper for Printed Library Materials, ANSI Z39.48–1984.

∞

Library of Congress Control Number: 2019944288

ISBN 978-0-8132-3244-7

COOPERATION WITH EVIL

To my sisters and brother: Mary Kathleen, Ellen, Ruth-Anne, Patricia, Noreen, Brian, Sheila, Sara-Beth, and Colleen

CONTENTS

ACKNOWLEDGMENTS

My thanks go out to Thomas Aquinas College (Santa Paula, California) which in November of 2013 invited me give a lecture on cooperation with evil. I thank the many people there who commented on and/or queried the arguments I made there. A few days later, I delivered the same talk at Ave Maria University (Ave Maria, Florida) and there also received many useful questions and comments. At Thomas Aquinas College, Joseph Hattrup was especially helpful; at Ave Maria, Michael and Catherine Pakaluk, William and Elizabeth Kirk, and Steven Long, were all very gracious and helpful.

When the book was in its final stages, I was at the University of Notre Dame, taking advantage of its wonderful library. For their kind hospitality at Notre Dame I am thankful to John O'Callaghan, director of the Maritain Center, and to Carter Snead, director of the Center for Ethics and Culture, where I am a permanent research fellow. I thank for their kindness all those at these centers, including Margaret Cabaniss, Ken Hallenius, and Tracy Westlake. Ideas that found their way into the book were presented at meetings of the Center for Ethics and Culture's annual Notre Dame Vita Institute. I profited from interaction with a number of the participants.

Many of the ideas contained in the present book were presented to the scholars who, like me, were part of the project entitled "Virtue,

Happiness, and the Meaning of Life," funded by the John Templeton Foundation and organized by Candace Vogler and Jennifer Frey at the University of Chicago and the University of South Carolina. I thank all who were involved in the project's meetings and who helped me to understand cooperation better, including – besides the main organizers – Nathan Cornwell, Valerie Wallace, and Jaime Hovey; also Talbot Brewer, Michael Gorman, Matthias Haase, Reinhard Hütter, Angela Knobel, Kristján Kristjánsson, Jean Porter, Nancy Snow, and Fr. Thomas Joseph White.

I thank my Jesuit superiors, in Rome and the United States, who have always and without hesitation supported me in my academic work. I thank my fellow professors in the Faculty of Philosophy at the Pontifical Gregorian University with whom I have discussed matters treated of in this book, especially Fr. Louis Caruana (who arranged for me to speak at an intra-faculty colloquium), Fr. Jakub Gorczyca, Fr. Ramon Lucas Lucas, and Msgr. Mario Pangallo.

I also thank the two anonymous readers of the manuscript recruited by the Catholic University of America Press. I thank all at the press, especially John Martino, the acquisitions editor, and Susan Needham, the book's very perceptive and precise copy editor, who has not only improved it stylistically but also sharpened its argumentation. I thank my sister Trish for the cover art. I thank Christine Jensen, who helped me with the indexes. I thank Daniel Gallagher and John DeJak for checking my Latin translations. I thank Steven Siebert at Nota Bene software, who is always very prompt and helpful when I have questions. I thank also Alasdair MacIntyre, Fr. Thomas Berg, Michael Bradley, Fr. Stephen Brock (who is not to be blamed for misinterpretations of Thomas Aquinas found in this book), Raymond Cardinal Burke, Fr. Ryan Connors, Fr. Andrew McLean Cummings, John Di Camillo, Rose and Bill DeCapite, John Finnis, Daniel Gallagher, Msgr. Hermann Geissler, Luke Gormally, Fr. José Granados Garcia, John Haas, Ryan Madison, and Msgr. Angel Rodriguez Luño. I am sure I am forgetting people who have helped me with this book and I hope that they understand.

ABBREVIATIONS

Works by Thomas Aquinas

De malo	*Quaestiones disputatae de malo*
in EN	*Sententia libri Ethicorum*
in Metaph.	*In duodecim libros Metaphysicorum Aristotelis expositio*
Sent.	*Scriptum super libros Sententiarum Magistri Petri Lombardi Episcopi Parisiensis*. For book 4, distinctions 23–50, not included in this edition, the Parma edition is used: *Commentum in quatuor libros Sententiarum Magistri Petri Lombardi*. (See bibliography.)
ST	*Summa theologiae*

Works by Aristotle

De an.	*De anima*
EE	*Eudemian Ethics*
EN	*Nicomachean Ethics*
Metaph.	*Metaphysics*
Phys.	*Physics*
Pol.	*Politics*

COOPERATION WITH EVIL

INTRODUCTION

I. Formal and Material Cooperation

Ever more frequently in the last few years, especially in Catholic contexts, one hears or reads the expressions 'formal cooperation' and 'material cooperation,' employed in order to argue that – or to explain why – certain actions are either moral or immoral, the basic idea being that it is always wrong to cooperate formally in the bad act of another person but that one can sometimes cooperate materially, provided certain conditions are met. The purpose of this book is to expound the meaning of these and related terms in the tradition, both magisterial and academic, of the Catholic Church, but also to suggest that scholars and others should be cautious in their use. More reliable tools in the analysis of cooperation can be found in the "toolbox" of Thomas Aquinas's moral theory.[1]

In 1679, Pope Innocent XI issued one the few magisterial teachings that exist regarding cooperation with evil. It took the form of a condemnation of what was generally recognized as a "laxist" position. The condemned proposition – known as Proposition 51 – runs as follows:

1. On the use of the term 'cooperation' in this book, see below, section IV.

A servant who offering his shoulders knowingly helps his master to climb through a window in order to violate a virgin and often assists him by carrying a ladder, opening a gate, or cooperating in some similar way, does not sin mortally if he does this out of fear of notable injury – lest, for instance, he be ill treated by the master, or be subject to angry looks, or be expelled from the house.[2]

In an essay that first appeared in 1961, Elizabeth Anscombe, in her characteristically shrewd manner, interprets Innocent's condemnation as a criticism of a strain of "Cartesian psychology" that has dominated the thought of philosophers and theologians, she maintains, since the seventeenth century. "According to this psychology," she says, "an intention was an interior act of the mind which could be produced at will." She explains:

Typical doctrines from the seventeenth century were that it is all right for a servant to hold the ladder for his criminous master so long as he is merely avoiding the sack by doing so; or that a man might wish for and rejoice at his parent's death so long as what he had in mind was the gain to himself; or that it is not simony to offer money, not as a price for the spiritual benefit, but only as an inducement to give it.[3]

2. "Famulus, qui submissis humeris scienter adiuvat herum suum ascendere per fenestras ad stuprandam virginem, et multoties eidem subservit deferendo scalam, aperiendo ianuam, aut quid simile cooperando, non peccat mortaliter, si id faciat metu notabilis detrimenti, puta ne a domino male tractetur, ne torvis oculis aspiciatur, ne domo expellatur" [Heinrich Denzinger et al., *Enchiridion Symbolorum Definitionum et Declarationum de Rebus Fidei et Morum* (San Francisco: Ignatius Press, 2012), §2151]. See Andrew McLean Cummings, *The Servant and the Ladder: Cooperation with Evil in the Twenty-First Century* (Leominster, Herefordshire [U.K.]: Gracewing, 2014), 3–32. See also John A. Di Camillo, "Organizational Cooperation with Evil: Conceptual Analysis and Renewed Understanding of the Principles Governing Cooperation with Implications for Catholic Health Care Collaborations in the United States" (Rome: Athenaeum Pontificum Regina Apostolorum, 2016), 36–38.

3. G. E. M. Anscombe, "War and Murder," in *Ethics, Religion and Politics*, vol. 3 of *Collected Philosophical Papers* (Minneapolis/Oxford: University of Minnesota Press/Basil Blackwell, 1981), 58–59. On Anscombe's criticism that the formal cooperation / material cooperation distinction has often presupposed a Cartesian approach to intention, see Charles F. Capps, "Formal and Material Cooperation with Evil," *American Catholic*

In her enormously important book *Intention*, Anscombe does not deny that what a man says to himself or the thoughts that go through his mind when performing a particular action sometimes provide insight—even for the person so acting—into what his intention is in doing what he does. It might even be the case that such thoughts can be verified by no one other than that man. But even given such possibilities, she insists: "The idea that one can determine one's intentions by making such a little speech to oneself is obvious bosh."[4] She concludes the section of *Intention* (§§23–27) in which she criticizes the Cartesian approach with the remark: "So intention is never a performance in the mind, though in some matters a performance in the mind which is seriously *meant* may make a difference to the correct account of the man's action."[5] Intention, of course, involves the mind—as Thomas Aquinas says, intention is an act of the will [voluntas] and the will is in the rational part of the soul—but what one intends is an action.[6] And so, in most cases, the best way of determining what it is that a man intends is to look at what he does. Certainly in theorizing and formulating principles about cooperation, one should, rather than considering the exceptional cases in which what goes through a man's mind makes a difference, instead look to what the cooperator actually does, since even the exceptional cases have to do with exactly that.

Needless to say, Innocent's condemnation did not succeed in

Philosophical Quarterly 89, no. 4 (2015): 681–98. See also Cummings, *The Servant and the Ladder: Cooperation with Evil in the Twenty-First Century*, 87–129.

4. G. E. M. Anscombe, *Intention* (Cambridge, Mass.: Harvard University Press, 2000), §25 (p. 42).

5. Anscombe, *Intention*, §27 (p. 49) (emphasis in the original). Anscombe adds at the end of this sentence the words, "e.g. in embracing someone." In the argument leading up to this concluding sentence, she acknowledges that, while embracing someone, the thought might go through a person's mind "you silly little twit!" and that this would have a bearing upon what the person is doing in embracing the other. Even in this case, however, what is intended is a certain type of embrace: an insincere one.

6. See *ST* 1-2.12.1 and also Thomas Aquinas, *Sentencia libri De anima*, vol. 45.1, *Opera omnia* (Rome/Paris: Commissio Leonina/Librairie philosophique J. Vrin, 1984), 3.8 111–18.

eradicating the problem of equating intention with performances in the mind. The authors belonging to what has become known as the manualist tradition, which took definitive shape after the Council of Trent (1545–63), often knotted up the Cartesian problem with their treatment of intrinsic evil. For instance, manualist authors sometimes used the production of false idols as an example of an intrinsically evil act of cooperation. The objection is then raised that it is possible to perform the very same actions in the production not of idols but of park ornaments. And so, the production of idols is not intrinsically evil and the only thing that is evil in this regard is the intention to further the worship of idols. When such discourses become the basis of moral analysis, the result – not to say, the cause – is an over-emphasis on intention, not infrequently understood in an erroneous manner. Again, this is not to say that intention is not – or cannot be – a factor in the moral analysis of such actions. It may even be the case that an agent's particular intention is the only thing that makes an otherwise indifferent act to be immoral. But too quick recourse to intention, at the expense of other factors (to be discussed in this book), often produces moral analyses that might have been made more complete and so more accurate.

As we shall see, differences in analyses of cooperation with evil invariably come down to differences in the way that morally indifferent acts are understood. Both the manualist tradition and Thomas Aquinas speak in the abstract of indifferent acts, and both eventually attend to concrete actions, which they characterize as either morally good or morally bad. The difference between the two approaches has to do with this second phase. The manualists in question tend, in a relatively simplistic manner, to associate the morality of the act of cooperation with the agent's (the cooperator's) intention. Thomas, on the other hand, associates the morality of all human actions with the voluntary, as understood by Aristotle, especially in that section of the third book of the *Nicomachean Ethics* which deals with what are spoken of in the Thomistic tradition as the "circumstances" of human acts. This is a much more complex theory, but one which has the advantage (among other advantages) of giving an explanation of how an act of cooperation, whether or not intended as an act of cooperation with evil, relates to justice in general. It is this more complex, Aristotelian/Thomistic approach to cooperation that will be expounded and defended in this book.

One further point regarding the example, mentioned by Innocent XI in Proposition 51, of the servant who is required to aid his master in some way in committing fornication or theft.[7] Investigating the moral implications of cooperation, as we shall do in this book, while bearing in mind primarily such individual cooperation has certain advantages: above all, this approach retains in close view the essential truth that all ethics comes down ultimately to the things that individual agents do – or, at least, ought or ought not to do. In today's world, however, many of the questions asked regarding cooperation present themselves in what might be called "corporate" contexts. It might be asked, for instance, whether – or with what conditions – a Catholic hospital might join a health care system that offers "reproductive services" such as sterilizations or even abortions. Or it might be asked whether and/or under what conditions a Catholic health system might take into itself a non-Catholic hospital. The moral issues in such situations have to do not with the relationship between one cooperator and one malefactor but (typically) with the relationship between a governing board, whose members may very well not have been on the board when decisions regarding cooperation were made, and a complex entity that might include thousands of employees and

7. In the manual compiled by St. Alphonsus Liguori, his *Theologia moralis*, which is fundamental for the present work, the material cooperation/formal cooperation distinction is introduced at book 2, n. 63, to which number he assigns the title, "What is licit for servants? And what is material and what formal cooperation?" (See appendix 1 and the list of titles given just after the title of the article there translated.) The edition of Alphonsus's manual used in the present work is Alphonsus Maria de Ligorio, *Theologia moralis*, ed. L. Gaudé (Rome: Typographia Vaticana, 1905–12 [4 vols.]); it will be referred to throughout as *Theologia moralis*.

multiple subdivisions. In such situations, although (again) everything comes down ultimately to individuals making decisions, the process of establishing guidelines in these regards is not immediately about the intention with which individual decision-makers act; it has to do rather with what is just and what unjust.[8]

II. St. Alphonsus Liguori

A pivotal figure, especially in the earlier pages of this book, is Alphonsus Liguori, the founder of the Congregation of the Most Holy Redeemer (the Redemptorists). Canonized in 1839 and declared a Doctor of the Church in 1871, he is the most prominent and esteemed "dedicated" moral theologian in the history of the Church. In the writings of moral theologians coming after him, one can often discern an effort not to contradict positions he has set out. And he is invariably referred to when the formal/material distinction is invoked. Accordingly, his remarks on that distinction will be the starting point for the present book and his judgments regarding cases of cooperation will be referenced throughout. As has already been suggested, much more reliable philosophically and theologically is Thomas Aquinas, whom Alphonsus himself cites constantly. With characteristic bluntness, Elizabeth Anscombe remarked in a lecture in 1989 that "St. Thomas is a strikingly good philosopher; St. Alphonsus not."[9] Once again she

8. Such guidelines can be found, for instance, in the following ecclesial documents: Congregation for the Doctrine of the Faith, "Some Principles for Collaboration with Non-Catholic Entities in the Provision of Health Care Services," *National Catholic Bioethics Quarterly* 14 (2014): 337–40 and United States Conference of Catholic Bishops, *Ethical and Religious Directives for Catholic Health Care Services, Sixth Edition* (2018), 23–27, Http://www.usccb.org/about/doctrine/ethical-and-religious-directives/. On these matters, see also Di Camillo, "Organizational Cooperation with Evil."

9. G. E. M. Anscombe, *Faith in a Hard Ground: Essays on Religion, Philosophy, and Ethics by G. E. M. Anscombe*, ed. Mary Geach and Luke Gormally, St. Andrews Studies in Philosophy and Public Affairs (Exeter, U.K.: Imprint Academic, 2008), 135. The chapter in which this remark appears is entitled "Sin"; it comprises the four McGivney lectures that Anscombe delivered in 1989 at the John Paul II Institute in Washington, D.C.

is right, but neither would she (or we) deny that Alphonsus's pastoral intuitions were characteristically sound.

Alphonsus was born in 1696 at Marianella, near Naples, into a politically well connected family. Although his birthplace was only about 140 miles south of Rome, in Alphonsus's time it was located in a political entity – or actually successive political entities – distinct from the Papal States. When he was born, Naples, as well as most of what is now the southern part of Italy, was under Spanish Hapsburg rule; in 1700 it came under Bourbon rule; in 1707 it came under Austrian Hapsburg rule; and by 1734 it was once again under Bourbon rule, until some years after Alphonsus's death in 1787. In this latter period, during which "the Kingdom of Naples" was ruled by Charles III and then his son Ferdinand IV, there was great tension between the kingdom and the Holy See.

This latter fact has a certain bearing upon the argument of the present book, since it meant for Alphonsus that much of his energy was expended negotiating approval of the constitutions of the religious congregation he was founding. The constitutions had to be approved not only by Rome but also by the Bourbon rulers, who demanded things that displeased the Holy See and which caused the latter occasionally to mistrust Alphonsus. Another major focus of Alphonsus's attention was the work of the nascent congregation itself. He spent enormous quantities of time and energy travelling around the kingdom – and, in particular, its more remote rural parts – conducting missions, such as involved a week of sermons, catechism, processions, and communal prayer, plus, for the missioners, including Alphonsus himself, hours in the confessional. Writes the Redemptorist Frederick Jones:

> [Alphonsus] laid down that the confessors should be available in the confessionals during a mission for seven hours a day and he frequently went round the church to see that they were in attendance. His own patience in the confessional was remarkable; it was there that he achieved his greatest triumphs

over his natural impetuosity and irritability. It is revealing that he described the confessional as *una lima sorda*, a file which silently but painfully smooths the irritability of one's character.[10]

The point to be drawn from all this is that the background to his major ethical work, his *Theologia moralis*, was not a life of study but one of relentless pastoral and administrative activity. His original academic formation was in law and, although he did read Thomas as part of his preparation for the priesthood, this period of study was not long. Writes Jones: "Alphonsus' theological studies prior to the priesthood lasted for just three years and two months, from October 1723 to December 1726; for three months of this period he was seriously ill."[11]

III. The Structure of the Book (with Chapter Summaries)

Chapter 1 of this book is about the distinction between material and formal cooperation as understood by Alphonsus. The first couple of sections (I and II) talk about Alphonsus's writing of the *Theologia moralis*, its relationship with the Jesuit Hermann Busenbaum's *Medulla theologiae moralis*, and the origins and eventual solidifying of the material/formal distinction. Section III is an exegesis of Alphonsus's definition of formal cooperation; the section argues against the thesis that, according to that definition, one does not cooperate formally unless one shares the overall intention of the main malefactor.[12] According to Alphonsus, in certain cases even someone who cooperates out of grave fear might cooperate formally.

Section IV of chapter 1 considers Alphonsus's account of material cooperation, into which he introduces the concept of indifferent acts—which concept, as indicated above, is either a source or a symp-

10. Frederick M. Jones, *Alphonsus de Liguori: The Saint of Bourbon Naples, 1696–1787* (Dublin: Gill and Macmillan, 1992), 247. On missions as conducted by Alphonsus and his colleagues (in groups usually of eleven or twelve), see Jones, *Alphonsus de Liguori*, 246–55.

11. Jones, *Alphonsus de Liguori*, 47. Jones does mention the influence of St. Thomas on a number of Alphonsus's teachers: see Jones, *Alphonsus de Liguori*, 47–49.

12. On the term 'malefactor,' see below, section IV.

tom of difficulties in the tradition of which Alphonsus is a part. In Alphonsus's own theory, it leads to inconsistencies. He apparently attempted to remedy this situation in a later edition of the *Theologia moralis* by including toward the end of the work an account of Thomas Aquinas's understanding of indifferent acts; but the problems in his own original account remain.

Sections V and VI of chapter 1 consider the way in which the problems associated with indifferent acts vex manuals of moral theology subsequent to Alphonsus's, in particular, the manual associated with the name of Hieronymus Noldin, a Jesuit, and the manual associated with the name of Joseph Aertnys, a Redemptorist. One advantage of examining Noldin and Aertnys is that doing so enables us to explore the theory behind what is stated in two major manuals regarding cooperation. Noldin has an essay on this topic which helps to explain why he takes the positions he does in the manual; he also mentions in his manual that the position he adopts with respect to cooperation differs from that of Aertnys. Examining this difference provides us with insight into Noldin's somewhat ambiguous appreciation of Alphonsus but also into his efforts not to distance himself too much from the newly created doctor of the Church.

Also involved in the debate described in chapter 1, especially in section VI, is an Augustinian named Nicola Cretoni, another Jesuit named Juan de Cardenas, and the Dominican Pius Thomas Milante. At one point Cretoni, upon whom Noldin draws, quotes Alphonsus to the effect that "another's wickedness cannot alter the nature of your action." He employs this principle in criticizing the understanding of cooperation put forth by both de Cardenas and Milante. If true and taken to its logical limits, the principle would render unsound any argument to the effect that an act of cooperation that stops short of sharing the malefactor's intention is immoral.

Chapter 2 takes up again the issue of indifferent acts, considering it, however, within the context of Thomas's action theory more generally. What this consideration reveals is that Thomas, unlike later writers on cooperation, does not exaggerate the moral significance of intention. Indeed, this is a characteristic of his general approach in ethics: he takes all such factors in stride, calmly showing how they fit into the larger picture—which, for him, is a basically Aristotelian universe, which opens up, for some individuals, to the light of Christ. Indifferent acts, he explains, exist in the abstract, but no human act is indifferent. Intention is just one factor in the analysis of human acts, albeit an important one. But in the end all such factors must be related to the larger and ultimate concern: whether a person's actions are consistent with justice and with reason.

Where this more comprehensive approach to ethics becomes most evident is in Thomas's treatment of the circumstances (mentioned just above), which include not just what an action *is* "in its species" and why it is performed but also other factors such as where and when and in cooperation with whom (or what) it is performed. As explained in section I of chapter 2, the circumstances are listed in Aristotle's *Nicomachean Ethics* but were also studied by rhetoricians after Aristotle, who saw very clearly that circumstances provide the theoretical basis for connecting individual acts to justice itself.[13] Within this larger context—which is the context presupposed by any courtroom argument or discourse before a political assembly—an act of cooperation might be judged more or less unjust as it is closer to or more distant from the act of the malefactor.

The one place where Thomas sets out most clearly his understanding of how the circumstances bear upon the moral character of human acts is in the sixth article of the second question of his *Quaestiones disputatae de malo*, the article that asks "whether a circumstance might give species to a sin or alter its species transferring it into a different type of sin." Because this article provides an overview of Thomas's theory of human action, to which constant reference will be made throughout this book, and because of the centrality of the circum-

13. Aristotle himself wrote extensively on rhetoric, not only in the work entitled *Rhetoric* but also in his *Topics*. Many of the classical rhetoricians also draw on these works.

stances to the present argument, sections II and III of chapter 2 are devoted to its detailed exegesis.[14]

Section IV of chapter 2 considers some remarks in Thomas that would seem to reduce circumstances to the motives or even intentions of individual agents and, therefore, to make them less societal by nature; but, it is argued, they do not do so. Rather, they point up the close relationship between individual human acts and the larger and objective moral universe within which they are performed. Section V comes back to the issue of indifferent acts and explains how Thomas's understanding of circumstances drastically reduces the relevance of indifference for the moral analysis of human acts. Because a human act is a human act only in as much as it exists within the context of its own particular circumstances, which are basically its relationship with the larger context of justice and charity, there are no indifferent acts. Every particular human act is (in a particular sense specified by Thomas) susceptive of moral goodness and badness; and how that susceptiveness is specified in practice is all that interests the ethicist. Section VI of chapter 2 relates the arguments of the earlier sections of the chapter to those of the scholars encountered in chapter 1, in particular, Noldin, Cretoni, de Cardenas, and Milante.

Chapter 3 is about scandal. Some scholars insist that scandal is a topic quite distinct from cooperation. This thesis is not addressed here, since, whether or not it is true, scandal is certainly of concern to those who consider – for theoretical or practical reasons – cooperation with evil.

Section I of chapter 3 is an exegesis of Thomas Aquinas's treatment of scandal in *Summa theologiae* [*ST*] 2-2.43 with particular emphasis upon a controversy regarding whether "per se scandal" requires that the one scandalizing intend to give scandal, for Thomas appears to say both that it does and that it does not. The controversy is resolved once one understands that in the passage where he appears to say that per se scandal requires intention he is speaking about the

14. A translation of *De malo* 2.6 is found in appendix 4.

"special sin" of scandal – not the sin of scandal understood more generally. The controversy sheds light not only upon Thomas's teaching regarding intention and its involvement in the morality of acts but also upon his larger project of organizing the various sins (and the various virtues) according to their definite species. He conceives of his task as somewhat similar to that of a biologist who assigns to each species of animal its proper place in a model of the biosphere. The analogy is not a strict one, for Thomas is well aware that human acts are much more ephemeral than animals; nonetheless, it is clear that his approach is quite different from the individualism typical of the moral manualists in their consideration of cooperation or, for that matter, of scandal. The moral sense of a human action *is* the way in which its fits into the larger ethical universe of which it is a part.

Section I also contains a detailed exegesis of a passage in Thomas's commentary on Peter Lombard's *Sentences* in which he (Thomas) employs, in his typically flexible manner, the terms 'material' and 'formal.' This passage contains a useful remark about how an act that is not intended to scandalize can still be "a certain circumstance of the sin." His implicit point is that the moral character of even a sin of scandal that is not the special sin (and so is not intended to be the occasion of sin to others) comes from its relationship to reason itself and not just from the reason (or reasons) of its agent.

Section II of chapter 3 is about Alphonsus's understanding of scandal, which depends upon that of a number of other moralists. One of these is Hermann Busenbaum, who dismisses Thomas's question regarding the special sin of scandal as having "scarce reference to practice." After the publication of the first edition of *Theologia moralis*, Alphonsus changed what he says in the main text about scandal and, in an appendix to the second edition (included also in later editions), he explains why he made the changes. In his remarks both before and after these revisions, it is apparent that he does not understand what Thomas means by a "special sin" (that is, a sin that constitutes a particular species of sin). In the end, his treatment of ways of scandalizing – indirectly and directly, "directly and formally" and "directly but not formally" – proves to be very similar to his treatment of the ways in which one might cooperate in evil. But he unfortunately suggests that the species of the act of the person who is influenced by someone's scandalous behavior somehow comes back into the scandalizer's action.

Section III of chapter 3 offers some preliminary concluding remarks drawing connections with ideas set out in earlier sections of the book. In particular, it is suggested that Alphonsus's presumption that the immorality of scandal is to be explained as the transfer of a moral species from one person to another is the consequence of a failure, by the intellectual culture of which he was a part, fully to appreciate that the morality of any human act depends upon its place in the larger moral universe.

Chapters 4 and 5 are entitled, respectively, "Factors in Reason and Justice: Part I" and "Factors in Reason and Justice: Part II." They are thematically less unified than the previous chapters, for they simply contain successive expositions of factors (in addition to those already expounded), derived from various places in the Thomistic corpus, that have a bearing upon cooperation regarding evil. This gathering together of factors is made necessary by the fact that in Thomas there is not to be found a free-standing treatise on cooperation, as there is in Alphonsus and other moral manualists. This absence is regarded by the present author as an advantage; indeed, he would argue that it makes sense that Thomas composed no such treatise, for actions possibly involving immoral cooperation are simply human actions and are thus to be analyzed in the manner any human actions are analyzed. That the factors pertinent to the analysis of cooperation are the same factors pertinent elsewhere provides assurance that they constitute a sound basis for issuing judgments also regarding cooperation.

Section I of chapter 4 is about an aspect of action prominent also in previous chapters, that is, the way in which an act stands in relation to the larger moral realm with its precepts and norms, etc. It considers, however, an objection that might be made to that approach. The objection would call attention to the fact that Thomas Aquinas recognizes two such realms: the realm of charity (accessible only through Christ) and the realm of justice, inhabited by all human beings capable of human (moral) action. This difference can indeed be an important factor with respect to the way in which an act is assessed morally. It is noted in this section that, according to Thomas, the two realms are not wholly distinct and that, even to the extent that they are distinct, the moral imperatives of either are not cancelled out by the other.

Section II of chapter 4 is about the distinction that Aristotle makes in the third book of the *Nicomachean Ethics* between voluntary acts and choices. The distinction provides us, in effect, with a definition of what in the Thomistic tradition will be termed 'human acts.' Since moral character can be attributed only to human acts, clearly, in a book about the morality of cooperation, it is important to understand what a human act is.

Section III of chapter 4 is about force or coercion and its bearing upon human acts. This is often a factor in the analysis of cooperation. An act of cooperation that would be immoral if undertaken wholly freely, might be permitted when performed in the presence of a certain level of coercion; and a particular act that might appear to be an act of immoral cooperation might not be such because of an internal part of it that is not subject to the agent's will. In these regards also Thomas draws heavily upon Aristotle, and this section does the same.

Section IV of chapter 4 is about omission and consent. The reason why the former is important is that it is quite possible to cooperate in an evil practice by doing nothing at all, that is, by neglecting to do what one ought to do. A hospital administrator, for example, might simply turn his attention away from immoral procedures performed in his hospital and so be as much a cooperator as one who assists at the procedures: indeed, he may be more of a cooperator than one who is physically closer to the evil procedures. Thomas does not fail to consider this possible way of acting immorally, using the example of a ship's pilot who fails to be at the helm when he ought to be there.

We see here (once again) that the morality of certain acts depends, at least partially, upon things independent of the immediate acts of will of their agents: it might depend, for instance, upon rules pertaining to organizational roles. The section concludes with remarks about consent, for it is important to bear in mind that it is possible for a person to commit an act of immoral cooperation by omission without consenting to the evil with which he cooperates. This is true also when the cooperation does not consist in an omission.

Section V of chapter 4 is about the bearing of ignorance upon the morality of human acts. Some ignorance, such as (in some cases) ignorance of particular circumstances, can make an action involuntary—and, therefore, not blameworthy—either wholly or in part. Other types of ignorance do not have any such effect. A person who does not believe that a particular type of immoral act is immoral and so, in this sense, does not know that such acts are immoral can still be blamed for acts that cooperate with those immoral acts. The same can be said of the person who holds that a particular type of act *is* immoral but also holds, erroneously, that his particular role does not require him to do anything to discourage such acts. Thomas recognizes that the obligation to know what is moral and what immoral applies variously to various people; the extent of the obligation depends upon their capacities and also their social roles and responsibilities. Here once again Thomas draws heavily upon Aristotle, and so does this section.

Section VI of chapter 4 looks at Thomas's remarks, especially at *ST* 2-2.62.7, on the responsibility to make restitution for acts connected in some way with acts of theft. The particular interest of the section (section VI) is not, however, restitution as such. Many of the things mentioned in *ST* 2-2.62.7 pertain not just to acts of theft but to unjust injury understood more generally and so also to cooperation with immoral acts other than theft. Of particular significance is Thomas's position that the morality of an act of cooperation depends upon there being a causal relationship between the cooperator's action and the action of the malefactor (or malefactors). The causal relationships calling (under certain conditions) for restitution include such direct cooperation as "ordering" that a theft be performed; Thomas, indeed, says that he who commands is "he who moves principally" and, for this reason, is more to blame. Other such causal relationships include "counseling" with regard to a theft, "praising someone as fearless for accepting what belongs to another," "expressly consenting" to an act of theft, offering shelter to thieves, and actually participating in the theft. Thomas also mentions ways in which a person might cooperate indirectly. A person so cooperates if he "does not impede when he can and ought to impede," if he "withdraws an order or counsel impeding the theft or robbery," if he "withdraws aid by means of which he might have hindered [a theft]," or if he favors a theft by concealment of some sort. Although Thomas does not say so explicitly, all these ways of cooperating with theft are also ways of cooperating with evil quite generally.

Section I of chapter 5 is entitled "Intention, Paths of Intelligibility, Proportionality." It is essentially an exegesis of *ST* 2-2.64.7, where Thomas considers the permissibility of killing in self-defense. It is sometimes considered the place where Thomas formulates the principle of double effect, which (given certain conditions) would permit the performance of an act with an evil effect as long as that effect is not intended. This principle is often cited as the basic reason for judging some cases of what is termed material cooperation permissible. The purpose of section I, however, is to cast doubt upon the idea that in *ST* 2-2.64.7 Thomas is formulating a principle of wide application such as might be the basis of such judgments.

The opening lines of *ST* 2-2.64.7 say that it can be permissible to kill someone in self-defense if intended is the conservation of one's own life, the killing of the aggressor remaining "beside [praeter]" one's intention. The relevant texts make it apparent that such intentions must be understood within their intelligible contexts. It is possible for someone who kills simply in order to conserve his life to intend only that, since there is an unbroken "path of intelligibility" between defending oneself, even by possibly lethal means, and conserving one's life. Such a path of intelligibility does not exist, for instance, when someone fornicates in order to conserve his life. As Thomas explains the point, fornication "is not ordered toward the conservation of one's own life from necessity, as is an act from which a killing sometimes follows"; and so, if one fornicates in order to conserve one's life, the fornication must be intended separately.

The path of intelligibility making it possible just to intend conserving one's life is part of natural law; other paths of intelligibility, however, are more bound up in positive law. It is also permissible, says Thomas, for a public official such as "the soldier fighting against foes" to kill in self-defense; such a person can in fact do so licitly even if he intends to kill the foes. It is apparent from this assertion that fundamental for Thomas in *ST* 2-2.64.7 is not intention as such – and so he is not formulating there a principle of double effect – but rather the paths of intelligibility, recognizable in a just society, such as determine when intentional killing is permitted and when not. But, as Thomas also maintains in *ST* 2-2.64.7, even given that an agent is operating within a path of intelligibility, if his action is not proportionate to the end toward which that path is directed, he acts illicitly.

Section II of chapter 5 discusses a couple of remarks in Thomas in which he recognizes that a person who might seem to be cooperating with evil is not doing so because he is in fact directing his efforts along a particular path of intelligibility. A judge, he says, who is obliged by law to issue judgments based upon evidence presented in court, might be constrained by the testimony of false witnesses to condemn to death a person he privately knows to be innocent. He must do all he can within the law to expose the false witnesses; but, if he is unsuccessful, says Thomas, "he does not sin in issuing a sentence consistent with the evidence because it is not he who kills the innocent but those who assert that he is not innocent" [*ST* 2-2.64.6 ad 3].

The same section also discusses Cajetan's (Thomas de Vio's) comments on this case—which discussion brings to the fore the idea that not all "professional" paths of intelligibility are alike. If it is clear that in a particular case a standard medical procedure will kill a patient immediately, the physician is obliged to refrain from using it. Were he to employ the procedure and were the patient immediately to die (as he knew would happen) because of the procedure, he cannot argue soundly that he was only following the rules of his profession. This section also contains an exposition of a principle employed by Thomas according to which an act is correct when "the middle does not pull away from the extremes." The idea is, again, that one acts correctly when one remains on the straight path of intelligibility to the end intended.

Section III of chapter 5 discusses another type (or set of types) of apparent cooperation explicitly considered by Thomas. In *ST* 2-2.78.4, he asks whether it is licit to accept a loan "under usurious conditions." This would seem to constitute immoral cooperation because by doing so one causes the usurer to perform an unjust act—that is, to extort unjust interest for the loan. Thomas's answer is that, if the act involves inducing the usurer to give a loan, then it is illicit; if it does not involve inducement, then it can be licit. As seen also in *ST* 2-2.62.7 (the article considered in chapter 4, section VI, about restitution), the type of causality required for immoral cooperation can be termed 'inducement.' In order for one's asking for a loan not to constitute inducing, the usurer must be in the business of usury and one must genuinely need the loan.

Things that Thomas says regarding usury are pertinent to other themes developed earlier in the present work: namely, consent, scandal, and intention. Thomas says clearly here that consent need not pertain to the whole of a malefactor's act: one might consent to receiving a loan but not to its character as usurious. Similarly, regarding scandal (that is to say, the presentation of the occasion of sin for another), given the proper conditions, asking for a usurious loan would not be to present the occasion for a sin of usury but to present the occasion for the granting of a much-needed loan. In such a case and given the proper conditions, the borrower's intention, says Thomas, is directed not at the bad effect of the usurer's sinning but at the good effect of relieving the need. As seen in earlier sections of the present work, however, one must be careful when speaking of intention as determinant of the moral character of acts. What is essential in the moral analysis of cooperation is rather causality. Accordingly, a connection is made in this section with what Thomas says in *ST* 2-2.62.7 regarding the causality required in an act of cooperation for it to give rise to the obligation of making restitution.

Section III of chapter 5 continues with a close look at Thomas's response to the third objection in *ST* 2-2.78.4, which focuses not so much on the morality of usury as on the morality of depositing money with a usurer: that is, with giving him the material for his bad act. Thomas here touches upon themes that eventually generated the expressions 'material cooperation' and 'formal cooperation,' maintaining that a person sins if he provides a usurer with the material of his trade "with the intention of making more money" by means of the usurer's bad actions.

Chapter 6 is entitled "Concluding Ideas: Cooperation and Justice." In section I, expounded in a fairly exhaustive manner, is the Aristotelian-Thomistic virtue of justice; its objective – and yet personal – nature is emphasized. Section II explains how an ideal legislature charged with dealing with cooperation would formulate laws in accordance with justice. In this connection, it speaks also of the advantages and challenges of adopting a Thomistic approach to such matters, arguing that in so doing one has at one's disposal all the tools for the analysis of human actions provided by Aristotle and Thomas and not just the limited and philosophically inadequate set of ideas employed by, for instance, Alphonsus Liguori – great saint though he was. This does not necessarily make the task of determining what constitutes immoral cooperation any easier, although the ethicist faced with such material can proceed with the confidence that his laboratory is equipped with the appropriate instruments of analysis.

The present book contains a number of appendixes. The first three are translations of those sections in Alphonsus's *Theologia moralis* most discussed in the book: the section on cooperation, the section on restitution, and the section on scandal. The other two appendixes are translations of articles by Thomas Aquinas used in the book. Appendix 4 is a translation of the article in his *Quaestiones disputatae de malo* on indifferent acts; appendix 5 is a translation of his article in the *Summa theologiae* on killing in self-defense.

In the sections of his *Theologia moralis* found translated in appendixes 1 through 3, Alphonsus makes reference to a huge number of other authors. A list of their dates and works cited can be found in volume four of the Gaudé edition of the *Theologia moralis*, pp. 785–817.

IV. Terminology and Other Matters

A few remarks about terminology. The first has to do with the person (or persons) who perform the evil acts that might be connected in some way with acts that can be termed cooperation. In order to avoid excessive circumlocution, I call such a person the 'malefactor.' This makes the person sound quite sinister, which the main agent in a case of cooperation sometimes – but not always – is; but the term is used here simply as a "tag," so that it might be immediately apparent to which of a number of possible agents reference is being made.

Regarding the word 'cooperation' itself, sometimes in what follows, when using the term 'cooperation' (as well as 'cooperates,' etc.), I refer to cooperation of any sort, whether moral or immoral, in good or in evil. Sometimes, however, in order to avoid constant repetition, when I mean immoral cooperation with evil, I speak simply of cooperation. The context in which such terms are used should make their meaning apparent.

I adopt the convention, now common in philosophical circles, of reserving double inverted commas ("...") for genuine quotations and for things to which I wish to call attention as surprising or nonstandard, that is, as scare quotes. In all other appropriate cases, I employ single inverted commas ('. . .'), such as for the mention of a term or a concept or for quotations within quotations.

In order to keep italic text to a minimum, quotations in foreign languages but written in the Latin alphabet appear in double inverted commas (without italics). Occasionally Latin phrases are inserted into a translation in square brackets; again, italics are not used. When discussing or mentioning particular foreign words or short phrases, I do use italics. Some Latin expressions commonly used in English and/or frequently used in this book (such as 'per se,' 'per accidens,' and 'praeter intentionem'), I do not put in italics; they appear as if they were English expressions.

For Aristotle, I use a condensed system of reference. A reference will begin with a standard abbreviation of the work's title (see the list of abbreviations below). The abbreviation is followed by a number corresponding to one of the largest divisions of the work (usually books); that number is followed by a number corresponding to one of the next largest divisions (usually chapters); then follows the so-called Bekker number, which makes reference to a nineteenth-century edition of Aristotle's works by August Immanuel Bekker, of which all later editions and scholarly translations make use in order to ensure consistent referencing. Thus, '*EN* 3.1 1111a3–21' refers to the *Nicomachean Ethics*, book 3, chapter 1, the lines of the text corresponding to the first column ('a') of page 1111 of Bekker's Greek text. (Each page of Bekker's edition has two columns of text: column 'a' and column 'b.') For the division of works into books and chapters (which sometimes – but rarely – varies depending on the edition or translation), I follow the Revised Oxford Translation, edited by Jonathan Barnes.

Also for Thomas Aquinas I use a condensed system of reference. As with Aristotle, a reference will begin with an abbreviation of the work's title (see the list of abbreviations below). The abbreviation is followed by a number corresponding to one of the largest divisions of the work; that number is followed by a number corresponding to one of the next largest divisions, and so on. For the *Summa theologiae*, the first element indicates the part of that work: '1' = the first part; '1-2' = the first part of the second part; '2-2' refers to the second part of the second part; and '3' refers to the third part. Thus, '*ST* 1-2.18.7' refers to the first part of the second part, question 18, article 7. An article in the *Summa theologiae* typically begins with a number of objections to the main thesis of the article: the abbreviation 'obi.' stands for 'objection.' The objections are followed by a contrary thought or authority, that section beginning with the words *Sed contra*. Then follows the main argument, known as the corpus or body. Then follow responses to the objections. These are indicated with Latin preposition *ad* ("response to" *x*). Thus, '*ST* 1-2.18.7 obi. 3' refers to the third objection in that article; '*ST* 1-2.18.7 ad 3' refers to Thomas's response to that objection.

The texts of Thomas used are those of the Leonine Commission, when such are available, although I usually change the Leonine orthography to standard Latin orthography. In cases where a Leonine edition does not exist, I use the Marietti text, with the exception of the commentary on Peter Lombard's *Sentences*, where I use the Paris edition, except for book 4, distinctions 23–50, where I use the Parma edition. (See the bibliography.) For the Greek text of the works of Plato and Aristotle I have used the texts found in the online *Thesaurus Linguae Graecae*. (These are usually the critical editions from the Oxford Classical Texts series.)

For translations from Aristotle, I typically make use of the Revised Oxford Translation, occasionally altering it, usually for the sake of terminological consistency. All other translations (unless otherwise indicated) are my own, including the translations of Alphonsus Liguori and Thomas Aquinas found in the appendixes. I have recently become aware of an English translation underway of Alphonsus Liguori's *Theologia moralis*; the translator is Ryan Grant and the publisher is Mediatrix Press. This translation may be of use to those who want to know more about Alphonsus's theology but are disinclined to plow through his Latin.

CHAPTER 1 FORMAL AND MATERIAL COOPERATION

I. St. Alphonsus Liguori and His *Theologia moralis*

Despite his many other activities (described in the introduction), Alphonsus Liguori managed between 1742 and the end of 1746 to carve out time to work on the *Theologia moralis*, the first edition of which was published in Naples in 1748, when he was fifty-two years of age. It was the first genuinely scholarly book he had ever published. The title page of that first edition did not bear the title *Theologia moralis* but rather *Medulla theologiae moralis*, and its author was given not as Alphonsus but rather as Hermann Busenbaum, SJ; Alphonsus is acknowledged as having penned "annotations."[1] This minimizing of the role of Alphonsus was not without reason. In this first edition, the

1. Hermann Busenbaum and Alphonsus de Ligorio, *Medulla theologiae moralis R.P. Hermanni Busembaum Societatis Jesu theologi, cum adnotationibus per Reverendum Patrem D. Alphonsum de Ligorio* (Naples: Alexius Pellechius, 1748). Busenbaum's name becomes in Latin 'Busembaum,' as seen in this title; he lived between 1600 and 1668. Some sources say that the first edition of his *Medulla theologiae moralis* appeared in 1650; others report that an earlier edition appeared in 1645; see Carlos Sommervogel, *Bibliothèque de la Compagnie de Jésus* (Brussels/Paris: Schepens/Picard, 1890–1932), v. 2 col. 445.

whole of Busenbaum's *Medulla theologiae moralis* is reproduced, each section of Busenbaum being followed by Alphonsus's annotations. The annotations by Alphonsus are often, however, of considerable length. By way of example, the chapter on cooperation as treated under the virtue of charity contains two and a half columns by Busenbaum, followed by four and a half by Alphonsus. The *dubium* on restitution (which, as we shall see, also has to do with cooperation) contains two columns by Busenbaum and just over two by Alphonsus.[2]

Alphonsus revised the work continually, nine editions appearing during his lifetime, its title becoming *Theologia moralis* with the second. Busenbaum's name was definitively pushed into the background with the fifth edition of 1763 – which was entirely appropriate, since the proportion of material by Alphonsus continued to increase with the various revisions. To use the examples just mentioned, in the chapter on cooperation, in the final edition of his lifetime (1785), Alphonsus's contribution is three times the length of Busenbaum's; and one short paragraph in Busenbaum's *dubium* on restitution – the paragraph on one who "participates in plunder [participans de praeda]" – receives a commentary more than twenty times its length.[3]

II. The Origins of the Formal/Material Distinction

It is difficult to say with whom the formal/material distinction as applied to cooperation originates. In the recent literature, Alphonsus is often cited as the original source; but, as just mentioned, his commentary consists of annotations on Busenbaum's commentary, and Busenbaum's section on cooperation begins with the words, "I re-

2. The chapter on cooperation ("An liceat alterius peccato materialiter cooperari?") appears at columns 92–98 of the 1748 edition; the *dubium* on restitution ("An qui cooperantur ad damnum alterius, teneantur ad restitutionem?") at columns 284–289. The ultimate versions of the chapter on cooperation and of a part of the *dubium* on restitution are translated in appendixes 1 and 2 of the present book.

3. Busenbaum's paragraph, along with Alphonsus's commentary, is translated in appendix 2.

spond that it is licit to cooperate only materially, furnishing only the material and means of sinning, or exhibiting the object, if the following conditions are present" (and he goes on to list the conditions).[4] Busenbaum does not use in that section of his manual the term 'formal'; but, later in the same work, while discussing idolatry, a sin that often figures in treatments of cooperation, he does say that participation in idolatry can be either material or formal.[5]

The fact that words like *formalis* or *materialis* come into arguments in this almost casual way is itself evidence that their appearance does not necessarily signal that a writer (especially an earlier writer) is wielding a canonical distinction, such as the formal cooperation/material cooperation distinction that is often treated in ethics today. Subsequent to the discovery in the West of Aristotle's major works, the terms 'formal' and 'material' (and so on) became so much a part of traditional Catholic academic culture that they could pop up in most any context: ethical, metaphysical, logical, or biological

4. Hermann Busenbaum [Hermannus Busembaum], *Medulla theologiae moralis facili ac perspicua methodo resolvens causa conscientiæ ex variis probatisque auctoribus concinnata* (Münster [Monasterium Westphaliae]: Bernhardus Raesfeldius, 1650), lb. 2 tract. 3 cap. 2 a. 3 (p. 95). (Busenbaum's remarks on cooperation are quoted by Alphonsus at *Theologia moralis* 2 §59: see the translation in appendix 1.)

5. "Idolatry is twofold: one such is material, or simulated, as when someone without internal desire, out of fear of death, exhibits devotion to an idol; the other is formal or proper [idolatry], and this is either perfect, as when some adores an idol which out of infidelity he believes to be God, or imperfect, when someone out of hatred of God or out of the desire to obtain something from a demon or other creature, bestows devotion upon it as if to God" [Busenbaum, *Medulla Theologiae Moralis*, lb. 3 tract. 1 cap. 1 dub. 3 (pp. 110–11)]. Noldin says that one searches in vain in the older theologians for the formal cooperation/material cooperation formulation, although you do get some hints [Hieronymus Noldin, "Über die Mitwirkung zur Sünde des Nebenmenschen," *Zeitschrift für Katholische Theologie* 3 (1879): 501]. He mentions de Valentia (ca. 1550–1603) and Sánchez (1550–1610), who speak sometimes of "direct" (= formal) cooperation. He also mentions Laymann (1574–1635), who does actually use the terms 'formal' and 'material' with respect to cooperation: see Paul Laymann, *Theologia moralis: In V libros distribuita, quibus materiae omnes practicae, cum ad externum ecclesiasticum, tum internum conscientiae forum spectantes, noua methodo explicantur* (Padua: J. Manfrè, 1733), lb. 2 tract. 3 cap. 13 §4.

(to mention some major ones).[6] They were used in order to indicate some aspect of something that was, in comparison with some other aspect, either more formal or more material, the formal often being associated with the end (and resulting intelligibility) of the thing under consideration, the material with that *of* which the form is form. In Aristotle it is perfectly legitimate to speak at one moment of, for instance, the form of an animal's body, as distinct from its matter (flesh and bones), and at another moment of the form of flesh as distinct from *its* matter.[7]

All this said, however, in moral theology after Alphonsus the formal/material distinction came to be associated in a special way with cooperation. The distinction itself, notwithstanding serious disagreements about its application, was often invoked as if referring to a difference as fixed and verifiable as the difference between soul and body.

III. Alphonsus on (Mostly) Formal Cooperation

But let us set aside these complications for the moment and begin with Alphonsus's position. In the paragraph from *Theologia moralis* 2 §63 usually quoted, having first mentioned the way in which certain others before him had distinguished formal from material cooperation,[8] Alphonsus writes as follows:

6. Aristotle points to form or matter wherever it suits him, including in his logic where a syllogism is said to have a certain form (universal affirmative, particular negative, etc.), its "matter" being the propositions someone presumably puts *into* that form. See his *Physics* 2.3 195a18–19. But it is also true that the propositions themselves are formal with respect to the terms appearing in them. This idea is much developed in the subsequent Aristotelian commentary tradition. See Jonathan Barnes, "Logical Form and Logical Matter," in *Logica, Mente e Persona*, ed. A. Alberti (Florence: Leo S. Olschki, 1990), 7–119; see also Kevin L. Flannery, *Ways into the Logic of Alexander of Aphrodisias*, Philosophia Antiqua, vol. 62 (Leiden: Brill, 1995), 109–45.

7. *De generatione et corruptione* 1.5 321b32–34. See also Thomas Aquinas, "In librum primum Aristotelis De generatione et corruptione expositio," ed. Raimondo M. Spiazzi, in *In Aristotelis libros De caelo et mundo, De generatione et corruptione, Meteorologicorum, Expositio* (Turin: Marietti, 1952), 1.15.4 (§107). See also Aristotle's *De partibus animalium* 2.1 646a12–24.

8. It is interesting that, according to the approach which Alphonsus rejects just

But it is better, with [yet] others, to say that that cooperation is *formal* which contributes to the bad will of the other and cannot be without sin, but that cooperation is *material* which contributes only to the bad action of the other, beside the intention of the cooperator.[9]

On first reading, it sounds as if Alphonsus is saying here that one cooperates formally with a malefactor only when one shares his intention; otherwise, one cooperates only materially (and possibly morally). Thus, a pro-life junior doctor who is forced to participate in an abortion because otherwise he will lose his job, would be cooperating in the abortion but only materially, since his intention is only to keep his job. This understanding of Alphonsus's distinction is, however, incorrect, for it fails to appreciate the Thomistic distinction, presupposed by Alphonsus, between the *will* [voluntas] of the malefactor and his intention [intentio]. The intention of an end is just one of several possible acts of the will, according to Thomas; an agent's will is, for instance, also borne toward those things that are done for an end (*ST* 1-2.12.4). In the passage from Alphonsus just quoted, he says that formal cooperation "contributes to the bad will [voluntas] of the other" and that the material cooperator does not share the same inten-

before offering his own formulation, formal cooperation either "per se or because of some adjoined circumstance leads proximately to the execution of the sin, even if per se it is indifferent" [§63]. Alphonsus attributes this to the Jesuit Juan de Cardenas (1613–84) and the Dominican Pius Thomas Milante ("Master Milante") (d. 1749). Reference to circumstances marks this approach as properly Thomistic, as we shall see in chapter 2.

9. "Sed melius cum aliis dicendum, illam esse formalem quae concurrit ad malam voluntatem alterius, et nequit esse sine peccato; materialem vero illam, quae concurrit tantum ad malam actionem alterius, praeter intentionem cooperantis" [*Theologia moralis* 2 §63]. When speaking of cooperation, Alphonsus uses repeatedly derivatives of the word *concurro* (as in *concurrit, est concursus cum* and so on). It is important to resist the temptation to use the word 'concur' in translating these expressions, for 'concur' might refer to a cooperator's standing *back* and consenting to a malefactor's action. All cooperation has some involvement in the action of the malefactor, although it may not amount to actively helping him in the very act. (I discuss the meaning of *concurrit* further below.) Many of the ideas set out in the present chapter can be found also in Kevin L. Flannery, "Two Factors in the Analysis of Cooperation in Evil," *National Catholic Bioethics Quarterly* 13, no. 4 (2013): 663–75.

tion [intentio] with him (the malefactor). But this says nothing about whether formal cooperation necessarily involves sharing the intention of the malefactor. Indeed, in the very section of his *Theologia moralis*, Alphonsus gives examples of formal cooperation in which the formal cooperator does not share in the other's intention. He speaks of a servant who writes or conveys amorous letters to his master's lover: even though the servant does these things out of "grave fear" that he will be punished, says Alphonsus, he cooperates formally.[10] In a work whose short title is *Homo apostolicus* and which appeared a few years after his *Theologia moralis*, Alphonsus gives a couple of other examples, including that of someone who acts as a lookout for a thief or an assassin. Such cooperation, he says, is intrinsically evil and can never be licit, no matter what the reason for cooperating, be it even the threat of death.[11]

10. In this number (*Theologia moralis* 2 §67), the question is "Whether it is licit for a servant, out of grave fear, to write or to convey amorous letters to the concubine of his master" ["An licet famulo, ob metum gravem, scribere vel deferre litteras amatorias concubinae domini"]. Alphonsus, citing a number of other prominent moral theologians, says that "these [letters] are never licit, since they contribute formally to the sin of the master, fostering his illicit love" ["haec nunquam licere; quia formaliter concurrunt ad peccatum heri, fovendo turpem ejus amorem"]. It is not immediately apparent what is meant by "writing" amorous letters to the concubine; but, in the first source that Alphonsus cites in this regard, the question is framed in the following manner: "Whether servants can licitly convey amorous letters to a concubine or write them upon the order of a master" ["An servi licite possint deferre litteras amatorias concubinae aut eas iussu domini scribere"] [Salmanticenses (Collegium Salmanticense), *Collegii Salmanticensis cursus theologiae moralis* (Venice: N. Pezzana, 1750), vol. 5 tract. 21 cap. 8 §67]. So, the letters would seem to be composed by the servant and not just written out as dictated by the master. Besides the Salmanticenses, Alphonsus cites as agreeing with him Thomas Sanchez (d.1610), Dominic Viva (d. 1710), Paul Laymann (d. 1653), Martin Bonacina (d. 1631), Thomas Tamburini (d. 1675), Claud Lacroix (d. 1714), "etc." (Tamburini is sometimes associated with the condemned school of thought known as "laxism," although Alphonsus defends him.) A few sections earlier in *Theologia moralis*, Alphonsus appears also to recognize as formal cooperation a servant's seeking out a concubine for his master and a person's fabricating idols [*Theologia moralis* 2 §59].

11. "Material cooperation is commonly admitted by the learned to be licit when there is present a just cause. Let it be understood here that one thing is *formal* cooperation, which comes about when one directly cooperates in a sin (as in him who

In the analysis of a particular human act, the most distant point in the "scenario" under consideration is called the agent's intention: what he intends.[12] Thus, when someone takes medicine in order to achieve health, health is that which is intended, although taking the medicine also issues from the will: it is done voluntarily in order to reach the end intended.[13] Consider the following situation. A senior

---

fornicates), or else when it flows into the bad will of one's neighbor who wills to sin, as would be serving as a lookout ['watching the back'] for an assassin so that he might steal or kill more securely: to write amorous letters for an adulterer or to convey gifts to a concubine; to accept gifts from him who would undermine your integrity. These and similar acts of cooperation are intrinsically evil, for by them a hand is given to one's neighbor in committing a sin – or, at least, the bad will of the latter is fostered – and so for no reason, not even that of death, can they be excused as not mortal sin. Quite another thing is *material* cooperation, which is when an action is indifferent and one's neighbor can make use of it without sin but out of his malice he makes ill use of it in order to sin, as when one borrows money from another who refuses to give it without interest: to serve wine to him who ill uses it to get drunk; to give keys to one who uses them in order to steal" [Alphonsus Maria de Ligorio, *Homo Apostolicus instructus in sua vocatione ad audiendas confessiones, sive praxis et instructio confessariorum* (Mechelen: H. Dessain, 1867–68 [3 vv.]), tract. 4 punct. 5 §31 (v. 1 pp. 120–21)].

12. See *ST* 1-2.12.1.

13. On the other hand, if we shift our attention so that the scenario under consideration is now 'going to the pharmacy in order to buy that medicine,' 'buying the medicine' becomes the agent's intention, and 'going to the pharmacy' is voluntary, with respect to that intention. See *ST* 1-2.12.2c: "intention regards an end qua terminus of a movement of the will. Within a movement, however, a terminus can be taken in two senses: first, the very last terminus, at which the movement comes to a halt; this is the terminus of the whole movement. Secondly, some midway point, which constitutes the beginning of one part of the movement and the end or terminus of another – just as in a movement which goes from *a* to *c* through *b*, *c* is the last terminus and *b* is a terminus but not the last. And intention can be of either and so, although though intention is always of an end, it need not always be of the last end." See also *Quaestiones disputatae de veritate* 22.13c, where Thomas explains that intention, since it is a "tending" and so has extension, involves both the end and that which is for the end: "And thus 'to intend' in this way differs from 'to will,' for 'to will' tends toward the end in an absolute sense but 'to intend' signifies order toward an end in as much as the end is that toward which are ordered those things that are for the end" ["Et ita intendere in hoc differt a velle, quod velle tendit in finem absolute; sed intendere dicit ordinem in finem, secundum quod finis est in quem ordinantur ea quae sunt ad finem"].

doctor performs abortions because he believes that doing so promotes the equal rights of women. He could be involved in other more prestigious and better-paying procedures such as heart or brain surgery; but he has chosen, for this ideological reason, to make abortions a significant part of his practice. So, his intention in willingly performing a particular abortion is to promote the equal rights of women. On the other hand, a pro-life junior doctor might be obliged by the terms of a contract to assist him in this abortion, performing actions that make sense only *as* finishing in the death of the fetus. He might be required, for instance, to help direct the instrument, with which the senior doctor will kill the fetus, toward the fetus. He knows that he will lose his job if he does not assist the senior doctor in this way. His intention, therefore, is quite different from that of the doctor – and yet he cooperates formally in the abortion. As Alphonsus puts it in *Theologia moralis* 2 §63 (in, that is, the passage quoted above), the junior doctor "contributes to the bad will" of the senior doctor even though he does not have the same intention as the senior doctor does. The "bad will" of the senior doctor is present not just in his intention of promoting women's rights but also in the abortion he performs voluntarily – and it is that with which the junior doctor cooperates formally.

But how, someone might ask, can this be called *formal* cooperation if, within the Thomistic tradition presumed by Alphonsus, form is associated with intention – and the intentions of the two doctors are quite different? The example already used of going to the pharmacy with the intention of buying medicine (which one then takes with the intention of achieving health) is, in effect, the answer to the question. Any stage in the extended analysis of an action, with the exception of the very first stage, can be considered what the agent intends in doing something else. It is simply a matter of shifting the focus of analysis. The senior doctor performed the abortion with the intention of promoting women's rights, but he also entered the operating room with the intention of performing an abortion. And so, when the junior doctor helps guide the instrument that will kill the fetus, he is cooperating with *an* intention of the senior doctor, even though, in the original description of the scene, the senior doctor willed to perform the abortion with the intention of promoting women's rights. Alphonsus's only concern in all of this is whether the act of the cooperator "enters into" some willed (or intended) act that is immoral; if it does, the act amounts to formal cooperation.

How Alphonsus thinks about such matters becomes more clear if one considers the Latin phrase "concurrit ad," which, in the above passage, is translated "contributes to": "that cooperation is formal which contributes to the bad will of the other ... but that cooperation is material which contributes only to the bad action of the other" [*Theologia moralis* 2 §63]. That translation is perfectly accurate; but, in order to understand the distinction that Alphonsus is making, it is helpful to attend to the literal meaning of "concurrit ad" – "runs (in a cooperative way) up to [something]"[14] – for in so attending we become aware that the difference between formal and material cooperation depends upon the type of thing toward which a particular piece of behavior goes. According to Alphonsus, the action of a formal cooperator runs up to the bad *will* of a malefactor; the action of a material cooperator runs up to his bad *action*.

Since formal cooperation runs up to a will, it runs up to that of which it can be an integral part *as* that other act is intended. Material cooperation, on the other hand, runs up to another, distinct action. With material cooperation, there is a sort of "intelligible barrier" between the cooperation and the intention of the act cooperated in; with formal cooperation, on the other hand, the intention of the cooperator enters right into the intention of the malefactor. Both types

14. The words in parentheses – "in a cooperative way" – represent the prefix 'con-'. Since in the present context "running up to" is invariably attributed to a cooperator (that is, his "running up to" is said to cooperate in some way with the malefactor), in what follows I drop those words, speaking more simply of running up to something. See Flannery, "Two Factors in the Analysis of Cooperation in Evil," 665–69. Cp. Di Camillo, "Organizational Cooperation with Evil," 44, n. 135.

of cooperation concern actions linked to actions (the action of a cooperator linked to the action of a malefactor); but, since formal cooperation runs up to the will of the malefactor's bad action, the cooperator's action is united internally with that action. The very *point* of the formal cooperator's action is the same as the point of the malefactor's action, informed as the latter is by a bad will.

This interpretation of Alphonsus's remarks on formal cooperation is confirmed by an expression he uses in his *Homo apostolicus*, where he says that formal cooperation "flows into the bad will of one's neighbor who wills to sin."[15] Again, the idea is that the cooperator's action enters into the very intelligibility of what the malefactor does.[16] The same does not happen with material cooperation, the intelligibility of which remains distinct from – although connected to – that of the malefactor's action.

So, it is important always to bear in mind that the intention of the action with which the formal cooperator cooperates is not necessarily the same as the malefactor's intention – at least, as specified within a particular scenario. At issue is the action that the malefactor performs, which falls under his will, as well as under his intention, although his will is distinct from his intention. The formal cooperator cooperates specifically with the will of the malefactor. The junior doctor may not share the senior doctor's intention, but he does contribute to the will embodied in the action that the senior doctor performs – and "to which" the junior doctor's own action runs as to a completing terminus. When the junior doctor directs the instrument that kills the fetus, his action gets its sense – its form – from the fetus's being killed, which is what the senior doctor does, with another intention. The act of cooperating runs up to and *into* what little sense

15. "influit in pravam voluntatem proximi volentis peccare." Formal cooperation is here not just a matter of *influencing* the will of the malefactor but of helping it to be the case that his will comes about by way of his bad act. The fuller text is quoted above, in note 11. We will find a similar expression in *Theologia moralis*, 3 §571.

16. I discuss the term 'intelligibility' in chapter 5, section I.

there is in the senior doctor's act of killing the fetus. If the fetus is not killed, neither the junior nor the senior doctor's act achieves what it is essentially — an act aimed at killing that fetus.

IV. Alphonsus on Material Cooperation

Let us now turn our attention more directly to material cooperation. This will lead us into a consideration of some difficulties in Alphonsus's ideas on how to distinguish material from formal cooperation, but we begin with things less problematic.

Material cooperation does not at its point or terminus become part of the malefactor's action, as it would were it formal cooperation. As Alphonsus puts it in *Theologia moralis* 2 §63, material cooperation "contributes only to the bad action of the other," not to his bad will. In other words, the act of material cooperation, qua act, does not enter into the bad act of the malefactor formally, finding its point there; it has, rather, a point and sense of its own. The willed act of the malefactor is one thing; the act of the material cooperator is another.

Alphonsus's most extensive explanation of how (or when) this occurs comes in another section of his *Theologia moralis*: book 3. The two passages — *Theologia moralis* 2 §63 and *Theologia moralis* 3 §571 — are closely related, even though the former is included in the treatise on the theological virtue of charity, the latter in the treatise on the seventh commandment (and therefore under justice, which is not a theological virtue).[17] In *Theologia moralis* 3 §571, the question is whether a person is required to pay restitution to the victim of a robbery if he has cooperated in the act of theft by such acts as holding a ladder for the thief, giving him keys or other instruments for opening a strong-box, making copies of keys, or breaking open gates. Alphon-

17. In *Theologia moralis* 3 §571, Alphonsus makes a back reference to the passage from *Theologia moralis* 2 §63 in which he defines material and formal cooperation; in *Theologia moralis* 2 §63, he makes a forward reference to *Theologia moralis* 3 §571. A translation of *Theologia moralis* 3 §571 can be found in appendix 2. I discuss the relationship between the theological and the moral virtues in chapter 4, section I.

sus's ultimate answer is that, no, the cooperator need not pay restitution, provided that he does not share the intention of the malefactor. He cannot, for instance, be a member of a team of thieves who just happens to have been assigned by the team a task sufficiently separated from the actual taking of the other's goods as to otherwise qualify as material cooperation. Also, says Alpnonsus, he must fear the infliction of an evil "of a superior order" should he not cooperate.[18] But, given that these conditions are in place, a cooperator is not obliged to pay restitution for having (for instance) held a ladder or opened a strong-box, since such acts are, writes Alphonsus, "truly indifferent, for, depending on the end toward which they go, they could be either licit or illicit."[19] Such cooperation is material.

But before setting out his own position – or, more precisely, the position he considers "more probable" [probabilior] – Alphonsus set outs another position. This "first position [prima sententia]" distinguishes two types of cooperation: the first type, in which "the actions of the cooperator remotely cooperate in the theft" and would include holding a ladder for a thief or helping to open a strong-box, comprises actions that are "per se indifferent"; the second type, in which "the actions are proximately flowing into the theft" and would include "breaking open gates" and "setting fire to a house," comprises actions that are "intrinsically evil" and "cannot be excused on account of whatever fear." But he notes that one group of authors maintaining this first position, the Salmanticenses, changed their minds because they came to see actions of the first type as also intrinsically evil since

18. Such an evil would be "superior" to the evil of someone's losing his goods. As Alphonsus explains, in the case of theft, such an evil would include death, mutilation, or grave infamy, but not loss of possessions [*Theologia moralis* 3 §571]. See also Alphonsus Maria de Ligorio, *Homo Apostolicus*, tract. 4 punct. 5 §32 (v. 1 pp. 121–22).

19. "Ratio, quia omnes praefatae actiones, tam primi quam secundi generis, sunt revera indifferentes: cum, juxta finem quo fiunt, vel licitae vel illicitae esse possint" [*Theologia moralis* 3 §571 p. 67ab]. The reference in the first clause to two groups of acts ("tam primi quam secundi generis") is to the types of acts listed at the beginning of the "first position [prima sententia]" [p. 66ab].

they too "flow proximately into the sin of injustice which the thief intends to commit." This change of mind by the Salmanticenses is indicative of some very fundamental problems in the use of the concepts 'indifferent' and 'intrinsically evil' as employed by Alphonsus and others.

In any case, the second position ("Seconda vero sententia . . ."), the position of both Busenbaum and Alphonsus, is that *any* such cooperators "do not sin if they contribute the aforesaid actions because of fear of great harm." Alphonsus, addressing the reader in the second person, explains why such cooperation cannot be considered formal:

> Nor is it true that, in this case [the case of material cooperation], you formally run up to the sin of theft, for this would be the case if you positively brought your influence into his bad will.[20] When, however, you contribute only those actions that the thief afterwards ill uses in order to inflict damage, your action will not be the cause of the damage but only the malice of the thief will be.[21]

In other words, an action that has its own point independently of the point of the malefactor's act (independently, that is, of the formal aspect of that act) and which the malefactor "afterwards" uses – such an act is not formal but material cooperation. Although Alphonsus says here that the malefactor's abuse of "your" act occurs "afterwards," his point has to do not with the temporal order of the different acts but rather with the relative independence of what we have been calling

20. See the remarks made just above about formal cooperation flowing into the will of the malefactor; see also the passage quoted in note 11.

21. "Nec verum est, quod formaliter tunc concurris ad peccatum furis: nam hoc esset, si positive tu influeres in ejus malam voluntatem; quando autem tantum actiones illas praestas quibus fur postea abutetur ad damnum inferendum, non erit quidem causa damni actio tua, sed sola malitia furis (juxta quae fusius diximus *de Carit.* lib. 2 §63, v. *Sed melius*)" [Alphonsus Maria de Ligorio, *Theologia moralis* 3 §571]. The latter is a back-reference to the passage where Alphonsus defines material and formal cooperation. I translate "concurrit ad" as "run up to" in order to bring out the point made above about the formal cooperator's act entering into the voluntary character of the malefactor's exterior act; material cooperation stops short of that.

such acts' "intelligibilities." The servant holds the ladder and then afterwards the thief takes the goods; but the servant might also stay with the ladder while his master is burgling the house and hold it again as he leaves.[22] This too would be a case of material cooperation. The key idea is that the type of action that the servant performs in material cooperation does not depend on thievery: the two acts have separate intelligibilities.

At this point, however, Alphonsus introduces into his own position the difficulties alluded to above. He offers what he regards as a compelling proof that actions of the type listed are all indifferent actions and, therefore, instances of merely material cooperation. Unless we say, for instance, that breaking into a strong-box in order to hand over its contents to a thief is an indifferent act, then, if a thief forces you to open your *own* strong-box and to hand over its contents, you would be cooperating formally—that is, immorally—in theft. "Who, however, of sound mind," he asks, "would be so audacious as to assert that?"[23]

Now, in the first place, this argument suffers from an internal weakness. Recall that Alphonsus places the example of breaking into a strong-box not under the second type of cooperation discussed under the first position—that is, not among the actions that come closest to formal cooperation, such as do "breaking open gates" and "setting fire to a house"—but rather under the first type: among the actions that "remotely cooperate in the theft." And yet he uses the strong-box example in order to argue that *both* types involve indiffer-

22. In the passage where Alphonsus speaks about the act of holding a ladder for a thief, he speaks also of the act of carrying away stolen goods [*Theologia moralis* 3 §571]; so the temporal order is not key here.

23. "Nam alias, si fur te cogeret ad arcam tuam confringendam, ut tradas ei pecuniam ibi contentam, non posses sine peccato hoc facere, quia formaliter cooperareris ad illius peccatum. Sed hoc quis sanae mentis asserere audebit?" [*Theologia moralis* 3 §571]. See the similar remarks at Alphonsus Maria de Ligorio, *Homo Apostolicus*, tract. 10 punct. 2 §57 (v. 1 p. 303), where Alphonsus uses the example of handing over to a thief the keys to one's own house.

ent acts. An objector can certainly respond: "But even the exponents of the first position acknowledge that the first type of actions constitute material cooperation; you have proved very little, if anything at all."

The argument also weakens the larger structure of which it is a part, which includes Alphonsus's understanding of formal cooperation as set out in *Theologia moralis* 2 §§ 63 & 67 and in *Homo Apostolicus*. For there, as we have seen, he uses as examples of formal cooperation a servant's writing amorous letters to his master's lover and a person's acting as a lookout as someone else commits a crime.[24] A servant, however, could without sinning compose love letters to a young lady that *he* is courting and a person might serve as a lookout lest evil men see that he and a colleague are shifting their *own* goods to a safer location.[25] In other words, an extrapolated version of Alphonsus's own argument could be used to argue that what he identifies as formal cooperation is material cooperation.

It appears to be the case that Alphonsus received criticism regarding this line of argumentation, for in an edition of *Theologia moralis* subsequent to the formulations of *Theologia moralis* 3 §571, he includes, just before the beginning of book 5, a *Tractatus praeambulus*, "On human acts in general," the fifth and final article of which

24. Alphonsus also clearly maintains that acts of formal cooperation are not indifferent: in *Theologia moralis* 2 §63, he says that "it is better, with others, to say that that cooperation is *formal* which contributes to the bad will of the other and cannot be without sin."

25. One of the standard examples of the time was the manufacture of pagan idols (also mentioned by Alphonsus as, it seems, a case of formal cooperation [Alphonsus Maria de Ligorio, *Theologia moralis* 2 §59]). Hieronymus Noldin points out that such an object *could* be used as an ornament in a park [Hieronymus Noldin, "Über die Mitwirkung zur Sünde des Nebenmenschen," 510]. See also Nicola Cretoni, "Nota I (to v. 1 §249)," in *Compendium theologiae moralis, auctore P. Ioanne Petri Gury, S.I., editio secunda romana, novis adnotationibus et SS. Congregationum resolutionibus locupletata*, edited by Nicola Cretoni (1875), 572–73; see also Eduard Stephinsky, "Über den Begriff der materiellen und formellen Mitwirkung zum Bösen," *Der Katholik* 56, no. 2 (1876, part 2): 346–47.

is about indifferent acts.[26] In article 4 of the Tractatus *praeambulus*, Alphonsus follows Thomas in maintaining that the object of an act of theft is a *res aliena* ("something belonging to another"), such as makes the act of appropriating it immoral and, therefore, not indifferent in species. On the other hand, using a *res sua* ("something that belongs to oneself") is good and also not indifferent as far as its object is concerned – although, considered individually [secundum individuum] and under certain circumstances, it could be immoral: if the object is used, for instance, when it ought not to be.[27] In article 5, Alphonsus offers an accurate account of Thomas Aquinas's position on indifference. He explains that, according to Thomas, some human acts – such as picking up a piece of straw – might be seen as indifferent if one looks *just* to their object, although no such act is indifferent if one considers all its moral characteristics.[28] Thomas's position on indiffer-

26. The indifference argument we have been examining is included in the 1757 (the third) edition's 3 §571, but there is no *Tractatus praeambulus* inserted before the beginning of book 5. (It is now found in volume 2 of the Gaudé edition, pp. 689–703.) The treatise does appear in the 1767 (the sixth) edition, which was the first edition to be published after Alphonsus became bishop (in 1762).

27. See *ST* 1-2.18.8–9. In *ST* 1-2.18.2, Thomas speaks of the contrary objects: "uti re sua" ("to use something your own") and "accipere aliena" ("to accept something belonging to another"). See also *De malo* 2.4 ad 5, 2.6c and 2.7c. I go into these matters in more detail in chapter 2.

28. "Actus indifferens in specie est actus spectatus in genere (abstrahendo a fine et circumstantiis individualibus).... Actus vero indifferens in individuo est actus consideratus prout est a parte rei, secundum suum objectum, finem et omnes circumstantias individuales" [*Theologia moralis* 5 tract. praeam. a.5 xli]. Alphonsus goes on to deny that there are acts that are indifferent "in individuo." In this number, Alphonsus uses as examples of acts that are indifferent in species: "walking, picking up a piece of straw, collecting flowers, etc." The examples of walking and picking up straw ["festucam levare"] comes from *ST* 1-2.18.8. The presumption is either that the straw (or the flowers) belong to no one in particular or that their use by another would be of no concern to their owner. As Thomas says at *ST* 2-2.66.6 ad 3, "that which is minimal, reason apprehends as practically nothing [quasi nihil], and so in things that are minimal a man does not regard himself as suffering injury and he who accepts [such a thing] can presume that this is not contrary to the will of him to whom the thing belongs" (see also *ST* 2-2.66.7 ad 2 and 186.5 ad 4).

ent acts – which Alphonsus now apparently espouses – is difficult to reconcile with his (Alphonsus's) earlier argument (in *Theologia moralis* 3 §571) regarding the strong-box.[29]

V. Jesuits, Redemptorists, and an Augustinian on Intention and Indifferent Acts

Alphonsus's use, therefore, of this means of distinguishing material from formal cooperation – that is, by looking to indifference – is fraught with problems. The indifference issue vexes also manuals subsequent to Alphonsus's. We shall consider two widely used manuals: the first, originally authored by the Jesuit Hieronymus Noldin (1838–1922), was first published in 1902 and republished in successive editions up until the Second Vatican Council.[30] The second, originally authored by the Redemptorist Joseph Aertnys (1828–1915), was first published in 1886–1887 and also saw successive editions, one appearing after the Council.[31] It is especially useful for our present purpos-

29. On Thomas's understanding of indifferent acts, see chapter 2, especially II, III, and V; see also appendix 4.

30. H. Noldin et al., *Summa theologiae moralis* (Innsbruck: Felizian Rauch, 1961–63). The latest versions of the work comprise three volumes, plus two separately numbered *complementa*, included in the first volume. (The first *complementum* is on chastity, the second on ecclesiastical penalties.) The published volumes contain components of different dates and editions. In the present work, the 34th edition of volume 2, published in 1963, is used. Later editions of the work were revised by Albert Schmitt, SJ, and Godefridus (Gottfried) Heinzel, SJ, whose names appear (but as editors) on the title page of later editions along with Noldin's. Another Jesuit by the name of A. Schönegger is listed as helping in adapting the second *complementum* to the code of canon law. For simplicity's sake, even though in this essay reference is to the 1963 version of volume 2, I speak of the manual simply as Noldin's.

31. Aertnys was known also as Jozef (sometimes Josef) Aertnijs; he was born in Eindoven. The edition referred to here will be the 1890 edition, authored just by Aertnys [Joseph Aertnys, *Theologia moralis secundum doctrinam S. Alfonsi de Ligorio Doctoris Ecclesiae* (Tornaci [Tournai]: Casterman, 1890)]. The ninth to sixteenth editions were produced by Cornelius Damen, the seventeenth and eighteenth by Johannes Visser. This last appeared in 1967 [Joseph Aertnys, Cornelius Damen, and Joannes Visser, *Theologia moralis secundum doctrinam S. Alfonsi de Ligorio Doctoris Ecclesiae*, 18th ed. (Turin: Marietti, 1967)]. See Di Camillo, "Organizational Cooperation with Evil," 55–59.

es since, besides adopting a division of cooperation similar to that of many other manuals, it claims – with good reason – to be a faithful interpretation of Alphonsus.

Cooperation, Noldin says, is formal "if the cooperator contributes both to the intention and to the bad action"; it is material "if he contributes only to the bad action."[32] He gives examples: "One who hands over keys to a thief *in order* that he might be *able* to steal cooperates formally – if one intends to help him in the sin of theft; one cooperates materially if one for another end, for instance, in order to save one's life, furnishes keys which the thief misuses in order to steal."[33] The emphasis here ("*in order* that he might be *able* to steal") is in the original and it is significant. Noldin – who is well aware of the distinction often missed by contemporary writers between intention and the voluntary – is saying that only those who actually *want* the bad act to succeed cooperate formally; if one supplies the keys for another reason, one cooperates only materially. The same act will have been performed – the keys are handed over and, as the cooperator knows, they will enable the thief to steal – but the cooperator does what he does only (for instance) in order to save his own life.

Noldin goes on immediately to say that cooperation might be formal in two ways:

> either α. *explicitly*, because of the intention of the cooperator, who expressly has the intention of participating in the other's sin, or β. *implicitly*, because of the nature of the act supplied – namely, when someone performs an act that, by its nature or attending to its circumstances, is ordered exclusively to the bad action, for then *ipso facto* the contrary intention is retracted and the intention of the bad action is had implicitly. For instance, if a man participates

32. "Cooperatio dividitur in formalem, si cooperans tum ad intentionem tum ad actionem pravam concurrit, et in materialem, si solum ad actionem pravam concurrit" [H. Noldin et al., *Summa theologiae moralis* v. 2 §117].

33. "Qui furi tradit claves, *ut* furari *possit*, formaliter cooperatur, si illum in peccato furti iuvare intendit, et materialiter cooperatur, si claves, quibus ille ad furandum abutitur, ex alio fine e. g. ad propriam vitam servandam subministrat" [Noldin v. 2 §117, emphasis in the original].

in the divine worship of heretics, he cooperates formally, even though he says that he does not intend this.[34]

The person mentioned by Noldin who "participates in the divine worship of heretics" is presumably not under great pressure to do so. Unless he is under great pressure to participate in the "divine worship of heretics" – as were, for instance, recusant Catholics in Elizabethan England – he does intend to participate, "even though he says that he does not intend this."[35]

In Noldin's subsequent remarks on material cooperation, he uses as examples certain instances of (1) cooperation with fornication or adultery and (2) cooperation with the killing of another.[36] Noldin's grounds for saying that they amount to merely material cooperation are that the cooperator does not have the intention – either explicitly or implicitly – of participating in the sin of the other. In a note appended to the title of this section on cooperation ("De

34. "Cooperatio duplici modo potest esse formalis: α. *explicite* ex intentione cooperantis, qui expresse voluntatem habet participandi in peccato alieno; β. *implicite* ex natura operis, quod praestatur; cum nempe aliquis opus exercet, quod natura sua vel attentis circumstantiis exclusive ad pravam actionem ordinatur: tunc enim ipso facto retractatur intentio contraria et habetur implicite intentio pravae actionis, ut si quis participat in functione sacra haereticorum, formaliter cooperatur, etsi dicat se id non intendere. . . ." [H. Noldin et al., *Summa theologiae moralis* v. 2 §117, emphasis in the original].

35. Noldin draws heavily upon a ten-page note composed by the Augustinian Nicola Cretoni upon the section on cooperation in another Jesuit's manual which he (Cretoni) edited [Cretoni, "Nota I (to v. 1 §249)"]. (The note is about v. 1 §249, p. 159, of I. Gury's *Compendium theologiae moralis*.) Cretoni says that one is culpable of implicit formal cooperation when one is without an excusing reason. He speaks of three ways in which something can be intended: "1) *actualiter* et *explicite*, 2) *habitualiter* seu *virtualiter*, 3) *interpretive* ac *implicite*." Of the latter he says, it "takes place when someone cooperates in the sin of another utterly without any excusing reason" ["Id tamen locum habet cum quis peccato alterius cooperatur absque ulla omnino causa excusante"] [Cretoni, "Nota I (to v. 1 §249)," 574].

36. H. Noldin et al., *Summa theologiae moralis*, v. 2 §117.2–118.3. The principal malefactor in the sexual cases would be the person with whom the cooperator has intercourse. Noldin probably has in mind as cooperator a woman who goes along with a man who is already determined to have illicit intercourse.

cooperatione"), reference is made to his 1879 article, "On cooperation with the sin of one's neighbor."[37] In this article, which goes more thoroughly into the theory behind his necessarily concise remarks in the manual, Noldin comes out decidedly in favor of those who would accept as formal only that cooperation in which the cooperator shares the intention of the malefactor.[38]

On this latter point, Noldin follows Nicola Cretoni.[39] Cretoni considers the case of a cooperator who performs an act that is intrinsically evil, "but in so cooperating in no way does he intend to be involved in the evil will of the other but [he intends] only to protect himself from injury." And he asks, "Will this cooperation then have to be called *formal* or *material*?" Invoking "the dictates of logic" and (less plausibly) Alphonsus, Cretoni answers his own question:

> such cooperation is not *formal* but *material*—although it is certainly illicit. Its character as illicit in this case comes entirely from the immediate object of the cooperator and the intrinsic end of the act and not from the extrinsic end, so that the cooperation in this case is illicit qua *action* and not qua *cooperation*.[40]

37. Hieronymus Noldin, "Über die Mitwirkung zur Sünde des Nebenmenschen." The note, which is at H. Noldin et al., *Summa theologiae moralis*, v. 2 §116, does not appear in the 1902 edition of the manual.

38. In the initial notes to the article [Hieronymus Noldin, "Über die Mitwirkung zur Sünde des Nebenmenschen," 495, nn. 3–4], Noldin refers positively to Nicola Cretoni [Cretoni, "Nota I (to v. 1 §249)"] and to Eduard Stephinsky [Stephinsky, "Über den Begriff der materiellen und formellen Mitwirkung zum Bösen"]. Both of these authors argue strenuously in favor of associating the formality of formal cooperation with the intention of the cooperator.

39. Cretoni (1816–1873) was member of the Augustinian order and a Consultor of what was called then "the Holy Office."

40. "Quid dicendum in casu quo actio ipsa cooperantis sit intrinsece mala, quin tamen sic cooperans ullo modo in tendat ad malam voluntatem alterius concurrere, sed tantum se indemnem servare? Erit tunc cooperatio dicenda *formalis*, vel *materialis*? Iuxta S. Doctoris loquendi modum et logicae dictamina, respondeo, cooperationem eiusmodi non *formalem* sed *materialem* dicendam esse, licet certo illicitam; quae quidem illicitudo tunc tota repetenda est ex immediato cooperationis obiecto et fine operis intrinseco, non autem ex fine extrinseco, ita ut cooperatio in hoc casu illicita sit qua *actio*, non qua

For Cretoni (followed by Noldin), the *only* thing that can bring an act into the category of formal cooperation is the cooperator's intention, which he speaks of here as the extrinsic end (extrinsic, that is, to the intrinsically evil action that amounts to merely material cooperation).

We find something quite different in Aertnys. He sets things out as follows:

Division. Cooperation is distinguished into:

1st *Formal*, which contributes to that which is *formal* in a sin, that is to say, to the bad *will* of the other, truly inciting it or otherwise having a positive influence upon it. This occurs (a) when one furnishes assistance to another – let it be in itself indifferent – with the *intention*, manifest to him, that the other realize his immoral will or that he might act more securely, more easily. And this is *direct* cooperation. I say that the intention is *manifest to the other* since otherwise, however evil the intention might be, the action does not have an influence upon the will of the other. Or it occurs (b) when one furnishes assistance which *by its very nature* is ordered toward evil or is part of it. Thus, cooperation is formal either *because of the end of the act* or *because of the end of agent*.

2nd *Material*, which contributes only to that which is *material* in a sin, or to the bad *action* of the other, beside the intention of the cooperator – which occurs in furnishing assistance to another which is in itself indifferent and which the other abuses in order to sin.[41]

---

cooperatio" [Cretoni, "Nota I (to v. 1 §249)," 569, emphasis in original]. See also Stephinsky, "Über den Begriff der materiellen und formellen Mitwirkung zum Bösen," 348–51. See also above, notes 35 and 38.

41. "Divisio. Cooperatio distinguitur: 1° *Formalis*, quae concurrit ad *formale* peccati, seu ad malam *voluntatem* alterius, eam nempe excitando aut aliter in eam positive influendo: quod contingit (a) alteri operam praestando, esto ex se indifferentem, *ea intentione* illi manifestata ut alter suam pravam voluntatem exsequatur, aut id securius, facilius faciat; et haec est cooperatio *directa*; dico: intentione *alteri minifestatata*; quia secus, quantumvis prava sit intentio, actio in alterius voluntatem non influit ; (b) praestando operam, quae suapte natura ad malum ordinata est, vel pars illius est. Cooperatio ergo formalis est vel *ex fine operis* vel *ex fine operantis*. [2°] *Materialis*, quae concurrit tantum ad *materiale* peccati, seu ad malam *actionem* alterius, praeter intentionem cooperantis; quod contingit praestando operam, quae ex se indifferens est, at qua alter abutitur ad peccandum" [Aertnys, *Theologia moralis secundum doctrinam S. Alfonsi de Ligorio doctoris ecclesiae*, 2.76 (v. 1 p. 149), emphasis in the original].

In the first phrase of the first section here, with its reference to the bad will [voluntas] of the malefactor, one already sees that Aertnys is making use of the will/intention distinction, as in Alphonsus. Noldin in fact acknowledges this, remarking after his own division of cooperation that Alphonsus's, as interpreted by Aertnys, speaks of formal cooperation as contributing to the will [voluntas] of the malefactor and having a positive influence upon it. As a consequence, he says, "many particular questions are resolved by the holy doctor [Alphonsus] – and also by other authors – not in the same way" (i.e., as Noldin resolves them).[42]

How Aertnys's approach diverges from Noldin's becomes especially apparent in the last sentence of the paragraph on formal cooperation. Aertnys includes within formal cooperation the cooperation of one whose intention manifestly coincides with that of the malefactor; but he also says that this might be effected simply by performing an act that is intrinsically ordered toward evil. This sounds not unlike Noldin's recognition of cooperation that is formal implicitly, "because of the nature of the act supplied." But Aertnys adds that formal cooperation is due either to the end of the act [ex fine operis] or to the end of agent [ex fine operantis]. For Noldin, the *only* thing that can bring an act into the category of formal cooperation is the cooperator's intention, acknowledgment of which might, however, be resisted by the agent himself. For Aertnys formal cooperation might be owing *either* to the end intended and shared by both malefactor and cooperator *or* to the end of the act that the cooperator performs.[43]

42. "Aliam notionem cooperationis formalis exhibet s. Alphonsus (n. 63), qui illam cooperationem dicit formalem, *quae concurrit ad malam voluntatem alterius*, 'eam nempe excitando aut aliter in eam positive influendo,' ut interpretatur *Aertnys*. Inde fit, ut complures quaestiones particulares a s. doctore non eodem modo atque ab aliis auctoribus solvantur" [H. Noldin et al., *Summa theologiae moralis*, v. 2 §117]. Noldin appears to concede that Aertnys has Alphonsus right. (This remark, incidentally, appears also in earlier editions of Noldin's manual, such as the 1906 edition, so the formulations referred to are not the ones that appears in later editions, such as the 1967 Aertnys-Damen-Visser edition.)

43. Editions of Aertnys's manual published after his death in 1915 move in the

VI. Into the Mix: Another Jesuit and a Dominican

As is acknowledged on all sides, then, what motivates Aertnys's thesis that formal cooperation includes acts of cooperation in which the cooperator does not share the malefactor's intention is his desire to follow Alphonsus – who, if occasionally confused, is at least *less* Cartesian than Noldin and Cretoni.[44] As we have seen, Alphonsus

---

direction of Noldin's manual. In the 9th edition (of 1918–19), the first under the editorship of Cornelius Damen, we read: "Cooperation is distinguished into formal and material cooperation.1. Foraml cooperation is that which 'contributes to the bad will of the other' [he gives a note here referring to Alphonsus's definition], that is, that which includes formal consent to the very sin of the other. This, however, can happen in two ways: first, by virtue of the agent's end, when someone contributes an action with precisely the intention that the other execute his vicious will or execute it more easily; secondly, by virtue of the end of the action, when someone contributes an action which by its nature is ordered toward the sin only, for then necessarily he implicitly gives consent to the sin, for the end of the action enters into the essence of the thing [done]. Who, therefore, wills the thing [done], necessarily wills the end of the action. Thus, for example, of the following each is formal cooperation: to construct an instrument suitable only for impeding generation [of a child]; to publish books against religion; on the order of a lord, to invite a concubine to get together with the master, and so on" ["Cooperatio distinguitur in cooperationem formalem et materialem. 1. Cooperatio formalis ea est "quae concurrit ad malam voluntatem alterius," i. e. ea, quae includit consensum formalem in ipsum peccatum alterius. Hoc autem contingere potest dupliciter: 1° ex fine operantis, quando quis operam praestat, ea praecise intentione, ut alter pravam voluntatem suam exsequatur seu facilius exsequatur; 2° ex fine operis, quando quis operam praestat, quae ex natura sua ad solum peccatum ordinatur; tunc enim necessario implicite dat consensum in peccatum; nam finis operis intrat in essentiam rei; qui ergo vult rem, necessario vult finem operis. Sic v. g. est cooperatio formalis conficere instrumenta, solum ad generationem impediendam apta, in lucem edere libros contra religionem, jussu heri invitare concubinam ut rem cum domino habeat, etc."] [Joseph Aertnys and Cornelius Damen, *Theologia moralis secundum doctrinam S. Alfonsi de Ligorio Doctoris Ecclesiae* (Galopia [Gulpen]: Alberts Filii, 1918–1919^{9}), 2.3.6.3 (§398)]. Similar language appears also in the 1967 (Aertnys-Damen-Visser) edition, except that the definition of formal cooperation (not presented as a quotation but with the same references to Alphonsus) runs as follows: "Cooperatio distinguitur in cooperationem formalem et materialem. 1° Cooperatio formalis ea est quae concurrit ad formale peccati alterius, seu ad ipsius malam voluntatem, ita ut necessaria includat consensum in ipsum peccatum" [Aertnys, Damen, and Visser, *Theologia moralis secundum doctrinam S. Alfonsi de Ligorio Doctoris Ecclesiae*, 2.3.6.3 (§353)].

44. On Cartesianism, see the introduction above, at (and including) notes 3 and 4.

states in *Theologia moralis* 2 n. 63 (1) that formal cooperation "cannot be without sin [nequit esse sine peccato]," (2) that, in material cooperation, the cooperating is "beside the intention of the one who cooperates [praeter intentionem cooperantis]," and (3) that acts of material cooperation are "per se good or indifferent." But he also says in *Theologia moralis* 2 n. 67 (and elsewhere) that actions such as writing amorous letters and serving as a lookout, even if one is forced to perform them, are formal cooperation.[45] All this would seem to entail that such actions are necessarily evil and not indifferent.[46] Accordingly, Aertnys insists that the second type of formal cooperation – described at (b) in the block quotation above from him – is the furnishing of "assistance which *by its very nature* is ordered toward evil or is part of it"; he says also that material cooperation is "in itself indifferent." Aertnys clearly holds that the difference between formal and material cooperation can be made precise by means of the notion of indifference (as he understands it).

Ironically, it is precisely this issue of indifference that leads Noldin to say that one cooperates formally only when one shares the intention of the malefactor. In this regard, Noldin again follows Cretoni, who exploits the very inconsistency in Alphonsus we noted earlier, although he hones in on another passage in the Theologia moralis. In the writing in question, Cretoni is always very deferential to Alphonsus (who had recently been declared a Doctor of the Church), never really saying that the saint was *wrong*; but he does put forward a way of understanding some of Alphonsus's assertions that is in tension with other of his assertions.[47]

45. At the very end of the passage quoted above and in note 41, Aertnys cites Alphonsus's *Theologia moralis* 2, §§59 and 63 as well as the passage quoted above in note 11 from *Homo apostolicus*.

46. If one supposes a sort of formal cooperation that is *praeter intentionem* and of an indifferent character, it would meet the criteria for material cooperation and so no longer be formal; the idea would also appear to be incompatible with Alphonsus's statement that formal cooperation "cannot be without sin" – for indifferent acts can be without sin.

47. As was mentioned in the introduction, Alphonsus was canonized in 1839 and declared Doctor of the Church in 1871. Cretoni's note was published in 1875.

At the start of the pertinent argument, Cretoni quotes first *Theologia moralis* 2 n. 63 (which speaks of acts that "cannot be without sin" and other acts that are "per se good or indifferent") and then *Theologia moralis* 2 n. 66, "Quaeritur 4°" ("It is asked 4thly"), "Whether, out of fear of death or grave injury, it is licit for a servant to lower his shoulders, or to carry a ladder so that his master might ascend and fornicate, or to open the door – and similar things?" Alphonsus, in his answer to this question, sides with those who would permit such cooperation:

> The reason is, as we said just above [in 2 §63], when you contribute an action per se indifferent – that is, which can be both good and evil – you are not obliged except in charity to abstain from it lest another misuse it in order to sin but, when you fear grave injury otherwise, you can licitly permit the sin of the other. For, on the one hand, charity does not oblige you with grave injury to avert his sin, while, on the other hand, another's wickedness cannot alter the nature of your action in such a way that from an indifferent action it becomes [evadat] intrinsically evil. [*Theologia moralis* 2 §66]

Cretoni puts the penultimate phrase, "another's wickedness cannot alter the nature of your action," in all caps: malitia alterius nequit mutare naturam tuae actionis.[48] He is asking implicitly, How can we not apply this principle also to those acts that Alphonsus calls formal cooperation and which yet involve acts that are not intrinsically evil – acts such as writing amorous letters and acting as a lookout? The only way to do so would be to say that they are intrinsically evil because of their connection with the bad actions of the malefactor; but that route is blocked by the principle that "the other's wickedness cannot alter the nature of your action."

Allowing that a mere circumstance – "that is to say, of a connection (sufficiently known and foreseen) between the cooperation and the sin of the other person" – could change an indifferent act into one that is intrinsically evil, would seem, says Cretoni, to create problems in the resolution of cases involving cooperation.[49] There is a way,

48. Cretoni, "Nota I (to v. 1 §249)," 572.

49. "Nevertheless, since a circumstance of this sort, that is to say, of a connection

however, he says, of saving the theory. One must introduce into the theory – which otherwise "limps" ["claudicat"] – a distinction between two types of circumstance: one that "affects the act itself intrinsically," the other that "only accompanies [the act], without affecting the substance of the same."[50] The latter type would include "a connection ... between the cooperation and the sin of the other person," so that such a connection could not affect the substance of the cooperator's act, making an indifferent act to be intrinsically evil.

Writes Cretoni:

(sufficiently known and foreseen) between the cooperation and the sin of the other person, especially in the case of great propinquity, so moves some that for this very reason they maintain that there would be certain actions, by virtue of their object and end either good or indifferent, which are, at least in the concrete, seemingly to be regarded as intrinsically evil, while, on the other hand, particularly in this regard, in the resolution of positions regarding cases, a difference of opinion becomes manifest, which in this regard seems hardly superfluous, [therefore] this question ought to be examined carefully also in some other respect and the doubt emerging therefrom resolved" ["Verum cum eiusmodi circumstantia, coniunctionis videlicet (satis cognitae aut praevisae) inter cooperationem et alterius peccatum, praesertim in casu magnae propinquitatis, adeo nonnullos moveat, ut ob hanc ipsam rationem habendas putent, saltem in concreto, tamquam intrinsece malas actiones quasdam, ex obiecto et fine vel bonas vel indifferentes, atque inde potissimum in casuum resolutione sententiarum discrepantia oriatur, idcirco haud superfluum videbitur, quaestionem hanc sub alio quoque respectu perpendere, ac dubium inde emergens resolvere" [Cretoni, "Nota I (to v. 1 §249)," 572].

50. "Added aspects that affect an act itself intrinsically are not to be confused with those that only accompany the act without affecting its substance" ["confundenda minime sunt adiuncta quae actum ipsum intrinsecus afficiunt, cum his quae eumdem tantummodo comitantur, quin afficiunt eiusdem substantiam"] [Cretoni, "Nota I (to v. 1 §249)," 573]. There is, in fact, a basis for this distinction in the passage in Aristotle's *Nicomachean Ethics* typically associated – also by Thomas Aquinas – with the "circumstances" of human acts. The passage is found at *EN* 3.1.1111a3–21, especially 1111a18–19; but see also Kevin L. Flannery, *Action and Character According to Aristotle: The Logic of the Moral Life* (Washington, D.C.: The Catholic University of America Press, 2013), 110–38. Note, however, that at this point Cretoni cites a passage in Salvator Tongiorgi that makes quite a different distinction from what is found in Aristotle and Thomas: see Salvator Tongiorgi, *Institutiones philosophiæ moralis Salvatoris Tongiorgi e Societate Iesu ab eodem in compendium redactae* (Rome: B. Morini, 1863), lb. 1 cap. 3 a. 3 §157. We will consider this passage – and Cretoni's use of it – in chapter 2.

And so it is also to be denied that the particular addition of a connection or a link – be it even quite close between the action of the cooperator and the sin of the other – might affect the substance of the cooperation to the extent that an action in itself good or indifferent might come out [evadat], on account of this addition, intrinsically evil, for such an addition is not of the type of additions which affect intrinsically the immediate object of the cooperation.[51] And so ... it appears that one can conclude that wholly false is the opinion that maintains that *actions by their very nature good or indifferent, on account of proximity of the cooperation to the sin of the other, become intrinsically evil.*[52]

Notable here are two things: first, the insistence that what is at issue is whether the substance of the act of cooperation can change because of its link to the bad act of the malefactor; secondly, that talk of proximity to the bad act of the malefactor is irrelevant.

In an earlier passage, Cretoni speaks similarly, although there he also identifies two of his opponents in these regards. In the passage he first says that, if one allows the link to change the species, it becomes impossible to say that any type of cooperation is licit. He then acknowledges that certain opponents of his would have an answer to this argument.

They indeed could respond that they are speaking not of any connection or link whatsoever but only of one that is more proximate or (in any case) of the highest degree. So argue, among others, de Cardenas and Milante, with

51. Perhaps Cretoni has in mind Thomas's *ST* 1-2.18.10c: "Et ideo quod in uno actu accipitur ut circumstantia superaddita obiecto quod determinat speciem actus, potest iterum accipi a ratione ordinante ut principalis conditio obiecti determinantis speciem actus."

52. "Deinde negandum etiam, quod peculiare adiunctum coniunctionis et nexus, licet propinquioris inter actionem cooperantis et alterius peccatum, cooperationis substantiam eo usque afficiat, ut actio de se bona vel indifferens, evadat ob eiusmodi adiunctum intrinsece mala, quia eiusmodi adiunctum non est de illoram genere quae immediatum cooperationis obiectum intrinsecus afficiunt. Quapropter ex dictis super hoc primo ac praecipuo theoriae capite, de intrinseca scilicet bonitate vel malitia actionis, concludi posse videtur, falsam omnino esse sententiam quae tenet, *actiones natura sua bonas aut indifferentes, ob proximitatem cooperationis peccato alterius, fieri intrinsece malas*" [Cretoni, "Nota I (to v. 1 §249)," 573, emphasis in the original].

respect to Innocent XI's 51st condemned proposition. But neither does such a distinction help them in any respect at all, for a different degree of connection – or in general, the more and the less – do not change the species, that is, the nature of an action, even if in some other respect the idea of greater or lesser proximity to a sin in cooperation ought to be considered (as will be seen below) and ought to be considered quite generally.[53]

The position maintained by Juan de Cardenas, SJ (1613–84) and Pius Thomas Milante, OP (d. 1749) in their commentaries on Pope Innocent XI's condemnation, is rejected also by Alphonsus, immediately before he gives his definitions of formal and material cooperation:

In distinguishing, however, when cooperation is material and when formal, others – such as de Cardenas and Master Milante – say that cooperation is material when it per accidens and remotely leads to the sin of the other, but formal when per se or on account of some adjoined circumstance it leads proximately to the performance of the sin, even if per se it might be indifferent. But it is better with others to say that that cooperation is formal which [and so on]. [*Theologia moralis* 2 §63]

53. "Possent ipsi quidem respondere, non de qualibet coniunctione aut nexu etiam remoto id se affirmare, sed tantum de proximiori, aut maximi saltem gradus. Sic, inter alios Cardenas et Milante, in prop. 52 [sic] ab Innoc. XI damnatam. Sed nec huiusmodi distinctio sub ullo prorsus respectu eisdem suffragatur; nam diversus coniunctionis gradus, seu generatim *magis et minus non mutant speciem id est actionis naturam*, licet sub alio respectu, maioris vel minoris propinquitatis ad peccatum in cooperatione, ratio quidem habenda sit, ut infra videbitur, eaque communiter habeatur" [Cretoni, "Nota I (to v. 1 §249)," 571, emphasis in original]. The last phrase in the quotation refers to Cretoni's later (pp. 575–76) treatment of proximity to the act of the malefactor; he cites there Alphonsus's *Theologia moralis* 2 §78 (on usury). Cretoni also speaks in the quotation of one of the propositions condemned by Innocent XI in the bull of 1679 *Sanctissimus Dominus*. Cretoni's text refers to proposition 52; he means proposition 51. (This has been corrected in the translation.) The passages in de Cardenas and Milante would be: (1) Juan de Cardenas, *Crisis theologica, in qua plures selectæ difficultates ex morali theologia ad Lydium veritatis lapidem revocantur ex regula morum posita a SS.D.N. Innocentio XI. P.M. in diplomate damnante sexaginta quinque propositiones* (Seville: Typis Thomœ Lopez de Haro, 1687), dis. 31 638–40 and (2) Pius-Thomas Milante, *Exercitationes dogmatico-morales in propositiones proscriptas a SS. Innocentio XI* (Naples: Ex typographia Januarii, et Vincentii Mutio, 1739), ex. 28 300–303.

We shall come back to these two figures and their ideas in the next chapter. For the moment, we simply acknowledge that Cretoni's approach is, of course, hard to reconcile with what Alphonsus says at *Theologia moralis* 2 §67 about the servant's writing or conveying amatory letters: that is to say, that such actions are "never licit since they cooperate formally in the sin of the master." It also lays the theoretical basis for Noldin's decision to limit formal cooperation to cooperation in which the cooperator either performs an action immoral by virtue of its object (an action such as murder itself or adultery itself) or has the same intention as the malefactor.

Following Cretoni, therefore, Noldin is decidedly adverse to declaring acts to be intrinsically evil. One of the standard examples of formal cooperation employed in literature was the manufacture of pagan idols. But Noldin, in his 1879 article, points out that such an object *could* be used as an ornament in a park.[54] He goes on in the same place to mention a number of acts that some regard as intrinsically evil: selling poison or a weapon to a murderer, calling people to an heretical sermon by ringing a bell ("an invitation to blasphemy"), constructing a temple for false gods ["Götzentempel zu bauen"]. None of these acts, he insists, is intrinsically evil, since all of them – selling a weapon, ringing a bell, constructing a building – can be performed quite faultlessly. He points also to what he clearly regards as the inadequacy of a thesis maintained by "the older moralists": that, if when a servant invites a woman to sin with his master that end is specified, he performs an intrinsically evil act, but, if that end is not specified, he does not. Finally, he mentions the moral problem of a Catholic attendant in a hospital who is asked by a non-Catholic "to fetch the minister of a false religion." Noldin is implicitly asking, Is this to perform an intrinsically evil act?

He concludes at this point that the following "is entirely true":

54. See Hieronymus Noldin, "Über die Mitwirkung zur Sünde des Nebenmenschen," 510; see also Stephinsky, "Über den Begriff der materiellen und formellen Mitwirkung zum Bösen," 346–47.

> That which is in itself evil has according to its nature only a bad use and is always and in every instance bad since it maintains its morally bad nature under all circumstances. That which can have also a good use must therefore in itself at least be indifferent and its sinfulness derive from a circumstance, from which one can abstract and in the assessment of which morality also must abstract.[55]

He goes on then explicitly to reject Alphonsus's position, as set out in *Theologia moralis* 2 §65, that it is intrinsically immoral for a servant to bear a gift to his master's lover or, as in *Theologia moralis* 2 §67, to convey letters to her. He allows, however, that "at the most" [höchstens] bearing the gift of a "pornographic picture [ein unschamhaftes Bild]" or a "provocative love letter [Sünde reizende Liebesbriefe]" is intrinsically bad – "even if," he says, "in a particular instance, it leaves the recipient cold." He says nothing about *writing* amorous letters.

So, emerging from a reading of the relevant texts in Alphonsus, Noldin, Aertnys, and Cretoni (not to mention de Cardenas and Milante, whose writings are here yet to be examined) are a number of problems. In the next chapter, these problems are again considered, but with the help of Thomas Aquinas's thoughts on indifference and related concepts.

55. "Aus der obigen Darlegung ergibt sich, daß folgender Satz ganz wahr ist: was in sich böse ist, das hat seiner Natur nach nur einen schlechten Gebrauch und ist immer und überall schlecht, weil seine moralisch schlechte Natur unter allen Umständen beibehalt; was auch einen guten Gebrauch haben kann, das muss daher in sich wenigstens indifferent sein und seine Sündhaftigkeit von einem Umstande herleiten, von dem man absehen kann and bei Beurtheilung der Moralität auch ablehen muß" [Hieronymus Noldin, "Über die Mitwirkung zur Sünde des Nebenmenschen," 511–12].

CHAPTER 2 CIRCUMSTANCES, HUMAN ACTS, AND INDIFFERENCE

One curious fact emerges in a prominent way from the previous chapter: that Alphonsus (followed by Aertnys), on the one hand, and Cretoni (followed by Noldin), on the other, employ the notion of act-indifference to quite contrary purposes. Alphonsus uses it as support for his more extensive category of formal cooperation, which includes some acts in which the cooperator does not share the intention of the malefactor (as when a servant writes amorous letters for his master but only out of "grave fear"); Cretoni uses it in order to argue against the inclusion of such actions and thus to restrict (by contrast with Alphonsus's treatment) the category of formal cooperation.

Another curious – and, as we shall see, connected – fact is that both Alphonsus and Cretoni reject the approach to cooperation they associate with Juan de Cardenas and Pius-Thomas Milante. As we have seen, just before introducing his own definitions of formal and material cooperation, Alphonsus notes that some moralists –

> such as de Cardenas and Master Milante – say that cooperation is material when it per accidens and remotely leads to the sin of the other, but formal when, per se or on account of some adjoined circumstance, it leads proxi-

mately to the performance of the sin, even if per se it might be indifferent. [*Theologia moralis* 2 §63]

Alphonsus then says, "But it is better with others to say . . . ," and then he follows his definitions of material and formal cooperation (examined above, in chapter 1). Cretoni quotes the same passage from Alphonsus; his whole subsequent argument, against the idea that proximity to a malefactor's act could alter the substance or species of an act of cooperation, is directed against de Cardenas and Milante.[1]

In Alphonsus's brief description of the de Cardenas-Milante approach, a couple of things stand out: circumstances and proximity (to the sin of the malefactor). We will consider here circumstances, the investigation of which also turns up ideas having to do with proximity. The particular point is that an approach that considers circumstances together with proximity is more useful than one that focuses upon act-indifference. More generally, although the formal/material distinction, especially as understood by Alphonsus, serves some purpose as an approximate way of indicating what cooperation is morally acceptable and what cooperation is not, more sustainable theoretically is the Thomistic approach, which obsesses neither about intention nor indifference. Thomas, as we shall see, clearly regards intention as an important factor in the analysis of human acts, but not in any sense that excludes the possible importance – even the predominance – of other factors in particular acts. While recognizing that any act might in the abstract be seen as indifferent, he also holds that an act might be recognized as not indifferent quite independently of either its object or the intention with which it is performed; it might, for instance, be recognized as immoral simply by virtue of the fact (the circumstance) that it is closely related to the evil act of another.

But, before getting into such matters, we must first understand what are the circumstances.

1. Cretoni, "Nota I (to v. 1 §249)," 571–74.

I. Circumstances: *Nicomachean Ethics* 3.1

In his remarks on the circumstances of human acts, Thomas is dealing with a complicated tradition, the basis of which is found in Aristotle, although the edifice itself was constructed by theoreticians of rhetoric. Thomas uses both these sources, although his account remains basically Aristotelian. The rhetorical understanding – and, in particular, the very concept of a circumstance as something that "stands around" another thing without entering into it – gives him the means of resolving certain ambiguities in Aristotle's presentation and of developing an account of how some factors, sometimes correctly described as extraneous to actions, can also attach to actions with various degrees of proximity. (For instance, the fact that Mr. X's act helps along another's bad act might not be Mr. X's responsibility; that is a circumstance, therefore, that does not enter into his act. But it could also be that that fact does enter into his act, either proximately or remotely.) Accordingly, Thomas insists that rhetoric is not wholly distinct from considerations of good and evil and so is not distinct from ethics.[2] But (again) his actual theorizing about human action is, at heart, Aristotelian.

Aristotle introduces the circumstances in the beginning section of the third book of his *Nicomachean Ethics*.[3] That book begins with the statement that involuntary are "those things that come about either because of force [βίᾳ] or through ignorance [δι' ἄγνοιαν]."[4] Obviously, the issue of force – which can sometimes be partial and therefore not wholly exclude the voluntary – is very often a factor in the analysis of acts of cooperation, and we shall have something to say about it in

2. *Sent.* 4.16.3.1.1 ad 1.

3. *EN* 3.1 1111a3–6. The circumstances are also mentioned in Aristotle's *Eudemian Ethics*: *EE* 2.9 1225b2–7. Most scholars regard book 2 of *EE* as earlier than book 3 of *EN*. One can find an extensive treatment of circumstances as Aristotle understood them in chapter 4 of Flannery, *Action and Character According to Aristotle*.

4. *EN* 3.1 1109b35–1110a1. I consider these two factors, force and ignorance, more extensively in chapter 4, sections III and V.

chapter 4 (section III). But for the moment we are interested simply in the circumstances, which have more particularly to do with one's ignorance — or knowledge — of what one is doing when performing an action. Depending on the type of ignorance involved, one's ignorance or knowledge of what one is doing has a bearing upon one's culpability for what one does. The type of ignorance that excuses actions that would otherwise be immoral is ignorance that is in no sense voluntary.[5]

Aristotle's list of the aspects of an act (the circumstances) of which one might be ignorant runs as follows:

> (1) who, (2) what, (3) about what — or (4) within what — someone acts; sometimes also (5) with what (e.g. what instrument), (6) to what end (e.g. for safety), (7) and how (e.g. whether gently or aggressively).[6]

Aristotle himself goes on immediately to say that one can hardly be unaware of who is acting when one acts [*EN* 3.1 1111a6], so it is apparent that, although they are introduced under the rubric of the involuntary by reason of ignorance, the things mentioned in this list might also be *known* — and, indeed, it is only when (in some sense) a circumstance is known that it becomes a genuine factor in the moral analysis of an act.[7] When a person knows that he is king of a sovereign realm — and, as Aristotle notes, he could hardly not know this — and utters the words "off with his head" at the end of a criminal trial, cir-

5. On this issue, see Flannery, *Action and Character According to Aristotle*, 113–18. See also *ST* 1-2.19.5–6 and the very good commentary on it by Richard Schenk, "*Perplexus supposito quodam*: Notizen zu einem vergessenen Schlüsselbegriff thomanischer Gewissenslehre," *Recherches de théologie ancienne et médiévale* 57 (1990): 62–95.

6. (1) τίς τε δὴ καὶ (2) τί καὶ (3) περὶ τί ἢ (4) ἐν τίνι πράττει, ἐνίοτε δὲ καὶ (5) τίνι, οἷον ὀργάνῳ, καὶ (6) ἕνεκα τίνος, οἷον σωτηρίας, καὶ (7) πῶς, οἷον ἠρέμα ἢ σφόδρα [*EN* 3.1 1111a3–6]. I have interjected the numbers for easier reference. The Latin version of this list that Thomas would have read is as follows: "(1) quis utique et (2) quid et (3) circa quid vel (4) in quo operatur, quandoque autem et (5) quo, puta instrumento, et (6) gratia cuius, puta salutis, et (7) qualiter, puta quiete vel vehementer."

7. The circumstances mentioned in the parenthesis at *EE* 2.9 1225b3–5 are presented as things of which the agent is aware.

cumstance (1), what we can refer to as 'the who,' is an essential aspect of what he does in saying "off with his head."[8]

Aristotle offers examples of the second element in the list, 'the what.' One might claim, for instance, that 'I did not know that it was a secret' or 'I did not know that it (the catapult) was loaded' (*EN* 3.1 1111a8–11): that is, I did not know *what* I was doing. In such cases, what one does is independent of what one intends to do. As with 'the who,' however, one might not be ignorant of what one is doing, even while 'the what' remains distinct from what one intends to do. A custodian, for instance, might know that, by opening a strong-box, he is helping a thief to steal its contents: he knows that that is *what* he is doing, helping the thief to steal, even though he may not want the thief to succeed in stealing. St. Thomas speaks of 'the what' as the "exterior act" (see *ST* 1-2.18.6).

The third and fourth elements in the list – 'the about what' and 'the within what' (one acts) – both make reference to what Thomas calls the object of the act. The two are not wholly distinct from each other, as is indicated by the syntax of Aristotle's list at this point: "about what – or within what – someone acts."[9] The theory behind them is set out in book five of Aristotle's *Physics*. A movement, such as a human act, goes toward something. 'Breaking a window,' for instance, goes toward a window, so the window (to some extent) gives that act its species or substance. (If there was no window there, neither would there be a breaking of a window.) On the other hand, there are various types of movement that might have a window as their end point: washing a window, for example, or removing a window. So, in order to correctly identify the object of 'breaking a window,' one must speak not only of the window but also of the context within which it is the terminus of a movement, that context being a breaking. Now one might break a window and be wholly (and non-culpably) igno-

8. To say, however, that something is an essential aspect of an act is not to say that such a circumstance enters into the substance of the act. (The importance of this distinction will become apparent below.)

9. καὶ περὶ τί ἢ ἐν τίνι πράττει [*EN* 3.1 1111a4].

rant of doing so; but, just as with the other elements in Aristotle's list, one might not be so ignorant: one might know that one is *breaking* a *window*. In this case, 'the about what' and/or 'the within what' are constitutive parts of what one is doing.

Elements (5) and (7), 'the with what' (instrument) and 'the how' (gently or violently or whatever) can be treated similarly, that is, as either what one is ignorant of or what one is aware of; we need not discuss them any further here. But the sixth element, 'the to what end' [ἕνεκα τίνος] is more complicated – and (of course) quite important for the moral analysis of cooperation. The end to which Aristotle refers here is not necessarily the end that the agent has in mind when he performs the act in question. We know this from an example he gives in the *Eudemian Ethics*, where he refers in this regard to the myth of the daughters of Pelias who, relying on Medea who wants Pelias dead, believe erroneously that in dismembering their father and boiling his body parts they will make him young again [*EE* 2.9.1225b2–3]. Here the true end is something of which the daughters are unaware: their end is rather to restore their father's health. It is also worth mentioning (again, since it is important for understanding cooperation) that, as with the other elements in Aristotle's list, an agent need *not* be ignorant of an end, whether it be his own or the end of another with whom the agent cooperates. When that is the case, that circumstance (the end) becomes a part of the act performed.

One final thing should be noted before moving on to Thomas. Having listed the aspects of actions of which an agent might be ignorant or aware and so with respect to which he might act either involuntarily or voluntarily, Aristotle says that two of them are "the most principal."[10] These are the object – alternatively referred to by means of the expression 'within what' (an action is) – and 'the to what end.'

10. κυριώτατα δ' εἶναι δοκεῖ ἐν ᾧ ἡ πρᾶξις καὶ οὗ ἕνεκα [*EN* 3.1 1111a18–19]. The text is corrupt; on this reading of it, see Flannery, *Action and Character According to Aristotle*, 130–31. In his commentary on this passage, Thomas says that these "most principal" circumstances "appear to be the things 'in which the act is,' that is, the object of the

II. Circumstances: *ST* 1-2.7.3 and *De malo* 2.6, Section I

That then is how Aristotle understands the elements in his list. As mentioned above, however, Aristotle's remarks in the *Nicomachean Ethics* are not the only source that Thomas cites in discussing the circumstances. Toward the beginning of his analysis of human action, that is, in *ST* 1-2.7.3, where he is basically setting out the vocabulary to be used later, Thomas asks, "Whether the circumstances are suitably enumerated in the third book of [Aristotle's] *Ethics*."[11] He quotes a mnemonic verse often found in one form or another in various medieval texts: "Quis, quid, ubi, quibus auxiliis, cur, quomodo, quando" ["Who, what, where, by what means, why, how, when"], which he attributes to Cicero's rhetorical writings, noting that Aristotle's list is somewhat different. (Aristotle adds "about what [circa quid]," which, Thomas says, Cicero includes under "what [quid].")[12] The verse does not appear as such in Cicero, although it does appear in, for instance, Boethius and Nemesius. Boethius calls the elements in the list 'circumstances'; Nemesius calls them "circumstantial particles [circumstantivae particulae]."[13]

---

material of the act, and that 'for which,' that is, the end" ["Et dicit quod principalissimae circumstantiae esse videntur in quibus est operatio, idest obiectum sive materia actus, et cuius gratia, idest finis"] [*in EN* 3.3 214–217 (§423)].

11. This is the title given to *ST* 1-2.7.3.

12. *ST* 1-2.7.3c; see also *in EN* 3.3 146-148 (§415) and *Sent.* 4.16.3.1.2 ad 5.

13. When in *ST* 1-2.7.3 Thomas refers to Cicero, the reference appears to be to his *De inventione* [Marcus Tullius Cicero, *Rhetorici libri duo qui vocantur De inventione*, ed. Eduard Stroebel, Bibliotheca Scriptorum Graecorum et Romanorum Teubneriana. (Leipzig: Teubner, 1915), I 24–28 (31b-37b)]. The word *circumstantia* is not used there; note, however, that in I 26 (and further in I 28) he speaks of "adiuncta negotio": "adjuncts" to the affair (or action). In *Sent.* 4.16.3.1, which is about the circumstances, Thomas quotes a passage from I 34 ("Confirmatio est per quam argumentando nostrae causae fidem et auctoritatem et firmamentum adiungit oratio"), although instead of the word 'confirmatio' he has 'circumstantia' [*Sent.* 4.16.3.1.1 obi. 3].

In Boethius (who does speak of circumstances), see Boethius, *De topicis differentiis, libri quatuor*, vol. 64 of Patrologia Latina (Paris: J.-P. Migne, 1847), 1205CD, 1212C–1213A; see also Boethius, *De topicis differentiis*, ed. and trans. Eleonore Stump

This rhetorical tradition is not easy to reconcile with what Aristotle says in *EN* 3.1. The problem is that, speaking literally, a circumstance is something that "stands around" something else without entering into it; but, when (for instance) a person reveals a secret, knowing that it is a secret, that knowledge – that element – does enter into what he is doing.[14] Or take the example of an instrument: if someone strikes someone with an instrument he knows will kill the other and there are other instruments available, his choice of *that* instrument is a factor internal to what he is doing.[15] Also awkward is the

(Ithaca, New York: Cornell University Press, 1978), 79–95. At *Sent.* 4.16.3.1, Thomas associates the circumstances with both Cicero and Boethius.

In Nemesius (whom Thomas thought was Gregory of Nyssa), see chapter 30 ("De involuntario quod est propter ignorantium" – sometimes numbered chapter 31) of his *De natura hominis* [G. Verbeke and J. R. Moncho, eds., *Némésius d'Émesè: De natura hominis, traduction de Burgundio de Pise*, Corpus Latinum Commentarium in Aristotelem Graecorum (Leiden: Brill, 1975), 122–24]. Nemesius attempts to combine Aristotle's talk of "particulars" (or "singulars") at *EN* 3.1 1110b33 (see below, note 14) with the rhetorical tradition that spoke of circumstances: "His ita determinatis deinceps dicendum est, quae sunt singularia. Haec autem sunt, quae vocantur a rhetoricis circumstantivae particulae: quis, quae, ubi, quando, qualiter, propter quid, puta persona, res, organum, locus, tempus, modus, causa."

See René-Antoine Gauthier and Jean Yves Jolif, *L'Éthique à Nicomaque: Introduction, traduction et commentaire* 2nd ed. (Louvain-la-neuve: Éditions Peeters, 2002), II.1 186. See also D. W. Robertson Jr. "A Note on the Classical Origin of 'Circumstances' in the Medieval Confessional," *Studies in Philology* 43, no. 1 (1946): 6–14.

14. See *ST* 1-2.7.1 – in particular, objection 2; see also *De malo* 2.6c: "Dicitur autem circumstantia quod circumstat actum, quasi extrinsecus extra actus substantiam consideratum." In the Aristotelian passage, there is no equivalent of the word 'circumstance' (or 'circumstances'). Aristotle refers to the traditional circumstances simply as the "particulars" (or "singulars") "in which and about which an action is": ἡ [ἄγνοια] καθ' ἕκαστα, ἐν οἷς καὶ περὶ ἃ ἡ πρᾶξις [*EN* 3.1 1110b33–1111a1].

15. In one place, Thomas says that a circumstance that gives a new species to an act is no longer, strictly speaking, a circumstance but is "a specific difference of the moral act." In the passage, Thomas is speaking about adultery: "for example, when a man, in addition to the fact that he approaches a woman not his own, approaches one who is the wife of another, and so there enters in the deformity of injustice, that circumstance thus gives to the act a new species and, properly speaking, it is not now a circumstance, but a specific difference of the moral act comes about" ["puta, cum aliquis super hoc quod accedit ad non suam, accedit ad eam quae est alterius, et sic incidit ibi deformitas iniustitiae; unde

fact that included in Aristotle's list is an act's object ('the about what' and/or 'the within what'). If a circumstance "stands around" the act, how can the circumstances include the element that gives an act its species, as Thomas, following Aristotle, says in *ST* 1-2.18.3?

Thomas is not at all dismayed by this apparent inconsistency between his two sources. On the contrary, he uses the idea of a circumstance as (in some sense) external to the act in order to explain how a factor in the situation in which an act is performed might enter into the act according to various degrees of proximity. The one place where he goes most schematically and deeply into these matters is question 2, article 6, of the *Quaestiones disputatae de malo* [*De malo* 2.6], on "whether a circumstance might give species to a sin or alter its species and thereby transfer it into a different type of sin." This work dates to approximately the same years as the *prima secundae* of the *Summa theologiae* [*ST* 1-2], where we find Thomas's most developed and detailed theory of human action.[16] Because of its importance, in what remains of the present section of this chapter and in the two subsequent sections, we shall examine this article in detail.

The body of *De malo* 2.6, divides in a fairly obvious manner into

---

illa circumstantia dat novam speciem, et proprie loquendo, iam non est circumstantia, sed efficitur specifica differentia actus moralis"] [*De malo* 7.4c]. See Joseph Pilsner, *The Specification of Human Actions in St. Thomas Aquinas* [Oxford University Press, 2006], 193–98.) See also Steven J. Jensen, *Good and Evil Actions: A Journey through Saint Thomas Aquinas* [Washington, D.C.: The Catholic University of America Press, 2010], 112] and Steven J. Jensen, "Do Circumstances Give Species?" *The Thomist* 70, no. 1 (2006): 20–21. Pilsner and Jensen use this (and similar) texts in order to argue that Thomas employed two senses of the word *circumstantia* and thereby to resolve the apparent contradiction between Thomas's sometimes associating the diversification of species with circumstances (as in *Sent.* 4.16.3.2.3), sometimes seemingly denying this association (as in *De malo* 14.3). I propose an alternative solution to this problem below, in section IV.

16. According to Jean-Pierre Torrell, *ST* 1-2 was put together in 1271 and "the Questions *De malo* would have been disputed in Paris during the two academic years 1269–71" [Jean-Pierre Torrell, OP, *St. Thomas Aquinas: The Person and His Work* (Washington, D.C.: The Catholic University of America Press, 1996), 333, 336]. Many of the ideas contained in *De malo* 2.6 are worked out first in *Sent.* 4.16.3.1.2; knowing this is useful for understanding some of the more obscure points in *De malo* 2.6. On circumstances in Thomas, see Jensen, "Do Circumstances Give Species?"

three sections, the topics of which he identifies at its very beginning. In the first section [I], he will consider the question, From what does a sin have species? In the second [II], he will consider the question, What is a circumstance? Having answered these questions, he will be in a position, he suggests, to explain in the third section [III] just how a circumstance gives species to a sin. The body is followed, as usual, by Thomas's responses to the various objections, a couple of which are of particular interest to us.[17]

Thomas opens section [I] with some remarks about the relationship between species and sin. Since moral acts are voluntary, he says, "it is necessary that a moral act have species according to something considered in the object that is related to reason." If this thing accords with reason, the act will be good according to its species; if not, it will be bad according to its species.

Thomas speaks about this relationship also in an earlier work. "Our acts," he says, "are moral according to whether they are ordered by reason with respect to the end of the will." He continues:

> But everything that is ordered toward an end must be proportionate to the end. And so reason, which orders our act toward the end, considers the act's proportion toward those things that might occur together with the act; and this correspondence is called a circumstance.[18]

Most notable here is the Latin word translated "might occur together": it is *concurrere*, the very word that appears in Alphonsus's (and others') definitions of formal and material cooperation.[19] Characterizing this "occurring together" is a proportion – for good or for

17. For a translation of *De malo* 2.6, see appendix 4. In that translation, the text is organized by means of the symbols employed in this chapter: [I], [II], [IIa], [IIa.1], [IIa.2], etc.

18. "Respondeo dicendum ad primam quaestionem, quod actus nostri dicuntur morales secundum quod a ratione ordinantur in finem voluntatis; ex hoc enim habent rationem boni vel mali. Omne autem quod ordinatur ad finem, oportet esse proportionatum fini; et ideo ratio quae actum nostrum in finem ordinat, attendit proportionem actus ad ea quae ad actum concurrere possunt; et ista commensuratio circumstantia dicitur" [*Sent.* 4.16.3.1.1].

19. *Theologia moralis* 2.63.

ill – with respect to the end, which Thomas goes on to identify as the "ultimate end."[20] A circumstance, says Thomas, *is* this proportion or, as he also calls it here, this *commensuratio*.[21] If we connect this passage with the issue of cooperation, it becomes apparent that, for Thomas, an act of cooperation's moral character depends upon its proportion, as determined by at least some circumstance, with respect to the ultimate end. For a particular act to be an immoral act of cooperation with evil would be for a circumstance – in this case, a *dis*proportion with respect to the ultimate end – to pertain to it.

This approach to cooperation is quite different from (although not wholly incompatible with) what we find in the moral manualists, including Alphonsus. There the focus is upon the relationship of the cooperator's act and that of the malefactor; here the act of cooperation is related to ethics itself. To employ again the example used in chapter 1, instead of attending simply to the relationship between the junior doctor assisting at an abortion and the abortionist (and asking, for instance, whether or not the junior doctor's intention coincides with that of the abortionist), an approach framed in terms of circumstances (as in *De malo* 2.6) considers the reasonableness – or, in this case, lack of reasonableness – of the whole event. This is ultimately to consider the injustice done to the innocent victim, the fetus, whether by the abortionist or by his assistant or by both. Regarding cooperation, then, the question would be whether and in what degree the fetus is done an injustice also by the assistant. The answer (as we shall see) depends on the proximity of his action to that of the primary

20. "Ad tertium dicendum, quod est duplex finis, scilicet ultimus et propinquus. Ultimus quidem non potest poni circumstantia, quia omnes circumstantiae sumuntur in proportione ad ipsum" [*Sent.* 4.16.3.1.2 ad 3].

21. Thomas takes the Latin term from Boethius [*De topicis differentiis* 3.1]; the corresponding passage in Aristotle would be *Topics* 3.1 116b26–30 (where the term translated *commensuratio* is ἀνάλογον). The argument has to do with what is relatively better and what is relatively less good. See also *ST* 2-2.6.2 ad 2: "for an act is called deformed on account of a privation of an intrinsic form, which is the appropriate proportion of the circumstances of the act" ["dicitur enim actus deformis per privationem formae intrinsecae, quae est debita commensuratio circumstantiarum actus"].

malefactor, either as an intelligible part of it and/or as enabling it.[22]

But let us consider once again Thomas's statement at the beginning of *De malo* 2.6c that a moral act has its species "according to something considered in the object that is related to reason." Noticeable here is that species, which can come from circumstances, are "in the object." Thomas is insisting here that, whatever role circumstances might have in providing species, the object is still basic. Just as any movement receives its species from its object (recall the example of the window above), so also do moral actions. He mentions eventually here – that is, toward the end of [Ia] – a trio of sins that appears also in *EN* 2.6 1107a11–12: murder, adultery, and theft.[23] Following Aristotle, Thomas regards such actions, qua types of actions, as being necessarily evil. What diversifies them one from the other, he says, is their different objects: their "matter." Murder goes toward an innocent man, adultery toward the wife of another, theft toward what belongs to another.[24] It does not matter with whom or against whom one acts or when or how one performs the act: "to perform any of these acts is simply to go wrong," says Aristotle [*EN* 2.6 1107a16].

But, Thomas goes on to say (in [Ib]), sins can receive species also from more formal considerations.[25] Receiving a species can depend, first, upon whether, with respect to a certain matter which *could* be

22. In chapter 4, section VI (on restitution), such enabling is associated with the concept of "concausality."

23. "*peccata* differunt specie secundum diversas *materias*, puta homicidium, adulterium et furtum" [*De malo* 2.6c] [Ia].

24. Thomas immediately interjects an argument against those who would claim that what are wrong are not murder, adultery, and theft specified according to their matter but rather "killings of the innocent that are prohibited by law," "sexual intercourse with another's wife that is prohibited by law," and "theft that is prohibited by law." "Nor ought it to be said," he interjects, "that these differ in species according to a difference of precepts but rather the converse: precepts are distinguished according to a difference of virtues and vices." On this issue and the passage in *EN* 2.6, see John Finnis, *Moral Absolutes: Tradition, Revision and Truth* (Washington, D.C.: The Catholic University of America Press, 1991), 31–34.

25. The following two considerations are called formal because qualities like "too much" hold *of* some matter; they are not the matter itself.

the matter of a virtue, one pushes things too far or (rather) not at all. The virtue of liberality, for instance, has as its matter money [*ST* 2-2.117.2] (i.e., money given to others). If one acts with respect to this matter either excessively or too rarely, that is a sin. The sin has a certain form or species (prodigality or stinginess) with respect to that matter (money given to others). Thomas makes no mention here of cooperation with evil but [Ib] at least suggests that he would not be adverse to the thesis that the fact that some otherwise good act helps a malefactor could enter into (as a formal factor) the object of that act.

The second formal consideration is more relevant to Thomas's overall argument, for it has to do with the way in which circumstances give species. He uses the example of the sin of gluttony and says that various species of gluttony correspond to the circumstances mentioned in another verse he knew from the tradition: "Precipitously, sumptuously, excessively, rapaciously, fastidiously."[26]

Here in *De malo* 2.6, he does little more than allude to gluttony and its species; in *ST* 2-2.148.4, however, he gives a usefully detailed analysis of what allows for these various species. Gluttony itself he defines as "an inordinate desire to eat." The morally relevant circumstances that might further specify this vice have to do with five aspects that any act must have: (1) its own substance or species given by its object, (2) the quality of that object, (3) the quantity of that object, (4) when the act itself occurs, and (5) how that act is carried out. Thomas notes that (1), (2), and (3) have to do with the object (in the case of gluttony, food), (4) and (5) with the act (here, eating gluttonously).[27]

In an answer to an objection that circumstances, being accidents,

26. "Praepropere, laute, nimis, ardenter, studiose." The verse appears in Alexander of Hales and in Albert the Great.

27. By dividing things in this manner (object/act), Thomas is alluding to the Aristotelian approach we saw above in which an act itself is constituted by its object (the περὶ τί), although that object is an object within a particular practical context (ἐν τίνι). Part of Thomas's reason for associating (2) quality and (3) quantity with the object might also be the fact that quality and quantity are not mentioned either in Aristotle's list or in that of the rhetoricians.

cannot diversify species, Thomas says that the disorder of diverse circumstances does indeed result in [facit] diverse species of gluttony, although it does this "on account of [propter]" diverse motives.[28] We can set out the points that Thomas makes in *ST* 2-2.148.4 (and implicitly in *De malo* 2.6) schematically:

1. If the food sought is extremely costly and that is what motivates one's eating, one's gluttony is specified (characterized) by sumptuousness.
2. If the food is very meticulously prepared and that is what motivates one's eating, one's gluttony is specified by fastidiousness.
3. If the quantity of food is large and one cannot control one's appetite, one's gluttony is specified by excess.
4. If one eats at the wrong time because one cannot stand to wait for one's food, one's gluttony is specified by precipitousness.
5. If one eats out of contempt for good manners, one's gluttony is specified by rapaciousness.

Again, what is important for us to note is that the circumstances that might put an action into a species of sin are aspects that necessarily belong to any act: what, what type, how much, when, how, etc. Sometimes they put the acts in question into particular species of sin, that is, when the particular character of the circumstance has a bearing upon the reasonability of performing that particular act.

28. "Ad primum ergo dicendum quod corruptio diversarum circumstantiarum facit diversas species gulae propter diversa motiva, ex quibus moralium species diversificantur. In eo enim qui quaerit lautos cibos, excitatur concupiscentia ex ipsa specie cibi; in eo vero qui praeoccupat tempus, deordinatur concupiscentia propter impatientiam morae; et idem patet in aliis" [*ST* 2-2.148.4 ad 1]. It is important to bear in mind that when Thomas speaks here of circumstances "diversifying" sins, he does not mean that a species is changed into another (see *De malo* 2.6 ad 7). He means rather that one sin (gluttony), defined by its own object which remains throughout, is diversified into different types: "the corruption of diverse circumstances effects diverse species of gluttony" ["corruptio diversarum circumstantiarum facit diversas species gulae"]. What he says in this (and related) articles does not apply to every instance in which a circumstance gives (or adds) a species; it has to do with the diversification of species.

One might read this argument as a rejoinder to Cretoni's insistence, mentioned in chapter 1, that a connection with "another's wickedness cannot alter the nature of your action."[29] Thomas would doubtless reply, But why not? If the connection (the cooperation) is such as to put your action in conflict with reason, that is what matters, since the morality of human actions depends wholly and entirely upon what is in accordance with reason or justice.

III. Circumstance: *De malo* 2.6, Sections [II] and [III]

In section [II] of *De malo* 2.6, Thomas answers the question, What is a circumstance? He begins by remarking that, "It is said that a circumstance is that which 'stands around' an act, considered as if extrinsically outside of [extrinsecus extra] the substance of the act."[30] His phraseology is doubly hesitant here ("considered as if" [quasi ... consideratum]) because he will go on to say that something which is extrinsic can become intrinsic. He goes on then to say that being a circumstance might occur in three ways: on the part of a cause [ex parte causae], on the part of a measure, on the part of the act itself. These three groupings are then themselves divided. When one compares what Thomas is saying here with the parallel passage in *Sent.* 4.16.3.1.2, one sees that these various divisions are part of an elaborate explanation of how the circumstances considered by the rhetoricians are basically the same things introduced by Aristotle in *EN* 3.1.[31] Accordingly, at the conclusion of this second section of *De malo* 2.6, he quotes the rhetoricians' verse: "Who, what, where, by what means, why, how, when." He immediately adds, however, that this list (the verse) must be understood "in such a way that not only

29. This is the remark he puts "in all caps": "malitia alterius nequit mutare naturam tuae actionis" [Cretoni, "Nota I (to v. 1 §249)," 572].

30. "Dicitur autem circumstantia quod circumstat actum, quasi extrinsecus extra actus substantiam consideratum" [*De malo* 2.6] [II].

31. The explanation can be found at *Sent.* 4.16.3.1.2c: "Ad secundam quaestionem dicendum, quod versus ille distinguit circumstantias secundum assignationem Tullii et Boetii, secundum quod a rhetore considerantur" and so on.

the effect but also the object is included in 'what,' so that both 'what' and 'within what' are understood." This latter point brings the rhetoricians' list into line with Aristotle's.[32]

The question that comes immediately to mind is, How can Aristotle's object ('the what' and 'the within what' someone acts) be understood as "extrinsically outside of the substance of the act"? It sometimes happens with other things, Thomas in effect replies, that "something which is extrinsic to something higher is intrinsic to something lower." For instance, the concept 'rational' is extrinsic to the genus 'animal,' but when we go down to the level of species, 'rational' is intrinsic to man. "In the same way," he says, "something is a circumstance with respect to an act considered more generally which cannot be called a circumstance with respect to an act considered more particularly."[33]

32. "quae omnia continentur hoc versu: 'quis, quid, ubi, quibus auxiliis, cur, quomodo, quando'; ita tamen quod in quid includatur non solum effectus, sed etiam obiectum, ut intelligatur et 'quid' et 'circa quid'" [*De malo* 2.6c] [IIa.3]. Regarding the last phrase, as mentioned, Thomas regards Aristotle's περὶ τί ('the in regard to what [*circa quid*]') as representing the object and would include it among the circumstances [*ST* 1-2.7.3]. There are a couple of differences between the account found in *Sent.* 4.16 and that found in *De malo* 2.6. In the former, Thomas says that the proportion of the act to the ultimate end might be "either according to that which is in the act itself or according to that which is outside" ["Proportio enim actus ad finem potest accipi vel secundum id quod est in ipso actu, vel secundum id quod extra"]. In the first group, he includes 'the what' and 'the how' but not the object and the effect (as in *De malo* 2.6 [IIa.3], where Thomas speaks of "the act itself"). But he also says in *De malo* 2.6 [IIa.3] that these two (object and effect) must be included in 'the what.' (He gives an example of such an effect: "whether striking, he wounded or also killed" ["sive etiam effectum quem agendo induxit, puta utrum percutiendo vulneraverit, vel etiam occiderit"] [IIa.3].) The second group includes all that which is described in *De malo* 2.6 as a circumstance with respect to the act itself: i.e., that which is a circumstance on the part of the cause and that which is such on the part of the measure ([IIa.1] and [IIa.2]). In *ST* 1-2.7.4 ad 3, Thomas appears to downplay the idea that 'the how' is to be associated with the act itself. It is "not the substantial form of the act, for in an act being the substantial form depends upon the object and terminus (or end), but it is a sort of accidental quality" ["Modus etiam non est substantialis forma actus, hoc enim attenditur in actu secundum obiectum et terminum vel finem, sed est quasi quaedam qualitas accidentalis"].

33. "[I]ta aliquid est circumstantia respectu actus communius considerati quod respectu actus magis in speciali considerati, non potest circumstantia dici" [*De malo* 2.6c]

The example he gives is theft. The concept 'belonging to another' [alienum] is extrinsic, for instance, to the act of accepting money. Once, however, we descend into particulars and see that this money belongs to another, 'belonging to another' moves into the act in such a way that it is not a circumstance at all.[34] We might even say that 'belonging to another' is "extrinsically outside of the substance of the act" and is therefore called a circumstance precisely because, once it *is* present in a particular act, it can no longer be called a circumstance.[35] That is, the concept 'belonging to another' in combination with *this money* no longer applies to the substance of the act as a circumstance but constitutes rather that substance itself, just as the *differentia* 'rational' enters into animal and constitutes man. As Thomas has mentioned previously, theft (as also adultery or murder) is an intrinsically evil act in the sense of being evil according to its species. It is so because of "the what" (what it is) and not on account of a circumstance that adheres to that act.

Thomas immediately adds, however, that not every time that something is extrinsic to something of a higher order (as 'rational' is

---

[IIb]. On this passage, see Pilsner, *The Specification of Human Actions in St. Thomas Aquinas*, 194.

34. Thomas's emphasis on particular acts is also seen in *De malo* 2.6 ad 13 "operationes morales sunt in singularibus."

35. See also *Sent.* 4.16.3.2.3 ad 1: "Regarding the first objection, therefore, it must be said that a circumstance that causes some species of sin to be in act pertains to the species of the act in as much as the act is moral; thus, at that point it does not have the character of a circumstance of the sin even though it stands around [circumstet] the substance of the act, as stated previously" ["Ad primum ergo dicendum, quod quaecumque circumstantia aliquam speciem peccati in actu causat, ad speciem actus, inquantum est moralis, pertinet; unde non habet jam rationem circumstantiae peccati, quamvis circumstet substantiam actus, ut prius dictum est"]. The latter reference is to the previous article, where (as in *De malo* 2.6) reference is made to the passage in *EN* about the three intrinsically evil acts (adultery, theft, murder). Thomas says that a circumstance that constitutes such a species of sin "is either not a circumstance (if considered is only the moral genus) or (referring it to the very substance of the act) it is included in the circumstance 'what?'" ["vel non est circumstantia, si consideretur tantum genus moris; vel referendo ad ipsam substantiam actus, includitur in hac circumstantia quid"] [*Sent.* 4.16.3.1.2 ad 3].

to 'animal') and one moves to a lower (more particular) level is the result an independently constituted species. The quality 'white' is also extrinsic to 'animal' and yet 'white animal' is not a particular species of animal. Thomas uses the same example (white) in extending the analogy to the moral field. If the object one accepts is identified as something *white* rather than as something 'belonging to another,' the accepting is not an intrinsically evil type of act. Just as the properly ordered divisions of biology go from a genus to the things that belong to that genus per se – a good biologist divides 'animal' into 'man,' 'horse,' 'dog,' etc., and not into 'brown,' 'green,' and 'white,' since the latter features are not ways of being an *animal* – so also the properly ordered divisions of human acts look to features that pertain to what human acts are per se: products of reason and will. As products of reason and will, their most basic division (that is, into good and bad) looks to whether they are "in accordance with or repugnant to reason."[36] Thus, accepting something that is white does not constitute a specific type of sin.

Thomas sees no theoretical difficulty in considering acts that he regards as evil in species as, in the abstract, indifferent. Taking something that belongs to another is just a taking, just as opening another's strongbox is just an opening. But this has no bearing upon whether in the end a particular act of taking something that belongs to another is intrinsically evil (i.e., evil in its species). Thomas, similarly, would see no theoretical difficulty in saying that an act of cooperation, which might be viewed under some angulation as indifferent, is (given particular circumstances) as bad as any bad act one might encounter. He would have no precise answer to the question whether it is formal or

36. "Iam autem dictum est, quod ad actum moralem aliquid per se pertinet, secundum quod comparatur ad rationem ut conveniens et repugnans" [*De malo* 2.6c] [IIb]. The back reference is to *De malo* 2.6 [I]: "if this thing is in accord with reason, the act will be good with respect to its species; if, however, it is discordant with reason, it will be bad with respect to its species" ["si sit conveniens rationi, erit actus bonus secundum speciem, si autem sit discordans a ratione, secundum speciem malus erit"]. See also *De malo* 2.5 and *ST* 1-2.18.5 and 7.

material cooperation — the question is, in any case, anachronistic — but that is no great disadvantage, for, as we have seen, there is little agreement about the theory standing behind those terms.

Let us get back, however, to *De malo* 2.6. As was announced at the beginning of the body of the article, the next section (section [III]) addresses the question, "Can it be made clear how a circumstance gives species to a sin?" Thomas realizes that he has not yet addressed this question, even in the immediately preceding argument, since the case discussed there does not really amount to a circumstance's *giving* a species to a sin; that argument falls under the general topic of what constitutes a circumstance.

Section III begins with the words: "But to be considered further is that an added circumstance pertaining to reason can constitute a *new* species."[37] The examples he uses are all examples of how a new species might be added to theft, which has its species from its object 'something belonging to another.' Here, though, his formulation of what constitutes theft is altered slightly in order to accommodate one of the examples he uses: adultery. That is, he sometimes speaks of "*using* something belonging to another" [uti re aliena] rather than accepting or taking such a thing since he will be speaking of adultery as a sub-species of theft so understood, i.e., as using something belonging to another.[38] He speaks also in this section of the sacrilege of stealing something from a sacred place. This provides him with an example of a circumstance — "the where" — that places an act within a particular species (sacrilege). Occasionally, however, while discussing the same issue, he will say simply that the object is sacred, not bothering to mention that it is sacred because of the place from which it is taken.

37. "Sed considerandum est ulterius, quod circumstantia addita ad rationem pertinens potest constituere novam speciem peccati dupliciter" [*De malo* 2.6c]

38. Thomas uses the 'uti re aliena' formulation also in *ST* 1-2.18.2; in the same article he uses the expression 'accipere aliena,' as if it were equivalent to the former. He recognizes the same equivalence in the passage from *De malo* 2.6 we are presently considering, i.e., in [IIIa].

There are two ways in which a new species might be added to another, says Thomas. In the first, the new species is a sub-species of the other species and the corresponding act is, therefore, also a member of the superior species; in the second, the new species is not a sub-species but a "disparate species."[39] The first way is itself divided into two; that is, the sub-species might be related materially to its superior species or it might be related formally. (Here as elsewhere, incidentally, we see Thomas's typical flexibility in his use of the terms 'material' and 'formal.') An instance of the former is adultery, for the wife of another *is* "something belonging to another." The specification concerns that matter: "something belonging to another." His example of a sub-species that is related formally to theft is sacrilege: "if, for instance, I should take something belonging to another [accipiam rem alienam] from a sacred place" [IIIa]. This is related formally to the other (superior) species because what is special (species-creating) here is not 'belonging to another' (although the object *does* belong to another) but rather its being in a sacred place or its sacredness. This is a "form" holding *of* that matter or object: holding, that is, of something that belongs to another and so bringing about a distinct species of sin.

Because sacrilege is related to its superior species, theft, formally—that is, because the circumstance 'where' is not the object itself—Thomas does not consider it an intrinsically evil act in quite the same sense that murder, adultery, and theft are. And yet it comes very close. In *ST* 1-2.18.10, he says that in the case of sacrilege, "place, which was first considered a circumstance"—that is, when it is considered quite generally—"is now considered a principal condition of the object such as is repugnant to reason [rationi repugnans]."[40] The

39. See also *De malo* 2.6 ad 2.

40. "Et ideo locus, qui prius considerabatur ut circumstantia, nunc consideratur ut principalis conditio obiecti rationi repugnans" [*ST* 1-2.18.10c]. In Aristotle's list, 'the where' does not appear; Thomas maintains, however, that it is implied in the fourth element, "in quo operatur." See above, note 6; see also *in EN* 3.3 148–150 (§415). Apparently, as in theft itself, the circumstance disappears (*as* a circumstance) once it is part of a

expression "repugnant to reason" is the same type of language we saw him using just previously in *De malo* 2.6 [IIb] when discussing circumstances that cease to be called circumstances.

In this case, 'the where' adheres so closely to the object that, even if the thief does not care whether the thing he steals is in a sacred place or not, he still commits the sin of sacrilege.[41] In the sixth objection of *De malo* 2.6, the argument is made that, when a thief is not interested in stealing a sacred object but only in having its gold, his will is directed not toward a sacred thing but toward the gold, and so the circumstance that the object is sacred does not give species to the act. Thomas replies: "Although the will of the thief is directed, not toward the sacred thing *principally*, but rather toward the gold, it is directed

---

particular act. On the other hand, the object remains what it was originally, for Thomas says earlier in the same article: "And so what in one act is regarded as a circumstance added 'on top of' the object that determines the species of the act, can again be regarded by ordering reason as a principal condition of the object that determines the species of the act" ["Et ideo quod in uno actu accipitur ut circumstantia superaddita obiecto quod determinat speciem actus, potest iterum accipi a ratione ordinante ut principalis conditio obiecti determinantis speciem actus"]. See also *ST* 1-2.18.5 ad 4: "A circumstance is sometimes taken as an essential difference of the object, in so far as it is compared to reason; and then it can give species to a moral act. And this is necessarily so whenever a circumstance transforms an act from goodness into evil, for a circumstance would not make an action evil, except in so far as it is repugnant to reason" ["circumstantia quandoque sumitur ut differentia essentialis obiecti, secundum quod ad rationem comparatur, et tunc potest dare speciem actui morali. Et hoc oportet esse, quandocumque circumstantia transmutat actum de bonitate in malitiam, non enim circumstantia faceret actum malum, nisi per hoc quod rationi repugnat"]. See also *De malo* 2.6 ad 2. In the latter, note that the Marietti edition has "fit species furti quae est sacrilegium, ex circumstantia loci, et non ex conditione obiecti" but Leonine has "fit species furti quae est sacrilegium, ex circumstantia loci, et tamen ex conditione obiecti." The latter is preferable.

41. *De malo* 2.6 obi. 6 argues that, since the thief does not care whether the object stolen is in a sacred place, that circumstance (or indeed any circumstance) cannot put his sin into the species of sacrilege. Since Thomas response concedes nothing to this argument, it follows that he holds that such a thief commits the "special" sin of sacrilege, that is, the sin belonging to that species. It is important to note, however, that nothing that Thomas says implies that all morally negative circumstances put one's sin into the corresponding special sin. (Just below we go into the matter of how one commits a special sin.)

upon the sacred thing by consequence [ex consequenti]: for he would rather take the sacred thing than be without the gold."[42] Important here, as we shall see, is the specification that the thief "would rather take the sacred thing than be without the gold." We might say that he is "committed" to taking that object, whether sacred or not. But equally important is the fact that this commitment has to do with a particular object belonging to another. The thief's act remains an instance of theft, a member of the superior species.

As an example of the second way of adding a new species – not, that is, a sub-species but a "disparate species" – Thomas mentions the case of a thief who takes something in order that he might commit a murder. He says that a similar phenomenon occurs "in other things" [IIIb]. Under the genus 'color,' one properly locates the species 'white,' since to be white is a way of being a color: 'color' divides per se into the various species of color. 'Sweet,' on the other hand, is not a species of color – it is a "disparate species," related to the other species only per accidens – although it is perfectly possible that a white thing might be sweet. Similarly, an act of accepting something might *be* an act of theft (since the object, the thing taken, belongs to another), to which is added the species of murder: not as a "principal condition of the object" [*ST* 1-2.18.10] but as a distinct, although attached, species.

42. "Ad sextum dicendum, quod licet principaliter voluntas furantis non feratur ad rem sacram, sed ad aurum, fertur tamen super rem sacram ex consequenti; magis enim vult rem sacram accipere quam auro carere" [*De malo* 2.6 ad 6]. Note that the thief *knows* that the thing is sacred; his avarice, however, makes him contemptuous of that fact. See Alasdair MacIntyre, "Social Structures and Their Threats to Moral Agency," in *Ethics and Politics: Selected Essays,* Volume 2 (Cambridge: Cambridge University Press, 2006), 200–202. See also *ST* 1-2.18.10, *de Malo* 2.4 ad 5, and *Sent.* 4.16.3.2.3 ("ad tertiam questionem"): "sometimes the species of a sin varies without the intention being brought to bear upon that circumstance, as when a thief would just as happily take a non-sacred golden goblet as a sacred one; and nonetheless the sin is changed into another species, that is, from a simple theft into sacrilege" ["aliquando variatur species peccati sine hoc quod intentio feratur ad circumstantiam illam; sicut fur ita libenter acciperet vas aureum non sacratum sicut sacratum; et tamen in aliam speciem peccatum mutatur, scilicet de furto simplici in sacrilegium"].

Thus, again, it is apparent that Thomas sees no problem in connecting one act or type of act with another, provided that the connection has a bearing upon reason or justice. In this case, the intention with which the act is performed adds a *new* species — but also a connection.

IV. Circumstances, Motives, and Intention

In the next section (V) these arguments will be developed further in connection with some of the issues raised in chapter 1. But, before developing the arguments, we will need to address a problem regarding Thomas's position regarding an agent's responsibility also for those aspects of his actions toward which his will [voluntas] is not directed principally, as in the example just mentioned of sacrilege committed by the thief who is interested only in the gold that happens to be in a sacred place. Such an act is not (or not necessarily) an act of cooperation, but there is an intimate connection with the theory of cooperation. The underlying and common issue is whether the very intelligibility of what one is doing can include something — that is, something bad — toward which one's *intention* is not directed — something, that is, toward which one's will is not directed principally.[43] As we have seen, with respect to cooperation and within the manualist tradition, depending on the author (or authors) followed, such an action might or might not be called formal cooperation. What interests us at the moment, however, is not this terminology but rather how, according to Thomas, even that which is not primarily intend-

43. I discuss the term 'intelligibility' in chapter 5, section I. In the present discussion I assume that that toward which one's will is directed principally is that toward which one's intention is directed; the question is, therefore, whether that upon which the will is directed "by consequence" can be included within the intelligibility of what one is doing intentionally. The language used here is, of course, the language used in *De malo* 2.6 ad 6: "Although the will of the thief is directed, not toward the sacred thing principally, but rather toward the gold, it is directed upon the sacred thing by consequence: for he would rather take the sacred thing than be without the gold" ["licet principaliter voluntas furantis non feratur ad rem sacram, sed ad aurum, fertur tamen super rem sacram ex consequenti; magis enim vult rem sacram accipere quam auro career"].

ed might fall within the intelligibility of what one does intentionally.

There are authors, both contemporary and considerably older, who have trouble with Thomas's remark that the thief interested in just the gold still commits the sin of sacrilege.[44] The difficulties stem from more general theoretical differences with Thomas on the part of at least some of these authors but also have to do with things that Thomas says in writings roughly contemporary with *De malo* 2.6. In *ST* 1-2.72.9, for instance, he says that "a circumstance never transfers an act into another species except when there is another motive."[45] Similarly, the first objection in *De malo* 14.3 argues that a circumstance, being an accident, cannot "diversify" a species (in particular, the species of gluttony). Thomas's response is that "the aforesaid species are not diversified because of the diverse circumstances but

44. Among contemporary authors, see Germain Grisez, *Christian Moral Principles*, vol. 1, *The Way of the Lord Jesus* (Chicago: Franciscan Herald, 1983), 247 n. 3. See also John Finnis, "Object and Intention in Moral Judgments According to St. Thomas Aquinas," in *Finalité et Intentionnalité: Doctrine Thomiste et Perspectives Modernes*, ed. J. Follon and J. McEvoy (Paris/Louvain: Librairie Philosophique J. Vrin/Éditions de l'Institut Supérieur de Philosophie, Louvain-la-neuve, 1992), 140 n. 43 (also to be found at John Finnis, *Intention and Identity: Collected Essays, Volume II* [Oxford: Oxford University Press, 2011], 164 n. 43. On this position, see Stephen L. Brock, *Action and Conduct: Thomas Aquinas and the Theory of Action* [Edinburgh: T & T Clark, 1998], 218 n. 57. At *Sent.* 4.16.3.2.3, Thomas makes a remark similar to the one at *De malo* 2.6 ad 6; he says, that is, that a thief, who would "just as happily take a non-sacred golden vessel as a sacred one" ["fur ita libenter acciperet vas aureum non sacratum sicut sacratum"], even still commits sacrilege. (He goes on then to say that "every circumstance can alter the species of a sin but does not always alter it" ["omnis circumstantia potest speciem peccati mutare, sed non semper mutat"].) Cajetan (Thomas de Vio) suggests that Thomas changed his mind between making that statement and writing *ST* 1-2.72.9, where he appears to state the opposite [Thomas Aquinas and Thomas de Vio (Cajetan), *Summa theologiae, cum commentariis Thomae de Vio Caietani Ordinis Praedicatorum*, in *Opera Omnia, Vv. 4–12*, Commissio Leonina (Rome: Ex typographia polyglotta S. C. de Propaganda Fide, 1888–1906), v. 7 23 (apud 1-2.72.9). On the role of circumstances in Thomas's action theory, see Jensen, "Do Circumstances Give Species?" and Jensen, *Good and Evil Actions: A Journey Through Saint Thomas Aquinas*, 103–16.

45. "Ad secundum dicendum quod circumstantia nunquam transfert actum in aliam speciem, nisi quando est aliud motivum" [*ST* 1-2.72.9 ad 2].

because of the diverse motives, as stated [in the body of the same article]."[46] It would seem that the only thing that counts here is the intention with which an act is performed, not the circumstance (e.g., the fact that the object stolen was in a sacred place).

Although what we are about to say does not address directly the issues raised by these authors, it is important to understand that, when Thomas speaks about the role of what he calls "motives" [motiva] and their connection with species, he is not analyzing *acts* but speaking about the way in which types of sin are defined (as species of sin). As we shall see in the next chapter (chapter 3), the sin of scandal gets its species from its central instance, the act in which someone intends to cause another to sin. This is not to say, however, that one who is interested only in satisfying a desire and incidentally gives scandal does not commit scandal: he does; the point is that the definition (or species) of scandal comes not from non-intended but rather from intended scandal – that is, scandal in which the agent's will is directed toward that specifying object: a scandalized person. The sin of one simply satisfying desire is not the special (species) sin of scandal. Similarly, a man might commit adultery with the wife of a superior simply because he finds her sexually attractive, all the while being aware (for instance) that he is thereby committing a sin of ingratitude toward his superior, her husband, but not caring about that fact one way or the other. The special sin of ingratitude itself looks, for its definition, to the act of deliberately – "specifically," we might say – withholding acknowledgment of a good done to oneself (see *ST* 2-2.107.2). That is not the act that this man is performing, although his act *is* an act of ingratitude.[47] Thomas's whole discourse about mo-

46. "Ad primum ergo dicendum, quod praedictae species non diversificantur propter diversas circumstantias, sed propter diversa motiva, ut dictum est" [*De malo* 14.3 ad 1]. On the "diversification" of species, see above, note 28.

47. See ad 1 of *ST* 2-2.107.2, where Thomas acknowledges that in every sin there is ingratitude toward God but the "special sin" of ingratitude is actually scorning (or "contemning") a benefit conferred: "In any sin there is material ingratitude to God, that is,

tives is not about individual acts and their constituents but about the origins of types (species) of sins. He consistently follows Aristotle's insight that movements are organized by species with respect to their termini and, in particular, that human acts are so organized with respect to the intentions or objects of certain acts.[48]

In *ST* 1-2.72.9 and *De malo* 14.3 ad 1, therefore, Thomas is not saying that the way a *particular act* is characterized depends solely upon what is within the agent's intention; rather, he is saying that, if we are going to speak about a particular species of sin at all, we have to find in the sphere of things that humans do an end or object that allows us to speak of a specific (delimited) type of sin. And so, it is entirely possible for an agent to be aware of (but not in the strict sense intending) certain bad aspects of what he is doing without what he is doing being characterized *specifically* by those aspects. In the example used just above, a man fully aware that he owes much to his employer might commit adultery with that employer's wife, without committing the special sin ingratitude. Thomas does recognize that it sometimes happens that bad aspects of an agent's act, aspects of which he is aware but toward which his will is not directed, are culpable aspects.

We must now, however, address more directly the issues raised by the above-mentioned authors regarding *De malo* 2.6 ad 6. In the opening of the corpus of *ST* 1-2.72.9, we read that, "as has been said, where there occurs another motive for sinning, there is to be found another species of sin, since the motive for the sinning is the end and the object."[49] The back reference here ("as has been said . . .") is to

---

in as much as a man does something that can pertain to ingratitude. Formal ingratitude, however, is present when the benefaction is actually contemned. And this is the special sin" ["Ad primum ergo dicendum quod in quolibet peccato est materialis ingratitudo ad Deum, inquantum scilicet facit homo aliquid quod potest ad ingratitudinem pertinere. Formalis autem ingratitudo est quando actualiter beneficium contemnitur. Et hoc est speciale peccatum"]. (In Thomas's Latin, unlike current English, the word *specialis* is still closely associated with the word *species*.)

48. See Flannery, *Action and Character According to Aristotle*, chapter 2.

49. "Respondeo dicendum quod, sicut dictum est, ubi occurrit aliud motivum ad

ST 1-2.72.8, where Thomas says that this object is "that toward which the intention of the sinner is borne [in quod fertur intentio peccantis]." This remark too might give the impression that that toward which a person's will is directed principally is the sole determinant of a particular act's species. And this impression might be strengthened by a superficial reading of an earlier article from that question. *ST* 1-2.72.3 (which *ST* 1-2.72.8 presupposes) asks whether sins are distinguished in species with respect to the causes (formal, material, efficient, and final); and Thomas's answer is that

> sins do not differ in species according to the diverse active causes or motives but only according to the diversity of the final cause. The end [finis], however, is the object of the will, for it was shown above [*ST* 1-2.1.3, 18.6] that human acts have their species from the end.[50]

Essential, however, for understanding this remark (and therefore also *ST* 1-2.72.8–9) is what Thomas goes on to say in response to the (second) objection. That objection argues that the material cause — or object — of an act pertains least to the species and so the other three causes are better suited to the role of distinguishing species. Thomas responds:

> Objects, in so far as they are part of exterior acts, have the character of "matter about which," but in so far as they are part of the interior act of the will they have the character of ends — and it is in this respect that they give species to an act. But even in so far as they are "matter about which," they have the character of termini — with respect to which movements are specified, as is said in *Physics* 5 and *Nicomachean Ethics* 10. But also termini give species to movements in as much as they have the character of an end.[51]

---

peccandum, ibi est alia peccati species, quia motivum ad peccandum est finis et obiectum" [*ST* 1-2.72.9c].

50. "Unde manifestum est quod peccata non differant specie secundum diversas causas activas vel motivas; sed solum secundum diversitatem causae finalis. Finis autem est obiectum voluntatis, ostensum est enim supra quod actus humani habent speciem ex fine" [*ST* 1-2.72.3c].

51. "Ad secundum dicendum quod obiecta, secundum quod comparantur ad actus

Even in associating species with the "intention of the sinner" in *ST* 1-2.72.8 and with motive in *ST* 1-2.72.9, Thomas is not rejecting the idea that a species might come from the object of the exterior act. This indeed is what we saw in *De malo* 2.6 [IIIa], where he says that an act might receive an additional species either from the "matter" (for example, the particular person with whom one has intercourse) or from a formal aspect holding of the matter, such as the circumstance that the thing stolen (or to be stolen) is in a sacred place.

What Thomas goes on to say in *ST* 1-2.72.9 confirms that, for him, an additional species might enter into an act by way of a circumstance. "It sometimes happens," he says,

> that the corruptions of diverse circumstances come from diverse motives. For instance, that someone eats precipitously can come from the fact that the man cannot put up with delay of food because of the easy consumption of the digestive humors; but that he desires an immoderate amount of food can come about because of a naturally strong capacity to digest much food; that, however, someone desires delicious foods comes about because of the desire for the enjoyment that is in the food. Thus, in such cases, corruptions of diverse circumstances introduce diverse species of sin.

It is not at all irrelevant that two of these motives — "the easy consumption of the digestive humors" and "a naturally strong capacity to digest much food" — are clearly physiological; and even the third, "the enjoyment that is in the food," might be understood as an objective quality of the food. In *ST* 1-2.72.3 Thomas is careful to say that the motives that specify sins always involve a final cause (an object of the will); even still, however, the "visceral" character of these motives

---

exteriores, habent rationem materiae circa quam, sed secundum quod comparantur ad actum interiorem voluntatis, habent rationem finium; et ex hoc habent quod dent speciem actui. Quamvis etiam secundum quod sunt materia circa quam, habeant rationem terminorum; a quibus motus specificantur, ut dicitur in V Physic. et in X Ethic. Sed tamen etiam termini motus dant speciem motibus, inquantum habent rationem finis" [*ST* 1-2.72.3 ad 2]. The references are to Aristotle's *Phys.* 5.4 224b7–8 and *EN* 10.4 1174a29-b5.

suggests that such motives need be at the forefront of the sinner's mind *as* his intention in eating.[52]

So, the various places in which Thomas says that a change of species depends upon motives [motiva] does not contradict what he says in *De malo* 2.6 ad 6 about the thief whose will is "directed not toward the sacred thing principally, but rather toward the gold." As he says, the thief "would rather take the sacred thing than be without the gold." His disdain – however minimal or unexpressed even to himself – for the laws regarding sacrilege is enough of a motive to add the species of sacrilege to his theft.[53] Moreover, as noted previously, nowhere in what Thomas says about the identification of special sins does he say that there cannot be sins that, although they might be characterized with *reference* to a special sin, are not instances of the special sin.

Pertinent here is an example that Elizabeth Anscombe uses in that section of her book *Intention* in which she argues against the Cartesian understanding of intention. She introduces two fictional characters: an employee, whose job it is to pump water "into the cistern which supplies the drinking water of a house," and his employer, who has contaminated that water with poison, convinced that the death of those in the house would be a good thing.[54] She supposes first that the employee, in pumping the water, is doing his normal job

52. In this connection, it is also worth mentioning that, in both *ST* 1-2.72.1 and *ST* 1-2.72.8, the disorder [inordinatio] of a voluntary act – which is associated with whatever circumstances might be "corrupted" [*ST* 1-2.72.9] – is said to be "per accidens with respect to the intention of the sinner" ["per accidens se habet ad intentionem peccantis"] and "beside the intention of the sinner" ["praeter intentionem peccantis"], in contrast, that is, with the voluntary act itself, which is always for some good. In *ST* 2-2.53.2, Thomas makes remarks which are also occasionally cited as (supposedly) inconsistent with passages such as *De malo* 2.6 ad 6. They can be dealt with in the same way we have dealt with *ST* 1-2.72.9.

53. MacIntyre would attribute this to the thief's contempt for the fact that the object is sacred. See MacIntyre, "Social Structures and Their Threats to Moral Agency," 200–202.

54. Anscombe, *Intention*, §§23–27. (See above, the introduction, section I.)

and that he maintains that his pumping poisoned water was not his intention but that he was interested only in collecting his wages. (She imagines the employee's saying, "I didn't care tuppence one way or the other for the fact that someone had poisoned the water....") She speaks of this as possibly a genuine case of someone's intention not being to bring about something that he knows will result from his action. Such a claim could be true, she says, but "there can be a certain amount of control of the truthfulness of the answer." Suppose, for instance, that "he distracts the attention of one of the inhabitants from something about the water source that might suggest the truth; the question 'Why did you call him from over there?' must have a credible answer other than 'to prevent him from seeing'; and a multiplication of such points needing explanation would cast doubt on his claim not to have done anything with a view to facilitating the poisoning." This possibility of verification is evidence that, as she puts it: "The idea that one can determine one's intentions by making such a little speech to oneself is obvious bosh" [§25]. She goes on to say: "On the other hand, if, say, this was not his normal job, but he was hired by the poisoner to pump the water, knowing it was poisoned, the case is different" [§25]. If the employee as described in this second scenario argues that the killing was not intentional because he was interested only in receiving his pay, very clearly he would be invoking what she describes as bosh: the false Cartesian understanding of intention.

Thomas's example in *De malo* 2.6 ad 6 of the thief who takes the sacred vessel and argues that he is interested only in the gold would seem to fall into the same category as this second, re-described employee. It may very well be the case that this thief doesn't care whether the object is sacred or not. But that is not what is crucial here. What is crucial is what Thomas says about sacrilegious theft in the corpus of *De malo* 2.6: that further specification of the act comes from the circumstance of the *object's* being in a sacred place. The sacrilegious theft is indeed sacrilegious but it is also theft, and the sacrilegious aspect cannot be separated off from that object: it is part of the act's very intelligibility. Similarly, the man who in Anscombe's example is hired explicitly in order to poison the occupants of the house has as his object poisoned persons. Unlike the employee as first described, any argument to the effect that he was only earning his keep clearly would be false.

V. Once Again, Indifferent Acts

We come back now to the question of indifferent acts. As we have seen, in *De malo* 2.6 Thomas does occasionally consider actions as indifferent in certain respects. We see this, for instance, in his remarks about theft: "if we consider this act which is to accept money, it is not part of that concept that the money belongs to another."[55] But this is just a prelude to his assertion that the money in question does belong to another and that this makes the particular act of accepting it not indifferent at all but intrinsically evil, for the circumstance so enters into the act that it can no longer be called a circumstance.

A somewhat similar thing can be said of any act considered in all its particularity. With respect to certain circumstances, an act might not be characterized morally: it may make no difference whether you whistle while walking through the streets or rather in the privacy of your home. But, if you whistle during a concert or while the judge is addressing you (i.e., in those circumstances), that is bad. "It is necessary," says Thomas, "that any individual act whatsoever have some circumstance by which it is drawn into the good or the bad, at least on the part of the intention of the end" [*ST* 1-2.18.9]. He speaks of certain acts that are indifferent according to their species, that is, with respect to the species that comes from their object. It can happen, he says, "that the object of an act does not include anything pertaining to the order of reason, such as to pick up a piece of straw from the ground or to walk through a field" [*ST* 1-2.18.8]. But even such an act, given that it is a human act and so is an act proceeding "from deliber-

55. "si consideremus hunc actum qui est accipere pecuniam, non est de ratione eius quod sit aliena" [*De malo* 2.6c] [IIb].

ative reason" [*ST* 1-2.18.9], will, as a particular act, not be indifferent. Even picking up a piece of straw, presuming it is not done inadvertently, falls within the moral realm. It is most likely morally good, unless done, for instance, in order to irritate another or to signal an assassin – in which case it would, of course, be bad. It is necessary, says Thomas, that any such act be "either ordered or not ordered toward the appropriate end."[56]

In book two of his commentary on the *Sentences*, Thomas provides a dense but also very helpful explanation of how this truth, that ultimately there are no indifferent human acts, is discoverable in the very meaning of the word 'evil.' Thomas, following Aristotle, distinguishes privation from contrariety. Privation is pure negation; contrariety has a foundation in something positive which, however, is subject to privation in some way.

He puts the matter in this way:

> [E]vil, in as much as it is evil, is not opposed to good in any other way than as a privation is opposed to the having; but the opposition of contrariety consists in the fact that that being upon which such a privation is founded is incompatible with some good that is good simpliciter, as immoderate delight in food is incompatible with the good of moderation with respect to food [sobrietas] – which is good simpliciter. And so, that immoderate delight is conjoined with the privation of good and is called evil.[57]

What causes immoderate delight in food to be called evil is the immoderation, for in itself delight is not a bad thing; what is bad about

56. "Necesse est autem quod vel ordinetur, vel non ordinetur ad debitum finem" [*ST* 1-2.18.9c].

57. "[Q]uia malum, inquantum malum, non opponitur bono, nisi sicut privatio habitui: sed oppositio contrarietatis est ex hoc quod illud ens supra quod fundatur talis privatio, non compatitur secum aliquod bonum quod est simpliciter bonum; sicut immoderata delectatio in cibis non compatitur secum bonum sobrietatis, quod est simpliciter bonum; et ideo illa immoderata delectatio adjungitur cum privatione boni, et sic mala dicitur" [*Sent.* 2.40.1.5c]. One could translate the word *sobrietas* as simply 'moderation,' but moderation is about more than one's attitude toward food, and Aristotle is being quite specific here.

the delight in this case is its incompatibility with moderation with respect to food.

According to Thomas, then, for a human act to be indifferent—that is to say, neither good nor evil—the indifference would have to come either from the contrariety of good and evil or from evil's being a privation.[58] With respect to this first option, the indifferent act would supposedly fall between these two extremes (the contraries, good and evil). But in so far as good and evil are contraries, they involve something positive: immoderation as the contrary of moderation attaches to something positive, delight in food. The intermediate contrary (the *medium* which is supposedly indifferent) located

58. "If, therefore, among actions there is found a *medium* between good and evil, this will not be other than (1) in as much as good and evil are contraries or (2) in as much as evil is the privation of a good. But not in as much as they are contraries can there be in actions a *medium* which is neither good nor bad. For they are called contraries in so far as in both something is considered positively [positive]—from which the *ratio* of evil cannot be drawn. Because a *medium* stands at a distance from both extremes precisely in as much as it posits [ponit] something positively [positive], it does not bring about distance from the *ratio* of good and evil in such a way that it would be possible to say that it is neither good nor evil. For in them the reason for the opposition of contrariety and the distinction between good and evil is not the same. The first is a consequence of the positing in each; the second, however, is a consequence of the privation in evil and the positing in good. If, therefore, there is a *medium* between good and evil in actions, this will not be except in so far as evil and good are opposed privatively [privative]" ["Si ergo in actionibus invenitur medium inter bonum et malum, hoc non erit nisi (1) inquantum bonum et malum sunt contraria, vel (2) inquantum malum est privatio boni. Non autem inquantum sunt contraria, potest in eis esse medium quod sit neque bonum neque malum. Dicuntur enim contraria, secundum quod in utroque aliquid positive consideratur; ex quo non potest sumi ratio mali; unde propter hoc quod medium distat ab extremis, inquantum aliquid positive ponit, non efficitur distans a ratione boni et mali, ut possit dici neque bonum neque malum; non enim ex eodem est in eis oppositio contrarietatis et distinctio boni et mali; sed primum est ex parte positionis in utroque; secundum autem ex parte privationis in malo, et positionis in bono. Si ergo sit medium inter bonum et malum in actionibus, hoc non erit nisi secundum quod malum bono privative opponitur"] [*Sent.* 2.40.1.5c]. For an account of Thomas's understanding of evil, especially as it pertains to human acts, see Kevin L. Flannery, "Aristotelian Resonances in Aquinas' Conception of Evil," in *Evil in Aristotle*, ed. Pavlos Kontos (Cambridge: Cambridge University Press, 2017), 205–21.

between the two extremes would also involve something positive: indeed, it is this positive aspect that allows it to have such a position. This very being an intermediate between the two extremes also depends upon the opposition of contrariety – that is, upon the positive character of the extremes good and evil – and not upon the distinction between good and evil. The idea, therefore, that because of the contrariety of good and evil this intermediate contrary might be indifferent – distancing itself supposedly from both good and evil in a way that keeps them both out – is excluded, since that distinction (the distinction between good and evil) is quite different from that which constitutes good and evil as contraries. In short, the pair good and evil, qua a pair of contraries, gives us a continuum of degrees of good and evil rather than a positive/privative juxtaposition.

Whether indifference might be borne of privation itself also proves to be a complicated question. Thomas acknowledges that some acts might be called indifferent because of privation. Just as a stone is not "susceptive" [susceptivus] of vision, so an act considered *as* "conduct [agere]" or *as* a "being [ens]" is not susceptive of moral goodness or badness. But this latter sort of abstract privation is not what interests Thomas; he is interested rather in whether *particular* acts might be not susceptive of moral good or moral badness in the way that a particular stone is not susceptive of vision. And he acknowledges that some particular acts *are* like stones in this respect. Just as stones are not susceptive of vision, so some acts, such as inadvertently scratching one's beard, are not susceptive of moral goodness and badness. But this is because they are not properly speaking human acts: acts, as he defines them, which are "ordered by the will, which follows upon the deliberation of reason."[59]

Human acts, by contrast, are *all* "susceptible of moral goodness" (or moral badness), says Thomas, and this makes them non-

59. "An act, however, is susceptible of moral goodness according as it is a human act; but an act is human according as it is deduced to some degree by reason: this occurs only in those acts which are commanded by the will, which follows upon the deliberation

indifferent. The key term here is 'susceptible' (*susceptibilis*) – or, alternatively, "susceptive" [susceptivus] (used by Thomas in the same passage). Certain acts – properly speaking human acts – are "susceptible" of characterization as either morally good or morally bad. Their being susceptible does not mean that they might or might not take on such a characterization: that would make them indifferent acts. The only thing that can prevent a genuinely human act from being either good or evil (and nothing in between) would be non-susceptibility. But human acts are susceptible; they cannot be indifferent.

It would be possible to translate the words *susceptibilis* and *susceptivus* (plus the genitive) not as, respectively, 'susceptible of' and 'susceptive of' but rather as 'subject to' – which would make more apparent the inevitability of the moral characterization; but that translation would obscure the contrast with the privation and indifference involved in acts that are not properly speaking human acts (and so are not susceptible or susceptive of moral characterization). The concept of susceptibility is also useful in bringing cases of cooperation out onto a stage larger than the one of recent tradition (Alphonsus et alii), in which the primary moral issue is whether the cooperator intends what the malefactor intends. That larger stage is the moral universe itself, within which a human act is bad if it is unjust or un-

---

of reason" ["Actus autem susceptibilis est bonitatis moralis, secundum quod humanus est: humanus autem est, secundum quod aliquatenus ratione deducitur: quod contingit in illis actibus tantum qui imperantur a voluntate, quae consequitur deliberationem rationis"] [*Sent.* 2.40.1.5c]. Thomas gives as an example of a non-deliberate act scratching one's beard [*ST* 1-2.18.9]. See also *De malo* 2.5.186–194: "This good and evil, however, is proper to the singular act, and so no singular human act is indifferent. And I call an act human which is from a deliberate will. For if it should be some act proceeding merely from imagination without deliberation – scratching one's beard, for example, or something of that sort – such an act is outside the genus of morals and so does not participate in moral goodness or evil" ["Hoc autem bonum et malum est proprium actus singularis; et ideo nullus actus humanus singularis, est indifferens; et dico actum humanum qui est a voluntate deliberata. Si enim sit aliquis actus sine deliberatione procedens ex sola imaginatione, sicut confricatio barbae, aut aliquid huiusmodi, huiusmodi actus est extra genus moris; unde non participat bonitatem vel malitiam moralem"]. On the definition of human action, see chapter 4, section II.

reasonable but otherwise it is good. All human acts are susceptible of one such characterization or the other.

In a passage we have already seen and discussed, Thomas speaks of human acts that, even independently of the species they receive from their objects, are susceptible of moral goodness and badness. He says there that "*everything*" (emphasis added)

> that is ordered toward an end must be proportionate to the end. And so reason, which orders our act toward the end, considers the act's proportion toward those things that might occur together with the act; and this proportion is called a circumstance.[60]

This approach in effect makes human acts dependent for their very being upon the larger context of justice and charity.[61] It is true that, in a certain sense, human acts' circumstances are not within them—they "stand around them" as the *way* in which they fit into practical reasonability itself; and yet no human act can exist without its particular circumstances. There is no human act that is not done by a particular person, at a particular time, and (especially) to a certain end; and these *are* the "proportions" (*commensurationes*) with respect to justice and charity that we call circumstances. The circumstances are morally relevant relations, either praiseworthy or not, with the ultimate end. Because a human act is a human act only in as much as it exists within this context of particular circumstances (relations within the larger context of justice and charity), every particular human act is susceptible—as Thomas says in *Sent.* 2.40.1.5—of moral goodness and badness. There are no indifferent human acts.

60. "Respondeo dicendum ad primam quaestionem, quod actus nostri dicuntur morales secundum quod a ratione ordinantur in finem voluntatis; ex hoc enim habent rationem boni vel mali. Omne autem quod ordinatur ad finem, oportet esse proportionatum fini; et ideo ratio quae actum nostrum in finem ordinat, attendit proportionem actus ad ea quae ad actum concurrere possunt; et ista commensuratio circumstantia dicitur" [*Sent.* 4.16.3.1.1].

61. On how charity and justice bear upon the assessment of human action, see below, chapter 4, section I.

This approach to the nature of human acts is subtly different from what we have seen in Alphonsus, Noldin, and Cretoni. For them all, the identification of indifference is tied up with the identification of cases of formal cooperation. They are not always in agreement regarding which acts are indifferent – and, as we have seen, Alphonsus is not always in agreement with himself – but they all hold that, in some sense, formal cooperation is a matter of adding intention (implicit or explicit) to an otherwise indifferent act. Thomas too says a number of times that, when in all other respects a human act is indifferent, it will, at least on account of the intention with which it is performed, not be indifferent.[62] But Thomas is as interested – if not more interested – in identifying all the circumstances of an act (including the intention with which it is performed), such as allow him to situate and assess the act within the larger context especially of justice. Cooperation with evil does not involve an indifferent act which turns immoral because of the cooperator's intention: in all cases, the cooperator is already in a situation in which his action is lending – or would be lending – aid in some way to the malefactor. If a person is completely cut off from any connection with the malefactor and in that situation performs an act that is indifferent except for its intention – if, to use Thomas's example [*ST* 1-2.18.8], he walks across a field and tells himself that he is doing this in order to encourage an evil act with which he has no connection – this is not a case of cooperation with evil but, in all probability, one of self-delusion.

Thomas does not recognize indifferent acts, nor does he even hold that acts evil in species (and, in that sense, intrinsically evil) are necessarily more evil than those that are evil because of a circumstance other than the one that Aristotle calls 'the what' and Thomas

62. See, for instance, *ST* 1-2.18.9c: "And it is necessary for whatever individual act to have some circumstance by virtue of which it is made good or bad, at least with respect to the intention of the end" ["Et oportet quod quilibet individualis actus habeat aliquam circumstantiam per quam trahatur ad bonum vel malum, ad minus ex parte intentionis finis"]. Thomas presumes here that an act is a human (or moral) act. He says similar things about circumstances also in *Sent.* 2.40.1.5.

calls the object. He cites repeatedly the pseudo-Dionysian adage that "any singular defect causes evil, but good is caused by a wholly sound cause."[63] An act evil because of the place where it is performed or the remote intention with which it is performed is not necessarily less evil than an act whose object makes it evil. Striking a match as a signal to initiate an assassination is a graver evil than lying to one's spouse about how much money one has given to an old friend who has fallen on hard times, even though the latter is intrinsically evil.[64] The circumstances – who, what, about what, with what, etc. – are useful to Thomas in the analysis of the structure and characteristics of human acts; but he is primarily interested in how such acts – as existing in *all* their circumstances – relate to the ultimate end and fit into morality itself.

VI. Cretoni versus de Cardenas and Master Milante

In the next chapter we will go more deeply into this idea that all acts are "susceptible" of moral goodness and badness. But at the moment we must bring some closure to the argument begun in the previous chapter regarding the indifference of acts, especially as this notion is understood and used by Nicola Cretoni with respect to cooperation.

To summarize briefly Cretoni's position (set out in chapter 1, sections V and VI): he would exclude from the category of formal cooperation – which is to say, from the category of acts that are necessarily wrong – any act in which the cooperator does not share the intention

63. "Quilibet singularis defectus causat malum, bonum autem causatur ex integra causa" [*ST* 1-2.18.4 ad 3]. See also, for instance, *ST* 1-2.75.1 ad 1 and *ST* 2-2.110.3. Thomas quotes pseudo-Dionysius from memory, not always using the same words. The original reads: Τὸ ἀγαθὸν ἐκ μιᾶς καὶ τῆς ὅλης αἰτίας, τὸ δὲ κακὸν ἐκ πολλῶν καὶ μερικῶν ἐλλείψεων [Pseudo-Dionysius the Areopagite, *De divinis nominibus*, vol. 1, *Corpus Dionysiacum* (Berlin: De Gruyter, 1990), 175.10–11].

64. For a further discussion of these matters, see Kevin L. Flannery, "Voting, Intrinsic Evil, and Commensuration," *American Journal of Jurisprudence* 60, no. 2 (2015): 181–97.

of the malefactor. He takes particular exception to the idea – which he associates with Juan de Cardenas and Pius-Thomas Milante – that a link with the act of a malefactor could affect the substance of the act performed by a cooperator and so turn an otherwise good or at least indifferent act into one that is intrinsically evil. He says that de Cardenas and Milante would respond to his objection by pointing out that they recognize degrees of connection with the act of the malefactor, only the most proximate effecting an alteration in the character of the cooperator's act. Cretoni will have none of this. "But neither," he says,

> does such a distinction help them in any respect at all, for a different degree of connection – or in general, the more and the less – do not change the species, that is, the nature of an action, even if in some other respect the idea of greater or less proximity to a sin in cooperation ought to be considered ... and ought to be considered quite generally.[65]

In support of his own position, Cretoni quotes the saying of Alphonsus – not applied consistently by Alphonsus himself – that "another's wickedness cannot alter the nature of your action."[66]

Now, one could – and we will – take issue with Cretoni's interpretation especially of Milante, for, as we shall see in chapter 3, the Dominican Milante does not ground the idea criticized by Cretoni simply on considerations of proximity to the malefactor's act. Alphonsus, from whom Cretoni clearly takes the two names de Cardenas and Milante, is more fair, acknowledging that the rejected position has as much to do with the per se/per accidens distinction as with proximity.[67] But Cretoni is on more solid ground in criticizing the

65. "Sed nec huiusmodi distinctio sub ullo prorsus respectu eisdem suffragatur; nam diversus coniunctionis gradus, seu generatim *magis et minus non mutant speciem id est actionis naturam*, licet sub alio respectu, maioris vel minoris propinquitatis ad peccatum in cooperatione, ratio quidem habenda sit, ut infra videbitur, eaque communiter hubeatur" [Cretoni, "Nota I (to v. 1 §249)," 571, emphasis in original].

66. "Malitia alterius nequit mutare naturam tuae actionis" [*Theologia moralis* 2.66].

67. Alphonsus says that some moralists "such as de Cardenas and Master Milante – say that cooperation is material when it per accidens and remotely leads to the sin of the

idea that cooperation with a malefactor might change the cooperator's act into one that is intrinsically evil.

One finds this idea in de Cardenas, although it is expressed in extremely tentative terms. The relevant passages in both de Cardenas and Milante concern Pope Innocent XI's 1679 condemnation of what was recognized as a "laxist" position (we encountered that condemnation above in chapter 1, section VI). The condemned proposition — known as Proposition 51 — runs as follows:

> A servant who offering his shoulders knowingly helps his master to climb through a window in order to violate a virgin and often assists him by carrying a ladder, opening a gate, or cooperating in some similar way, does not sin mortally if he does this out of fear of notable injury — lest, for instance, he be ill treated by the master, or be subject to angry looks, or be expelled from the house.[68]

De Cardenas does say that, in the condemned proposition, "it appears to be supposed" that the actions listed by Innocent — which, according to de Cardenas, are in themselves indifferent — "in those circumstances, are intrinsically evil." He goes on, however, almost immediately to say that "I do not presume to decide this issue according to my own judgment; I hold that the Holy See is to be consulted."[69]

---

other, but formal when, per se or on account of some adjoined circumstance, it leads proximately to the performance of the sin, even if per se it might be indifferent" [*Theologia moralis* 2.63]. Alphonsus prefers another formulation.

68. "Famulus, qui submissis humeris scienter adiuvat herum suum ascendere per fenestras ad stuprandam virginem, et multoties eidem subservit deferendo scalam, aperiendo ianuam, aut quid simile cooperando, non peccat mortaliter, si id faciat metu notabilis detrimenti, puta ne a domino male tractetur, ne torvis oculis aspiciatur, ne domo expellatur" [Denzinger et al., *Enchiridion symbolorum definitionum et declarationum de rebus fidei et morum,* §2151].

69. "Ex alia vero parte cum in propositione supponantur, eas actiones adjuvare ad exercedam turpitudinem, et per eas cooperari ad luxuriam, ut denotant ea verba, *aut quid simile cooperando,* videtur supponi eas actiones in illis circumstantiis esse intrinsece malas, atque ex nullo metu etiam gravissimo possint honestari. Et quidem ego non audeo hoc dubium meo judicio decidere; censeo enim consulendam esse Romanam Cathedram" [Cardenas, *Crisis theologica, in qua Plures selectæ difficultates ex morali theologia ad*

"Master Milante," however, is something of a better target. Milante argues in a spirited manner that the advocates of the position described in Proposition 51 hold that

> in such a case the servant could rectify his intention – and, hey presto, he could carry the ladder or convey amorous letters for the purpose of serving his master and avoiding personal harm, without, however, cooperating with the sin of another. For shame! Would this not, therefore, on the same grounds, allow one to commit any enormous crimes whatsoever provided one proposes to oneself some extrinsic good end?[70]

These concerns, which are valid enough in themselves, lead Milante, however, to assert the following: "Although, therefore, the servant acts out of fear, he acts voluntarily; but this, in the present case, is intrinsically evil, prohibited by divine natural law."[71] He also asserts that those who cooperate in fornication, murder, or theft, etc., providing means that are per se or proximately conducive to the crime in question, "in fact are guilty of the very species of sin in which the principal agents are entangled."[72]

Someone might attempt to exonerate Milante by arguing that in

---

Lydium veritatis lapidem revocantur ex regula morum posita a SS.D.N. Innocentio XI. P.M. in Diplomate damnante sexaginta quinque propositiones, dis. 31 639].

70. "Dicunt enim, quod in tali casu famulus posset rectificare intentionem: nimirum posset scalam bajulare, litteras amatorias deferre ex fine solum inserviendi domino et evitandi proprium damnum, secus vero cooperandi alterius delicto. Proh scelus! Ergo ne ex eisdem liceret quaecumque enormia crimina patrare solum extrinseco bono sibi proposito fine?" [Milante, *Exercitationes dogmatico-morales*, ex. 28 300–301].

71. "Igitur quamvis ex metu agat famulus, voluntarie agit quod facit. Sed hoc in casu intrinsece malum est, divina naturali lege prohibitum" [Milante, *Exercitationes dogmatico-morales*, ex. 28 301]. A couple of paragraphs later he says similarly: "Therefore, with regard to struck-down thesis [i.e., the thesis contained in Proposition 51 and struck down by Innocent XI], it is not licit for the servant to cooperate with the fornicating lord, etc., for an act of this sort is intrinsically evil and by virtue of itself against the law of nature; from this, no fear excuses" ["Ideo enim in casu confixae thesis famulo non licet cooperari hero fornicanti, etc., quia huiusce opus est ab intrinseco malum et ex se contra legem naturae; hinc metus nullus excusat"] [pp. 301–302].

72. "Quinimmo eiusdem specie peccati sunt rei, quo principales sunt irretiti" [Milante, *Exercitationes dogmatico-morales*, ex. 28 303].

the latter assertion he need be saying only that the circumstance that the servant's act is an aid to his master's sin *adds* a species to the act of carrying the ladder (or whatever), so that the situation according to Milante would be something like that of the thief who is interested only in gold but nonetheless commits sacrilege. But the fact that Milante says that in such situations an indifferent act becomes intrinsically evil is hard to reconcile with Thomas's action theory, which Milante certainly presupposes and Cretoni can be presumed to presuppose in this, his encounter with the arguments of the Dominican. As we have seen, according to Thomas, an intrinsically evil act would be one in which an inappropriate object – in theft, something belonging to another; in fornication, a person not one's spouse – determines for ill the very substance of the act.[73] In the present case, the object does nothing of the sort: the servant is simply carrying a ladder.

None of this is to say, however, that the Cretoni approach is to be recommended for the analysis of cooperation with evil. Indeed, his approach shares with the approaches of Noldin and several others in the manualist tradition a certain obsession with indifference that, taken to its logical extreme, sets aside all considerations other than intention (understood in a particular way) in the moral analysis of acts. This approach plays into the hand of those who might grant that formal cooperation is always immoral but maintain that material cooperation – which would include any cooperation in which the cooperator does not share the intention of the malefactor – is permissible, as long as a level of duress can be demonstrated or, at least, argued for.

Moreover, since *any* action – even an action that Thomas might be willing to call intrinsically evil – can be considered in an abstract way, a theory that uses indifference as its key principle lacks analytical "robustness": it explains very little for purposes of moral decision making. As we have seen, for Thomas there is no such thing as an indifferent human act. To consider an act as indifferent is to place it outside of

73. *ST* 1-2.18.2.

the realm of ethics, since "moral activities are in singulars, in which the various circumstances are considered."[74] It is, therefore, only in considering human acts as *not* indifferent (that is, when they are taken together with all their circumstances) that moral analysis can begin.

An example taken from Noldin will perhaps make this point more clear. Noldin, whose distinction between formal and material cooperation is much bound up with the notion of indifference, acknowledges that frequently "it is understood only with great difficulty whether some action is in itself evil or rather indifferent."[75] He puts forward, therefore, definitions of these terms: "The concept of an intrinsically evil thing or action is that it can have no good use; things and actions that, because of the end of the agent, could be good or bad are in themselves indifferent." As examples of non-indifferent acts, he lists the following: "utterly obscene images, utterly obscene writings, books utterly offensive to God and to religion, instruments that are only apt for impeding generation, medical means that can serve only for the procuring of an abortion."[76] The repeated word 'utterly' (*prorsus*) is already an indication that identifying intrinsically immoral acts is going to be, for Noldin, largely subjective.[77] But consider the last example: "medical means that can serve only for the procuring of an abortion." Let us say that the medical means adopted might indeed serve other purposes – that, for instance, the potion an assistant hands to the abortionist might also be used to sedate the

74. "Nam operationes morales sunt in singularibus, in quibus diversae circumstantiae considerantur" [*De malo* 2.6 ad 13].

75. H. Noldin et al., *Summa theologiae moralis*, 2.119.

76. "Admodum paucae sunt res (artificiales) in se malae, quae bonum usum habere non possunt; eiusmodi sunt imagines prorsus obscoenae, scripta prorsus obscoena, libri in Deum ac religionem prorsus contumeliosi, instrumenta, quae solum ad frustrandam generationem apta sunt, remedia quae solum ad procurandum abortum inservire possunt" [H. Noldin et al., *Summa theologiae moralis*, 2.120].

77. It also suggests that Noldin is in fact speaking about acts that are immoral on account of their end (a circumstance). An *utterly* obscene image, for instance, is one that is constructed in such a way that its only possible end is sexual arousal.

fetus. This fact has nothing to do with the gravity of the act that the assistant is performing and is of little help in the moral analysis of this act of cooperation.

Thomas Aquinas would never have taken this approach, for, as we have seen, he conceives of human actions as in every case having their existence within the larger moral universe. Like Alphonsus, Noldin, and Cretoni (and others), he does recognize that any indifference associated with a human act will disappear when the act is considered in all its particularity – "at least with respect to intention of the end" [*ST* 1-2.18.9c]. But in genuine cases of cooperation with evil that latter scenario will not present itself since, even "before" the intention of the end is a consideration, the intelligible proximity of the cooperator's act to that of the malefactor – in other words, the circumstance of cooperation – determines that the act is not indifferent. If, given such a circumstance, the cooperator does actually intend that his action help the malefactor – perhaps only in the way that Anscombe's water pumper, hired explicitly to poison the occupants of the house, intends to cooperate in the poisoning – that is a significant moral factor.[78] The character of one who does so cooperate is, by that act, more corrupted than one who does not so intend. But they both have a problem, and the problem is better understood by attending to the respective acts' strained relationship with reason and justice. Such an approach has the advantage of drawing attention away from the relationship between the cooperator and the malefactor and toward those who suffer injustice as a result of the cooperative action.

In the first book of the *Nicomachean Ethics*, Aristotle says that the human good "is the same thing for the individual and for the city [polis]," although he immediately puts the emphasis upon the good of the city (the common good) [*EN* 1.2 1194b7–9]. In the ninth book of the same work, he says that the good man is a lover of himself but that this means he understands that his own good is the common

78. On Anscombe's example, see the introduction, section I, and the present chapter, section IV.

good, in which he participates through his virtuous deeds [*EN* 9.8 1168b28–1169a11]. Thomas accepts all this. In his commentary on the first passage, he connects Aristotle's thesis with the "final cause" to which (as we have seen) all individual upright human acts must be proportionate. Thomas's approach, therefore, is always to look at the particular act being performed, for a person is responsible for that in all its relevant aspects; but those aspects are what they are because of their relationship with the common good of the polity within which the act is performed.

CHAPTER 3 SCANDAL

We saw in chapter 2 that Thomas Aquinas's idea that there are no particular indifferent human acts points us to the idea that any evaluation of a human act must be with respect to how well they fit into the moral universe itself. An act's status within the moral universe depends upon its circumstances, which Thomas defines as proportions [commensurationes] with respect to the "ultimate end" – and which, in fact, might be disproportions if they display incompatibility with the ultimate end and with the virtues that direct rational agents toward the ultimate end. Since no human act is without circumstances – that is, without a position within the larger moral universe – no human act is morally indifferent. Put another way, since human acts are rational entities, they must be evaluated morally with respect to the larger rational context within which they are performed, which inescapably calls for consistency with respect to the ultimate, rational end. Our understanding, therefore, of the moral universe itself – of its structure and the way in which acts fit into that structure – is the proper theater for the analysis of cooperation, since the pertinent questions invariably have to do, not with acts' substantial or special characteristics, but rather with how well they contribute to – or detract from – order in the moral universe.

Thomas's remarks on cooperation are not copious. We do, however, find in his writings quite a number of discussions having to do with the way in which acts relate to the moral universe. One such discussion – indeed, one that provides considerable insight not only into the way that acts in general relate to the moral universe but also into how acts of cooperation do so – is his discussion of scandal. For this reason, it merits our attention. Some fairly recent scholars have insisted that the issue of scandal is quite distinct from that of cooperation.[1] That is not a question that will concern us here. Even were it true that no instance of giving scandal constitutes immoral cooperation, Thomas's treatment of scandal would still merit attention because scandal is so similar to cooperation (as these others would have it) "strictly speaking." (The similarity – if not the overlap – is apparent once one understands that scandal is, by definition, the provision of the occasion for another's sin.) And, in any case, practically any situation in which immoral cooperation is an issue is also a situation in which scandal is an issue. The questions that we are attempting to answer in this book all have to do with what we should or should not do in such situations.

In the present chapter, we look first at Thomas's understanding of scandal and then at Alphonsus's.

I. Scandal according to Thomas Aquinas

The primary locus of Thomas's thought on scandal is *ST* 2-2.43, especially the first and third articles. In the first, he gives his precise

1. See especially Roger Roy, "La cooperation selon Saint Alphonse de Liguori," *Studia Moralia* 6 (1968): 383–89. See also G. J. Waffelaert, *Étude de théologie morale sur la coopération surtout en matière politique et religieuse, suivie d'une dissertation sur l'espèce morale du scandale* (Bruges: Vandenberghe-Denaux, 1883), 5–13, and G. J. Waffelaert, *Dissertations morales. 1ère série comprenant une étude sur la cooperation au mal surtout en matière politique et religieuse et une dissertation sur l'espèce morale du scandale (2e édition, entièrement revue)* (Bruges: C. Beyaert, 1892), 5–10. See also H. Noldin et al., *Summa theologiae moralis*, v. 2 §116, and Dominicus M. Prümmer, *Manuale theologiae moralis secundum principia S. Thomae Aquinatis* (Barcelona: Herder, 1961), v. 1, §617.

definition of scandal: "some less than correct remark or deed that provides occasion for another's ruin" (that is to say, their spiritual or moral ruin).[2] Scandal is said to involve something "less than correct" since what is done by the one genuinely giving scandal might only give the appearance of being in itself a bad act. In *ST* 2-2.43.1 ad 1, Thomas cites 1 Corinthians 8:10, where St. Paul asks, "For if any one sees you, a man of knowledge, at table in an idol's temple, might he not be encouraged, if his conscience is weak, to eat food offered to idols?"[3] Those who are knowledgeable know that eating food offered to pagan gods in itself is not wrong since such gods do not exist (1 Corinthians 8:4–6). One cannot honor beings one knows do not exist. Others, however, who do not fully understand this and whose consciences are correspondingly weak, when they see such persons eating food offered to these "gods," might be led to eat such food *as* an act of honoring the gods – and indeed that is what such an act would *be* morally, since that is what the person, in his relative ignorance, believes he is doing. Thus, one can provide the occasion for another's sin even if what one does, in itself, is not a sin; it can, however, be a sin in so far as it provides the occasion for the other's sin.

Thomas divides scandal into active and passive scandal – which is really just a way of distinguishing scandal qua existing in the scandalizer from scandal qua existing in the scandalized. When a man's fornication is known to his sons, the active scandal is the scandal that he "does" (whether he intends to do it or not); the passive scandal is his sons' being scandalized. It can happen that active scandal does not result in passive scandal – when, for instance, the sons already despise their father's general deportment. If the passive scandal occurs

2. "Et ideo convenienter dicitur quod dictum vel factum minus rectum praebens occasionem ruinae sit scandalum" [*ST* 2-2.43.1c]. Thomas also calls scandal "an obstacle conducing to ruin" ["obex disponens ad ruinam"]. Noldin will use the image of ripe fruit hanging from a tree, which, by its very presence, provides for someone the occasion of stealing [H. Noldin et al., *Summa theologiae moralis*, v. 2 §102c].

3. Thomas speaks here [*ST* 2-2.43.1 ad 1] of such actions as having "the appearance of sin" [habet speciem mali].

solely because of the weakness or ignorance of the scandalized, it is often called 'scandal of the little ones.' Thomas says that, in some cases in which "little ones" might be scandalized, even a spiritual good ought to be deferred until an explanation can be made.[4] It can also happen that passive scandal has no agent independent of the person scandalized. Take, for instance, the case of someone who performs a good action and others, out of maliciousness, use this as an occasion for ruin. The scandal stirred up is called 'pharisaical scandal,' after the Pharisees who, in reaction to Christ's rejection of their dietary regulations, stirred up within themselves negative dispositions and so provided the occasion for their own (passive) ruin – not to mention the occasion for the ruin of others.[5]

There is a controversy regarding the relationship between some remarks in *ST* 2-2.43.1 and some others in *ST* 2-2.43.3, the resolution of which will eventually be of help in understanding the various distinctions within cooperation (strictly speaking). In *ST* 2-2.43.1 ad 4 Thomas speaks of active scandal in the following manner: "One person's remark or deed can be the cause of another's sin in two ways: per

4. Pharisaical scandal [*scandalum Pharisaeorum*] and scandal of the little ones [*scandalum pusillorum*] are discussed in *ST* 2-2.43.7. The difference between Christ's rejection of the dietary regulations of the Pharisees and someone's eating food offered to idols (as in 1 Corinthians 8:4–6) is Christ's explaining why the regulations are not binding: "Hear and understand: not what goes into the mouth defiles a man but what comes out of the mouth, this defiles a man" (Matthew 15.10–11). Regarding scandal of the little ones, Thomas also says in *ST* 2-2.43.7 that if, once one's upright actions are explained, the scandal continues, it is likely that its cause is maliciousness; that is, the active scandal is in the person (or persons) scandalized.

5. In *ST* 2-2.43.7c, he speaks of the Pharisees's "stirring up scandals" ["scandala concitando"] and calls this "the scandal of the Pharisees" ["scandalum Pharisaeorum"]. In *ST* 2-2.43.6 ad 1, Thomas says that scandal is always the consequence of some active scandal, although the latter may be in the person scandalized. Regarding Peter's withdrawing from the gentiles in order to satisfy the Jews who criticized his living like a gentile, Thomas says in *ST* 2-2.43.6 ad 2 that in this case Peter sinned venially, although what he did ought not to have scandalized the gentiles. "Thus, they were subject to passive scandal; in Peter, however, there was not active scandal" ["Unde patiebantur scandalum passivum, non autem erat in Petro scandalum activum"] (see also *ST* 2-2.43.6 ad 3).

se and per accidens. It is per se when someone by an evil remark or deed [facto] either intends to induce the other to sin or also, if he does not intend this, the very thing he does [factum] is such that of its own intelligibility [ratione] it is an inducement to sin: for instance, when a person commits a sin publicly or does what has the appearance of sin."[6] So, per se scandal might involve just the "condition of the thing done," without the intention. He goes on then to say that per accidens cooperation occurs when the remark or deed is "beside the intention of the agent *and* beside the condition of the act."[7] Thomas gives an example of giving scandal per accidens: one person allows it to be known that he has certain goods and this causes another, who is "ill disposed [male dispositus]," to desire them. The connection here between allowing the goods to be known and that being the occasion of sin is different from, for instance, the connection between a father's fornication and a son's following suit. The former connection is per accidens, the latter per se, even if unintended by the father. The con-

6. "Ad quartum dicendum quod dictum vel factum alterius potest esse alteri causa peccandi dupliciter, uno modo, per se; alio modo, per accidens. Per se quidem, quando aliquis suo malo verbo vel facto intendit alium ad peccandum inducere; vel, etiam si ipse hoc non intendat, ipsum factum est tale quod de sui ratione habet ut sit inductivum ad peccandum, puta quod aliquis publice facit peccatum vel quod habet similitudinem peccati." It is important, at least in this context, not to translate *fatum* as 'act' or 'action' but rather to use a translation conveying the idea of a deed or a thing done. It is the thing qua done (and not qua act) that constitutes the scandal.

7. "But a person's word or deed is the cause of another's sinning per accidens when, even beside the intention of the agent and beside the condition of the act, some ill-disposed person, on account of such an act, is induced to sinning, for instance, when he covets the goods of others" ["Per accidens autem aliquod verbum vel factum unius est alteri causa peccandi, quando etiam praeter intentionem operantis, et praeter conditionem operis, aliquis male dispositus ex huiusmodi opere inducitur ad peccandum, puta cum aliquis invidet bonis aliorum"] [*ST* 2-2.43.1 ad 4]. Thomas's use of a linguistic pair — intention of the agent [*operantis*] / condition of the act [*operis*] — also makes it clear that he is deliberately juxtaposing the interior act of the agent and the exterior act that the agent performs. Earlier in the *Summa* Thomas associates the interior act with form, the exterior act with matter. See *ST* 1-2.18.6. Note, however, that Thomas does not mean matter in the physical sense; indeed, he says that the exterior act "has, in a way, the intelligibility of form — in as much as it gives species" [*ST* 1-2.18.2 ad 2].

dition of the thing he does in itself provides the occasion of sin. Even granting for the sake of the argument that scandal is not an instance of cooperation with evil, it is apparent that what Thomas says here about the non-intended giving of scandal is pertinent to the question of how central intention ought to be in the moral analysis of acts, including acts of cooperation.

That then is the position set out in *ST* 2-2.43.1 ad 4. Two articles later, however, Thomas offers what appears to be an incompatible analysis. In *ST* 2-2.43.3, he addresses the question "whether scandal is a special sin."[8] The objections maintain that it is not; the first, for instance, argues that scandal is "some less than correct remark or deed" and that this applies to all sins – so scandal is not a special sin. Thomas argues that, although scandal in the broad sense he has used so far is not the species-giving sin, one part of it is. He first excludes passive scandal as the special sin and then says of active scandal that it

> can be understood in a twofold manner: that is, per se and per accidens. It is per accidens when it is beside the intention [praeter intentionem] of the agent, as when someone by his inordinate deed or remark does not intend to give to another the occasion of ruin but intends only to satisfy his will [*ST* 2-2.43.3c].

This indeed appears to contradict *ST* 2-2.43.1 ad 4, where unintended active scandal was considered per se scandal. But the contradiction is indeed only apparent. Thomas follows Aristotle in wielding the expressions 'per se' and 'per accidens' (in Aristotle, καθ' αὑτό and κατὰ συμβεβεκός) in an extremely free manner, as instruments for making whatever distinctions having to do with intelligibility an argument might call for.[9] In a sense they are simply pointers, indi-

8. As mentioned above, in Thomas's Latin, unlike in current English, the word *specialis* is still closely associated with the word *species*. Thomas often points out that the idea of species of acts (including bad acts or sins) is found in Aristotle; here he refers to *EN* 5.2 1130a16–22.

9. I discuss the term 'intelligibility' in connection with the per se and the per accidens in chapter 5, section I.

cating "this here" and "that there," although 'per se' always indicates in some way a more direct or intelligible connection between two elements.[10] In the earlier passage, Thomas wished to call attention to the fact that active scandal, whether intended or not but related directly (per se) to its possible bad effect upon a scandalized person, is distinct from scandal in which there is no such relation. He did this by referring to the latter type of scandal as per accidens, the former *two* types as per se. Here in *ST* 2-2.43.3, however, the argument calls for a different distinction, although one he in effect recognized in *ST* 2-2.43.1 ad 4 by distinguishing intended from non-intended active per se scandal. He now "points" to the former by means of the phrase 'per se' and to the latter by means of the phrase 'per accidens.'

So, Thomas's answer in *ST* 2-2.43.3 to the question whether scandal is a special sin is that the actual role of constituting the special sin is played not by scandal in the broadest sense – which includes also non-intended active and passive scandal – but by a subcategory of it: active per se scandal that is intended. The species-giving cannot be done by passive scandal, since someone might be "scandalized to do" any number of things: fornicate, steal, lie, etc., etc.; there is nothing "special" (that is, specifying) here. But neither can it be done by active per se scandal that is not intended: scandal in which the mere "condition of the thing done" makes it to be scandal. This latter cannot be the special sin since, once again, what the scandalizer does – his *opus* – might be of various species: fornication, theft, lying, etc.

The role of special sin falls, therefore, to active per se scandal that is intended, for the *intention* of one committing scandal in this way is to occasion the ruin of another person; and that is a specific act, distinct from the species of act by means of which he scandalizes. It is one thing to fornicate; it is quite another to fornicate so that another might fall into sin – and this latter captures the essence of what it is to give scandal. Active per se scandal that is not intended is "some

10. On Thomas's and Aristotle's use of the per se/per accidens distinction, see Flannery, *Action and Character According to Aristotle*, chapter 5.

less than correct remark or deed that provides occasion for another's ruin" – so it *is* scandal: it does to the other exactly what active per se scandal that is intended does. But that name 'scandal' belongs properly to active per se scandal that is intended.[11]

A parallel passage in Thomas's commentary on Peter Lombard's *Sentences* confirms this account of the relationship between *ST* 2-2.43.1 ad 4 and *ST* 2-2.43.3;[12] it also gives us a fuller explanation of how, for instance, even active scandal that is not intended, although it is not the special sin, can still be called 'scandal.' The objections in *Sent.* 4.38.2.2.2 defend the same position defended by the objections in *ST* 2-2.43.3, that is, that scandal is not a special sin. The most important of the objections (the first and second) argue in effect that any type of sin can scandalize; therefore, scandal lacks specificity.

Thomas uses throughout his response the distinction between that which is "elicited" [elicitur] and that which is "commanded" [imperatur].[13] Earlier in *Sent.* – that is, in *Sent.* 3.27.2.4.3 – he gives a succinct account of this distinction:

> This is the difference between eliciting an act and commanding one: a habit or power elicits with no intermediate [nullo mediante] that act which it produces with respect to an object, but [a habit or power] commands the act which is produced by means of [mediante] an inferior power or habit, with respect to the object of that power.[14]

11. For Thomas, an act's getting its species is the same as its getting its name. See, for instance, *ST* 2-2.59.2, where he says that an act of injustice "receives its species and name from its per se object and not from its per accidens object." In this article Thomas recognizes that a person might genuinely do what is unjust ["facit iniustum"], even though, strictly speaking, he is not *being unjust*: he might, for example, not know what he is doing or do it out of anger but not with the intention of being unjust.

12. *Sent.* 4.38.2.2.2 refers to the second sub-question – or *quaestiuncula* – of the second article of the second question of distinction 38 of the fourth book of Thomas's commentary on the *Sentences*.

13. On this distinction, see Alan Donagan, "Thomas Aquinas on Human Action," in *The Cambridge History of Later Medieval Philosophy*, ed. Norman Kretzmann et al. (Cambridge: Cambridge University Press, 1982), 642–54.

14. "Hoc enim interest inter elicere actum et imperare, quod habitus vel potentia

The particular habit that Thomas is discussing here in *Sent.* 3 also plays a part in *Sent.* 4.38.2.2.2: it is the habit known as the virtue of charity, which is "compared to all the other virtues as mover and as end and as form."[15] Since this is "the mother of the other virtues," it commands the lower virtues, for it "causes them to operate for its end" (that is, is charity's end: happiness in Christ).[16] Knowledge

---

elicit illum actum quem producit circa objectum nullo mediante: sed imperat actum qui producitur mediante potentia vel habitu inferiori circa objectum illius potentiae" [*Sent.* 3.27.2.4.3].

15. On charity in relation to justice, see chapter 4, section I.

16. "Regarding the third question it must be said that charity is compared to all the other virtues as mover and as end and as form. That it should be the mover of all the other virtues is apparent from the fact that the good itself, which is the object of charity under the ratio of an end, is the end of the virtues. Now, in all ordered potencies or arts, it turns out that an art or potency that is for an end orders the acts of other arts or potencies to its proper end—just as the military art, which aims at victory, toward which every office of war is ordered, orders the cavalry, the navy, and all such offices to its end. And so charity is called the mother of the other virtues in as much as it produces their acts from the conception of the end, which functions as a seed, since it is 'the principle in actions,' as the Philosopher says. And in this way charity is said to command the acts of the lower virtues, according as it causes them to operate for its end; and in this way it moves the other inferior arts toward its end. And so charity also moves all the other virtues toward its end, and in this way it is said to command their acts" ["Ad tertiam quaestionem dicendum, quod caritas ad omnes alias virtutes comparatur et ut motor et ut finis et ut forma. Quod autem motor sit omnium aliarum virtutum, ex hoc patet, quia ipsum bonum, quod est objectum caritatis sub ratione finis, est finis virtutum. In omnibus autem potentiis vel artibus ordinatis ita accidit, quod ars vel potentia quae est circa finem, ordinat aliarum actus ad finem proprium; sicut militaris, quae est propter victoriam, ad quam omne officium bellicum ordinatur, ordinat equestrem et navalem et omnia hujusmodi in suum finem. Et ideo dicitur caritas mater aliarum virtutum, inquantum earum actus producit ex conceptione finis, qui habet se per modum seminis, cum sit 'principium in operabilibus,' ut dicit Philosophus: et secundum hoc dicitur imperare actus inferiorum virtutum, secundum quod facit eas operari propter finem suum; et secundum hoc movet alias artes inferiores ad finem suum. Unde caritas etiam omnes alias virtutes ad suum finem movet, et secundum hoc dicitur earum actus imperare"] [*Sent.* 3.27.2.4.3]. In replying to the second objection of *ST* 2-2.23.4 (which asks whether charity is a special virtue), Thomas says similarly: "The virtue or art which pertains to the ultimate end, commands the virtues or arts which pertain to other, secondary ends; thus the military art commands the art of horse-riding [*Nicomachean Ethics* 1.1 1094a9–13]. And so, since charity has for its object the ultimate end of human life, i.e., everlasting happiness, therefore, it

of the specific end of charity comes only with divine revelation, but Thomas makes it apparent in both places (both *Sent.* 3.27.2.4.3 and *Sent.* 4.38.2.2.2) that the same sort of analysis can be conducted when the agent involved knows nothing of Christ. He cites the Aristotelian idea that the acts of any person stand in relation to a "first principle" [ἀρχή]. For Aristotle this was simply happiness [εὐδαιμονία]; through revelation we know that happiness is specifically in the love of Christ.[17]

Thomas's answer in *Sent.* 4.38.2.2.2 to the question whether scandal is a special sin is as follows:

An act is determined to a moral species in two ways. One way is on the part of the object, as fornication is [determined] in so far as it is about the pleasures of touch. This determination is material and regards the habit that elicits the act. Another way is on the part of the end: this is formal specification and regards the commanding habit.

It can happen occasionally, however, that an act is determined to the same species on either part, as when some act is both elicited and commanded by the same habit, as when someone fornicates for the sake of pleasure.[18] Sometimes, however, an act is determined from either part but to diverse species, as when an act is elicited by one habit and commanded by another, as when someone fornicates for profit; this act is determined to the species of luxury because of its object but to the species of avarice because of its end.

---

extends itself to the acts of the whole of human life by way of command, not as if eliciting immediately all acts of virtue."

17. In *Sent.* 3.27.2.4.3, in support of his point that the end is like a seed, Thomas cites Aristotle: "since it is 'the principle in actions,' as the Philosopher says." (See the larger translation in the previous note.) The reference is likely to *EN* 7.8 1151a16: ἐν δὲ ταῖς πράξεσι τὸ οὗ ἕνεκα ἀρχή. In *Sent.* 4.38.2.2.2, the first objection, which introduces the idea of a special sin, he also makes reference to Aristotle: " "For, according to what the Philosopher says in book 5 of the Ethics, every special act of injustice at some time is found separate from all other acts of injustice" ["Quia secundum philosophum in 5 Ethic., omnis specialis injustificatio quandoque invenitur separata ab omnibus aliis injustificationibus"]. The reference here is probably to *EN* 5.2 1130a16–22. See also Thomas Aquinas, *in EN* 5.3 16–54 (§§914–15).

18. Here the vice of "luxury" comes into the act immediately but also commands the physical movements that bring the person to fornicate.

(There are not here, however, two sins but one "double sin," since the act is one.)

Sometimes it also happens that some act is determined to a *particular* species not on the part of the object but on the part of the end, in so far as it has a determinate habit by which it is commanded but not by which it is elicited, as in the case of edifying one's neighbor – which act charity does not elicit since it belongs to charity only to elicit interior acts, by means of which edification does not occur. But charity does command edification and it is elicited by the other virtues materially: not determinately by any one virtue but by them all since charity can issue commands to them all.[19]

And because active scandal is the sin opposed to edification of neighbors, therefore, materially speaking, on the part of the material and of the eliciting habits it is not a special sin – but [it is such] only speaking formally, on the part of the end and the commanding habit, which is the habit opposed to charity, that is, the vice of hatred. And so when someone makes a less than correct remark or performs a less than correct deed intending to present the occasion of ruin to a neighbor, he commits the special sin by scandalizing. If, however, this occurs beside his intention, the active scandal will not be the special sin. Nonetheless it will be a certain circumstance[20] of the sin because, just as whatever act of virtue *has* an order toward the end of charity, although the act is not *ordered* toward that end, and just as it has an aptitude to be commanded by charity, so also whatever sin, with respect to what it is in itself, *has* an order to the contrary end, although that end is not intended by the agent.[21]

19. As becomes clear toward the end of the argument where he speaks of "whatever act of virtue" [*quilibet actus virtutis*] and "whatever sin" [*quodlibet peccatum*], Thomas does not mean that an act that edifies one's neighbor necessarily involves all the other subordinate virtues; rather, he means that it involves no particular subordinate virtue.

20. Thomas speaks here of a circumstance because of the third objection, which argues that a circumstance such as "before another" [*coram alio*] cannot add a new species to an act (as the special sin of scandal would do to whatever act causes the scandal). *ST* 22.43.3 obi. and ad 3 contains similar language. One could express Thomas's point here by saying that the *scandalousness* attaching to the bad act (e.g. the father's fornication) is a certain circumstance of that bad act; but it is important not to lose sight of the fact that, even when the scandal is unintended, there is *scandal* there – not just some abstract quality called scandalousness. (I go into these matters more thoroughly below.)

21. "Ad secundam quaestionem dicendum, quod actus aliquis determinatur ad

Any human act has a material aspect and a formal aspect, referred to respectively as the exterior act and the interior act.[22] Each is elicited by a habit (or power) that is good or bad. Sometimes both exterior act and interior are elicited by the same object, as when a man fornicates, i.e., goes "materially" toward the object 'pleasure of the flesh,' because he intends to have pleasure of the flesh. Here the matter and the form of the act coincide. Sometimes the two do not coincide, as when a man fornicates (goes materially toward pleasure), but for money (this intention providing the form of the act). As Thomas says elsewhere, the two aspects of this particular act are related per acci-

---

speciem moris dupliciter. Uno modo ex parte objecti, sicut fornicatio ex hoc quod est circa delectabilia tactus; et haec determinatio est materialis, et respicit habitum elicientem actum. Alio modo ex parte finis; et haec est formalis specificatio, et respicit habitum imperantem.

Contingit autem quandoque quod ad eamdem speciem determinatur actus ex utraque parte, sicut quando aliquis actus ab eodem habitu elicitur et imperatur, ut cum quis fornicatur propter delectationem. Quandoque autem ex utraque parte determinatur, sed ad diversas species, ut quando actus ab uno habitu elicitur, et ab alio imperatur, sicut cum quis fornicatur propter lucrum; determinatur enim ad speciem luxuriae ex objecto, sed ad speciem avaritiae ex fine; non tamen sunt ibi duo peccata, sed unum peccatum duplex, cum sit unus actus.

Quandoque etiam evenit quod aliquis actus non determinatur ad aliquam certam speciem ex parte objecti, sed ex parte finis, eo quod habet determinatum habitum a quo imperatur, sed non a quo eliciatur, sicut aedificare proximum, quem actum caritas non elicit, quia ejus non est elicere nisi interiores actus, per quos non fit aedificatio, sed imperat eum, et ab aliis virtutibus elicitur materialiter, non determinate ab aliqua, sed ab omnibus, quia caritas omnibus imperare potest.

Et quia scandalum activum est peccatum oppositum aedificationi proximorum; ideo, materialiter loquendo, ex parte materiae et habituum elicientium non est speciale peccatum, sed solum loquendo formaliter, ex parte finis et habitus imperantis qui est habitus caritati oppositus, scilicet vitium odii; et ideo quando aliquis dictum vel factum minus rectum facit intendens occasionem ruinae proximo praestare, speciale peccatum scandalizando committit. Si autem praeter intentionem suam accidat, non erit scandalum activum speciale peccatum; tamen erit circumstantia quaedam peccati, eo quod sicut quilibet actus virtutis habet ordinem ad finem caritatis, etiamsi actus non ordinetur in finem illum, et sicut habet aptitudinem ut imperetur a caritate; ita quodlibet peccatum, quantum est de se, habet ordinem ad contrarium finem, etiamsi ille finis non intendatur ab agente" [*Sent.* 4.38.2.2.2c].

22. *ST* 1-2.18.6.

dens: there is no intelligible link between fornication and financial gain.[23]

It can happen that a genuine distinction between the material and the formal aspects involves not a per accidens relationship, as in the relationship between fornication and financial gain, but simply the fact that the end sought can also motivate other types of bad acts. Hatred, the end of active per se scandal that is intended, might be the end not of an act of fornication that one hopes will lead another to ruin but of an act of theft that one hopes will have a similar result. Because the material is not specific (it could be fornication, theft, lying, or whatever sin), the act considered at that level cannot be the special sin of scandal. That role falls rather to the act at the formal level – provided that there *is* such an act. When a man intends to scandalize another, there is such an act, and that act makes the act he performs in order to provide the occasion for the ruin of the other the special sin of scandal.

This does not mean, however, that an act in which someone provides the occasion for the ruin for another but does not intend to do so – as when the father provides the occasion for the ruin of his son by fornicating sheerly for pleasure – is not an act of scandal. For there is also here a certain connection with the end of disedification (which is, of course, the contrary of edification). Just as any act of virtue, even if not performed in order to edify, has a connection with edification in so far as it *could* be performed for that reason, so also an act such as the father's has a connection with disedification, even if he does not intend to disedify (or to give scandal), since it could be performed for that reason. As Thomas suggests in the above quotation, the act "has an aptitude [habet aptitudinem]" to be commanded by hatred.

This does not, however, make the connection with the vice of hatred (by way of disedification) anything less than a moral connection; it certainly does not make it, for instance, a merely physical connection. The connection has to do with reason – what it is reasonable or

23. *ST* 1-2.18.7.

not reasonable to do – and that makes the connection a moral connection. The father's act is scandalous since it is not good to disedify others, even unintentionally, and especially not one's own sons. This aptitude to disedification does not make the father's active scandal the special sin of scandal; it does, however, make it "a certain *circumstance* of the sin," as Thomas says in *Sent.* 4.38.2.2.2c.[24]

What does it mean for something to be a circumstance of a sin? One needs to bear in mind that in Thomas's vocabulary an end might be a circumstance. As we have seen in chapter 2, section I, Aristotle, upon whom Thomas is partially reliant in what he says about circumstances, speaks in this regard of the daughters of Pelias who, misled by the sorceress Medea, believe that in dismembering their father and boiling the body parts, they will make him younger.[25] The unintended end of their action is, of course, their father's death. Let us suppose for the moment that the daughters of Pelias were blamably feckless in trusting Medea. Even if the end of their action (their father's death) was unintended, that end *might* have been intended – in the sense, that is, that their act had an aptitude to having as its intended end the death of their father. This is enough – given their fecklessness – to characterize their act as immoral, although it does not make it to be the special sin itself: they have not *murdered* their father. Similarly, although a person's act of fornication might not be intended to scandalize others, since that act could and ought to have been avoided, scandal becomes a circumstance of the act, that is to say, a morally significant characteristic attaching to the act.

The third objection in *Sent.* 4.38.2.2.2 argues that a circumstance such as "before another [coram alio]" – or, for that matter, "secretly [occulte]" – does not add to a particular sin a specifying differentia. Thomas responds:

24. See above, notes 20 and 21.

25. See *Eudemian Ethics* 2.9 1225b2–3; see Flannery, *Action and Character According to Aristotle*, 120–21, 135–37, 155. The list of elements traditionally called the circumstances appears at *EN* 3.1 1111a3–6.

This circumstance "before another" adds to the sin a new species, not by virtue of its own character [ex sui ratione], but by virtue of the end toward which, through [per] such a circumstance, it [the sin] is orderable [ordinabilis]. Thus also, to sin in secret [in occulto] does not draw the sin into a new species, since the sin does not in this way receive an ordering toward another end.

So, the circumstance "before another" can be the means by which a sin becomes also the special sin of scandal, on the condition that "before another" attaches itself somehow to the agent's end. This condition is fulfilled when, for instance, a man commits fornication so that another man might do the same. If the sin is not so ordered, the circumstance "before another" functions only as a circumstance. As such, the sin can be scandalous but not the special sin of scandal. In as much as "before another" does remain a mere circumstances, it is like the circumstance "secretly," although it is also different from it, since the circumstance "secretly" *cannot* be the means by which a sin becomes the special sin of scandal.

A related and illuminating remark is found in *ST* 1-2.73.8. The question asked in the article is whether harm done increases the gravity of a sin. Thomas makes various remarks to the effect that the gravity depends on whether the harm was intended and/or foreseen. He eventually says that, when the harm is neither intended nor foreseen, we must make a distinction. If the harm is per accidens related to the sin, it does not directly add to the gravity, although the attendant negligence does do so. "If, however, the harm follows per se from the sin," he says, "even though it is neither intended nor foreseen, it directly aggravates the sin, for whatever things follow upon a sin per se pertain, in a certain sense [quodammodo], to the sin's very species." In this case, the extra harm done does not *quite* affect the sin's species although it does something quite similar to that. He gives the example of someone who fornicates "publicly" [publice] or in a way known to others generally. Sinning publicly – we might call this sinning in the circumstance "before all" – is related per se to giving scandal. From such an act it follows, he says, that many are scandalized—that is to say, the public nature of the act is such that they are possibly led into sin themselves—and for this reason the gravity of the sin is increased directly.[26] And so, even if, because it is unintended and unforeseen, the circumstance "before all" does not add the special sin of scandal to the other sin (fornication, in the example Thomas gives), its per se connection with widespread scandal augments the gravity of that sin.

One cannot help but to be struck by the strength of Thomas's language here. The harm possibly done "*directly* aggravates the sin"; it attaches to "the sin's *very species*." The reason for this is not that scandal stirs up emotions or creates a public furor but rather that there is a per se connection between the bad act performed and the bad acts that quite possibly follow from it. In a certain sense, the first person is *involved* in the possible subsequent bad acts. And yet it is also true that no new species is added to the act of fornication: the scandal attaching to the act is not a species but a circumstance.

That Thomas is willing to talk about augmentation in these contexts suggests that such talk would not be inappropriate with reference to cooperation—even when the cooperator does not share the intention of the malefactor.

II. Scandal according to Alphonsus Liguori

How much of this finds its way into Alphonsus? That is a complicated—but useful—story, for it confirms ideas put forward in the first chapter of the present work regarding Alphonsus's conception of formal and material cooperation, even while it points to his failure, not entirely his own fault, to understand Thomas's remarks on scandal and therefore also his account of how the morality of human

26. "Si vero nocumentum per se sequatur ex actu peccati, licet non sit intentum nec praevisum, directe peccatum aggravat, quia quaecumque per se consequuntur ad peccatum, pertinent quodammodo ad ipsam peccati speciem. Puta si aliquis publice fornicetur, sequitur scandalum plurimorum, quod quamvis ipse non intendat, nec forte praevideat, directe per hoc aggravatur peccatum" [*ST* 1-2.73.8c].

acts depends upon their place within the larger context of the moral universe itself.[27]

In the first edition of his *Theologia moralis*, in the article on what scandal is, how multiform it is, and what sort of sin it is, Alphonsus repeats (as he does also in later editions) what he finds in Hermann Busenbaum and then adds two remarks of his own, each beginning with the word *quaeritur* (*Quaeritur* I and *Quaeritur* II), the first of which interests us.[28] Busenbaum himself is somewhat dismissive of Thomistic inspired speculations on whether scandal is a special sin. "Every active scandal," he says, "directly intending the ruin of a neighbor, is a special sin contrary to charity, this being maintained by all. But whether the same holds when it is intended indirectly, this is debated by the scholastics, with scarce reference to practice" [*Theologia moralis* 2.43]. He cites Thomas Sánchez [1550–1610], Juan Azor [1535–1603], Martin Bonacina [d.1631].

In Alphonsus's first *quaeritur* — which begins, "It is asked first, When is scandal a special sin?" — he distinguishes two opinions. The first he calls "probable" [probabilis], the second "more probable" [probabilior]. Here is his account of the first:

The first, probable opinion asserts that scandal is the special sin against charity only when the spiritual ruin of one's neighbor is expressly intended.[29]

27. Useful in this regard, but taking a position in various respects different from that presented here, is G. J. Waffelaert, *Dissertations Morales. 1ère série comprenant une étude sur la coopération au mal surtout en matière politique et religieuse et une Dissertation sur l'espèce morale du scandale* (Bruges: Beyaert-Storie, 1892, 2e édition, entièrement revue), 79–151. (The cited pages contain his *Dissertation sur l'espèce morale du scandale*.)

28. Busenbaum and de Ligorio, *Medulla theologiae moralis R. P. Hermanni Busembaum Societatis Jesu Theologi, cum adnotationibus per Reverendum Patrem D. Alphonsum de Ligorio*, coll. 84–86. This is book 2, tract 3 ("De praeceptis caritatis"), *dubium* 5, article 1; it corresponds to what is found in the Gaudé edition [Alphonsus Maria de Ligorio, *Theologia Moralis*] at pp. 336–44 of vol. 1. The relevant part of the latter is translated in appendix 3. In that translation, Busenbaum's words are in all caps, Alphonsus's in standard type. As will be explained, there are considerable differences between what Alphonsus says in the first edition and what he says later.

29. This ("expresse intenditur") differs from later editions, which have "directe

Thus Sánchez, Bonacina, along with, according to the Salmanticenses, Palaus, Azor, Bañez, Trullench, and so on. The reasoning is that,[30] in order for some sin to be distinct in a special way it must have a special end contrary to the corresponding virtue. But, when the ruin of one's neighbor is not intended, charity is not harmed; harmed rather is that virtue which the neighbor is induced to harm.[31] And so such scandal is reduced to that species of sin toward which the neighbor is induced, whether directly by order or by counsel, or indirectly by example or by word.[32]

This description of the first opinion is virtually identical to what we find in later editions of *Theologia moralis*. Alphonsus appears to have primarily in mind Sánchez, against whom he explicitly argues in this regard in the subsequent paragraph. Noticeable here is one idea that does not appear in Thomas's *ST* 22.43.3 (the article about whether scandal is a special sin): the idea that, when the special sin of scandal is not present, whatever sinfulness *is* present "is reduced to that species of sin toward which the neighbor is induced." This additional idea comes from Sánchez.[33] Thomas Aquinas would never have said such

intenditur." The former expression comes from the Salmanticenses [Salmanticenses (Collegium Salmanticense), *Collegii Salmanticensis cursus theologiae moralis* (Venice: N. Pezzana, 1715), tom. 5 cap. 8 punct. 5 n. 51 (p. 177)], whom Alphonsus is closely following here. That he is using the Salmanticenses is evident in the severely truncated quotation from Thomas's *ST* 2-2.43.1 he quotes in setting out the second opinion. It corresponds word-for-word to what the Salmanticenses give in n. 53 (p. 178) as part of their second opinion.

30. In later editions, Alphonsus speaks of the reasoning "of these learned men": "Ratio horum DD," the abbreviation 'DD' standing for *doctores* (or here *doctorum*).

31. Later editions have "charity is not harmed in a special way [non specialiter laeditur caritas]."

32. "sive directe, jussu, consilio; sive indirecte, exemplo, dicto."

33. "Therefore, if by counsel or persuasion or example someone induces another to a sin, not in order that he might fall into the sin but for some other purpose (whatever that might be), that is not the special sin of scandal but scandal as generally accepted, and it is reduced to that species toward which it induces the other" ["Quare siue consilio, sive suasione, sive exemplo quis alium ad peccatum inducat, non eo fine ut in peccatum incidat, sed alio quocunque, non est speciale scandali peccatum, sed scandalum generaliter acceptum, & reducitur ad eam peccati speciem, ad quod inducit"] [Thomas Sanchez [Tomás Sánchez], *Opus morale in praecepta decalogi* (Madrid: L. Sanchez & I. Hasreij, 1613), 1.6.3 (p. 31b)].

a thing. When a man's fornication causes another also to fornicate, whether or not he intends to bring about the ruin of the other man, he does commit fornication by his fornicating but *not* by his scandalizing.

Alphonsus's paragraph on the second opinion actually includes further remarks in rebuttal of the first (i.e., the position of Sánchez). It reads as follows:

> The second, more probable opinion holds that the sin of scandal against charity is given always — and indeed directly or indirectly the occasion of ruin is given to a neighbor, although the ruin is not intended.[34] Following this opinion are the Salmanticenses, Lugo, Navarrus, Soto, de Valentia, Suárez, etc., and St. Thomas appears clearly to teach this. And, although Sánchez cites him for his own opinion (*ST* 2-2.43.3), nonetheless in *ST* 2-2.43.1 ad 4 the holy teacher so speaks: "When someone by an evil deed or remark intends to induce the other to sin or also, if he does not intend this, [and] the very thing he does is an inducement, then he gives the occasion of ruin; and thus it is called active scandal." To be noted is that in that case [tunc], besides the sin of scandal, which according to the second opinion is perpetrated, committed is also another sin of that species toward which the other is induced, as note the Salmanticenses,[35] along with Busenbaum [*Theologia moralis* 2.44 "3rd"], together with Lugo and Laymann.[36]

34. The Latin here — "Secunda probabilior sententia tenet, dari peccatum scandali contra caritatem, semper ac directe, vel indirecte datur proximo occasio ruinae, etsi ruina non intendatur" — is very awkward. Part of the wording — in particular, the idea of "giving" the sin of scandal — originates with the Salmanticenses: "The second opinion asserts: the special sin of scandal is given when it is estimated that probably the utterance or deed will be the occasion of ruin, even though this is not expressly or directly intended" ["Secunda sententia asserit: dari speciale peccatum scandali, quando probabiliter existimatur, dictum, aut factum futurum esse occasionem ruinae, licet haec expresse & directe non intendatur"] [Salmanticenses (Collegium Salmanticense), *Collegii Salmanticensis cursus theologiae moralis*, tom. 5 cap. 8 punct. 5 n. 52 (p. 177)].

35. Salmanticenses (Collegium Salmanticense), *Collegii Salmanticensis cursus theologiae moralis*, tom. 5 cap. 8 punct. 5 n. 56 (p. 178).

36. "Secunda probabilior *sententia* tenet, dari peccatum scandali contra caritatem, semper ac directe, vel indirecte datur proximo occasio ruinae, etsi ruina non intendatur. Hanc sequuntur Salmanticenses, Lugo, Suarez, etc., et hanc videtur clare docere S. Thomas. Et quamvis Sanchez citet ipsum pro sua sententia (2.2 q. 43 art. 3), tamen art. 1 ad 4 sic loquitur S. Doctor: *Quando aliquis suo malo facto vel verbo intendit alium ad*

Worthy of note here is the (as we shall see, relatively simple) distinction between directly and indirectly scandalizing. This second (more probable) opinion maintains, somewhat similarly to the first, that the scandalizer who does not intend to scandalize (that is, who scandalizes indirectly) does commit the sin of scandal and also "another sin of that species toward which the other is induced." As to the interjected argument against Sánchez, it is apparent that Alphonsus does not understand that, as we have seen, *ST* 2-2.43.1 ad 4 has nothing to do with identifying the special sin of scandal, the subject of *ST* 2-2.43.3; indeed, it seems unlikely that he understands the very point of the question, what determines a special sin.

In the second edition of the *Theologia moralis*, which appeared in the years 1753–55, Alphonsus included an *Elenchus quaestionum* ["list of questions"] in which he speaks very briefly of changes made to the first edition and refers the reader to the appropriate places in both the first and second editions. One of these questions, the 6th, has to do with the *quaeritur* we have been considering.[37] Alphonsus acknowledges that in the earlier edition he had said that the opinion held by "Palaus, Sánchez, Bonacina, Azor, etc.," was "probable," that is, the first opinion, according to which, as he explains it now, "one does not sin against charity unless one expressly intends the spiritual ruin of the other." "But in this book," he says, "the affirmative opinion is seen to be true," i.e., that one *does* sin against charity whether one expressly intends the ruin of the other or not.[38]

---

peccandum inducere, vel etiam si ipse hoc non intendat, [&] ipsum factum est inductivum ad peccandum, tunc ille dat occasionem ruinae; unde vocatur scandalum activum. Et notandum, quod tunc ultra peccatum scandali, quod patratur juxta secundam sententențiam, committitur etiam aliud peccatum ejus specie, ad quod alius inducitur, ut notant Salmanticenses, cum Busenbaum hic (n. 3), cum Lugo et Laymann" [Busenbaum and de Ligorio, *Medulla theologiae*, coll. 85–86].

37. It has to do, that is, with his first remark on Busenbaum's article on what scandal is, how multiform it is, and what sort of sin it is [see appendix 3, nn. 43–45]; in that remark, Alphonsus sets out the two opinions.

38. "Qu. 6. An, qui inducit sive directe sive indirecte proximum ad peccandum, semper peccet peccato scandali. In primo libro (col. 85, v. *Quaer. I*) dictum est cum Palao,

Accordingly, in the second and later editions, the first opinion is no longer described as probable. Neither is the second opinion described as "more probable," as it was in the first edition, and Alphonsus's description of that position has changed somewhat. Moreover, whereas earlier, in the second opinion, scandal was divided into direct and indirect, in this revised version also direct scandal is divided into two: "directly and formally, intending the [other person's] spiritual ruin" and "directly but not formally," as when a man seduces a woman not with the intention that she be spiritually ruined but simply in order to satisfy his lust. Indirect scandal continues, as in the first edition, to concern "the occasion" of ruin or sin; but, whereas earlier Alphonsus spoke of someone's giving occasion, here he says that "the other *draws* the occasion of sinning from one's example."

Alphonsus then offers a third opinion, which is clearly the "affirmative opinion" he describes as true in the *Elenchus quaestionum*, question number 6; his succinct statement of this third opinion reads as follows:

> The *third opinion,* to which I subscribe, holds that one who directly or indirectly induces a neighbor to sin sins *in two ways*: that is, both against charity and against the virtue toward the harming of which he induces the neighbor [emphasis in the original].

So, Alphonsus accepts the threefold division of the revised second opinion but rejects the idea that only directly scandalizing involves a sin against "the virtue which the neighbor is induced to harm."

Alphonsus then, in successive numbered points, explains why he does not accept the first opinion and why he does not accept the second. Regarding the first, he repeats his ill-conceived use of *ST* 2-2.43.1 ad 4 as a counter to *ST* 2-2.43.3 (the article about the special sin of scandal). He also mentions the sin that Thomas mentions so often: that of sacrilege. The relevant text reads as follows:[39]

Sanchez, Bonacina, Azor, etc., probabile esse, quod is non peccet contra charitatem, nisi expresse intendat ruinam spiritualem alterius. Sed in hoc visa est vera sententia affirmativa. Vide *Lib. II, n. 45*" [Alphonsus Maria de Ligorio, *Theologia moralis*, vol. 4, 699].

39. For the full passage, see appendix 3, at §45, question 1, "the *third opinion.*"

If charity obliges us, when we can, to correct or impede our neighbor lest he fall ruined into sin, how much more does it oblige us not to impel him into sin by counsel or example! Nor does the argument adduced – that in order to harm charity required is a special end of harming it – stand in the way of this position, for speaking generally it suffices to place something destructive of whatever virtue for that virtue to be offended – even though this is not intended. For instance, if someone kills an enemy in a church, even though he might not intend to commit an offense against religion, nonetheless he sins not only against justice but also against religion, since by the very act he harms it.[40]

A reasonable response to this argument would be that, although Thomas never discusses the question directly, it would be contrary to his common practice – not to mention the principles of logic as

40. For present intents and purposes, this latter example is equivalent to the example that Thomas uses in *De malo* 2.6 ad 6: "although the will of the thief is not directed toward the sacred thing principally, but rather toward the gold, it is directed toward the sacred thing because of what is implied." See also *Sent.* 4.16.3.2.3 ("ad tertiam questionem"): "sometimes the species of a sin varies without the intention being brought to bear upon that circumstance, as when a thief would just as happily take a non-sacred golden goblet as a sacred one; and nonetheless the sin is changed into another species, that is, from a simple theft into sacrilege" ["aliquando variatur species peccati sine hoc quod intentio feratur ad circumstantiam illam; sicut fur ita libenter acciperet vas aureum non sacratum sicut sacratum; et tamen in aliam speciem peccatum mutatur, scilicet de furto simplici in sacrilegium"]; see also the discussion in chapter 2. The sin of sacrilege has primarily to do not so much with the thing violated (the matter) as with the violating (the form) – although, of course, some matter is required in order to receive the form. In *ST* 2-2.99.2c, Thomas says that the species of anything (such as a sin) depends primarily upon "its formal character" rather than "its matter or subject" ["species cuiuslibet rei praecipue attenditur secundum formalem rationem ipsius, non autem secundum materiam vel subiectum"]. He goes on then to say: "In sacrilege, however, there is found a special character of deformity – because, that is, a sacred thing is violated by way of some irreverence." In *ST* 2-2.99.2 ad 2, Thomas says that "by whatever type of sin one goes against the reverence due to sacred things, one commits sacrilege formally, although materially there might be present diverse types of sins" ["quocumque genere peccati aliquis faciat contra reverentiam debitam sacris rebus, sacrilegium formaliter committit, licet materialiter sint ibi diversa genera peccatorum"] [*ST* 2-2.99.2 ad 2]. (In *De malo* 2.6c, Thomas similarly associates sacrilege with form rather than with matter: see appendix 4, at [IIIa].)

applied in the moral realm – to say that unintended (but knowing) sacrilege is the special sin. Again, Thomas's concern in *ST* 2-2.43.3 is simply to determine what *is* the special sin of scandal, and his answer to that question is clearly that the special sin is active scandal that is intended. He does not say that the non-intended active scandal of *ST* 2-2.43.1 ad 4 is not a sin. It is a sin: a sin of scandal and a sin that goes against charity. It is just not the special sin, since, not only can it be committed by committing any type of sin,[41] but it is not the *type* of general sin that might also be a special sin. It is not, for instance, a generic sin containing species of sin under itself in the way that, to use Thomas's example, imprudence does.[42]

In the second numbered point, Alphonsus says that he differs also with the second opinion in so far as he holds that even indirectly scandalizing entails that the scandalizer "sins also against the virtue he induced ... the neighbor to harm." He explains why:

> The reason is that any virtue not only prohibits contrary acts but also prohibits providing occasion that is inductive of others to sin, for then that occasion, although it is not in itself an inflowing cause, is however a moral cause to the effect that the neighbor sins. That is called a *moral cause* which is substantially equivalent to a cause directly inducing to sin since, without it, the neighbor would not sin.

The resemblance between what Alphonsus says here and what he says about the distinction between formal and material cooperation is striking. It is true that, in his reformulation of the second opinion, the two more serious types of scandalizing – which would be parallel to what are sometimes called explicit and implicit formal cooperation – are referred to as scandalizing "directly and formally" and "directly but *not* formally." But otherwise his analysis is remarkably similar: in these two more serious types of scandal, the scandalizing

41. *ST* 2-2.43.3c: "Passivum quidem scandalum non potest esse speciale peccatum, quia ex dicto vel facto alterius aliquem ruere contingit secundum quodcumque genus peccati."

42. See *ST* 2-2.53.2c.

"flows into" the act of the other person; in the less serious, indirect scandal, the flow of causality somehow stops short of that. As we saw in chapter 1, in the *Theologia moralis* treatment of formal cooperation, Alphonsus says similarly that the cooperator's action "runs up to" [concurrit ad][43] the bad will of a malefactor; and, in *Homo apostolicus*, he says that formal cooperation of whatever type "flows into the bad will of one's neighbor who wills to sin."[44] The action of the material cooperator runs up only to the other's bad action; it does not flow into it.

Despite, however, the difference he recognizes between directly and indirectly scandalizing, or between inflowing and "moral causes," Alphonsus insists – against the second opinion he previously embraced – that even the person who indirectly scandalizes commits "a double sin." Alphonsus continues, therefore, to understand the relationship between scandalizer and scandalized as the species of the scandalized person's sin somehow coming back into the scandalizer's action. One understands what Alphonsus is trying to say here; but strictly – or, at least, Thomistically – speaking it means that, whenever an instance of scandal leads, for instance, to an act of adultery, that act of scandalizing *is* an act of adultery (which, as noted, is false).[45]

43. "Sed melius cum aliis dicendum, illam esse formalem quae concurrit ad malam voluntatem alterius, et nequit esse sine peccato; materialem vero illam, quae concurrit tantum ad malam actionem alterius, praeter intentionem cooperantis" [*Theologia moralis* 2 §63].

44. "influit in pravam voluntatem proximi volentis peccare" [Alphonsus Maria de Ligorio, *Homo Apostolicus*, tract. 4 punct. 5 §31 (v. 1 pp. 120–21)].

45. One can make the same point even when the sin at issue is not, as is adultery, a sin of a particular species on account of its object (*ex genere*). For instance, one person's scandalous behavior (whatever it might be) might be the occasion of another's giving alms, but for the sake of vainglory. The latter's sin falls within the species of vainglory because of the act's end, even though *ex genere* the act is an act of giving alms. But (again) the original scandalous behavior does not thereby become an act of vainglory.

III. Concluding Ideas and Connections

What conclusions with respect to the theory of cooperation can we draw from all of this? They are two, it seems to me, although they are intimately connected. The first is that Alphonsus, at least with respect to cooperation and scandal, is locked into an approach to such issues that looks to particular two-person relationships: the cooperator-malefactor relationship and the scandalizer-scandalized relationship. He does not think to look elsewhere: not to any third (fourth, fifth, . . .) person (or persons) who might be involved and/or harmed by the cooperation or scandal, and not to the larger issue of how the actions performed relate to the ultimate end and order of the moral universe. The consequence of this is that the only way he has of explaining where the immorality of immoral cooperation comes from is to say that it – as represented by the species of the sin committed – is transferred from the malefactor back to the cooperator.

This latter point is connected with the second conclusion: that Alphonsus's writings on these issues suffer from a failure even to understand why Thomas is interested in such concepts as special sins. Had he understood this, he would have seen that there was another way of explaining why cooperation with evil is immoral – a way, that is, other than by speaking of a transfer of moral species from one agent to another. For *any* act is immoral in so far as it is not compatible with reason.

The two saints, Thomas Aquinas and Alphonsus Liguori, pursued quite different vocations. Thomas was a philosopher.[46] As a philosopher, his major concerns were metaphysical, which meant that, also when considering ethics, he was primarily concerned with ordering: determining what fit where and why.[47] One sees this in the language

46. There is nothing incompatible between this statement and the statement that Thomas was also a theologian.

47. The opening remark of Thomas's commentary on the *Nicomachean Ethics* is: "As the Philosopher says at the beginning of the *Metaphysics*, it belongs to the wise to

he uses even in ethics, which is borrowed often enough from biology. He speaks, for instance, of actions that are good or evil *ex genere* ("from their genus"), genera combined with *differentiae* to give species of actions, and, of course, special virtues and special sins. Biology, of course, is not metaphysics; but Thomas, following Aristotle, sees the task of any science as the putting in order of the relevant matter and its principles.

Alphonsus was not a philosopher. He was a scholar, certainly, but he would certainly have described his primary concerns as pastoral – which concerns gave rise to his composition of numerous books on the way that Christians should behave. In writing the *Theologia moralis*, he was dependent upon other scholars who, like Alphonsus himself, did not see why Thomas places such emphasis upon determining the order of ethics: the various species and subspecies of virtues and vices, virtuous and vicious acts. This dependence is evident in the section of Alphonsus's *Theologia moralis* on scandal. There he makes use, as always, of a large number of his predecessors in the field, including the Jesuit Hermann Busenbaum, who, as we have seen, spoke of the debate by "the scholastics" regarding the special sin of scandal as having "scarce reference to practice."

None of this is to say that Thomas did not understand that justice is about relationships among individuals. In this matter too he follows Aristotle: in particular, his remarks early in his treatise on justice where he says that, "alone of all the virtues, justice appears to be the good of some other, for it is directed toward another since it acts for

---

order. What causes him to say this is that wisdom is the most powerful perfection of reason, whose proper role is to recognize order" ["Sicut Philosophus dicit in principio *Metaphysicae*, sapientis est ordinare. Cuius ratio est, quia sapientia est potissima perfectio rationis, cuius proprium est cognoscere ordinem"] [Thomas Aquinas, *Sententia libri Ethicorum*, 1.1.1–4]. Thomas is referring to *Metaph.* 1.2 982a17–19. It is probably true, however, that this understanding of ordering – that is, putting in order as distinct from giving orders – looks more to Aristotle's *Metaph.* 12.10 1075a11–15 than to *Metaph.* 1.2 982a17–19. On this controversy, see René-Antoine Gauthier, *La morale d'Aristote* (Paris: Presses universitaires de France, 1958), 89.

another's well being, whether for a ruler or for a companion."[48] But Aristotle also says in the same chapter that, in a sense, justice is the same thing as ethics itself (*EN* 5.1 1129b25–31). This statement cuts both ways—or, perhaps, more in one way than the other. Justice *is* about our relationships with others (including with rulers) but it is not just that. If acting unjustly with respect to others is wrong, it is wrong because it is unethical—which is to say, unreasonable.

Accordingly, Thomas would resist any attempt to reduce either cooperation or scandal to the standard bipolar relationships: the co-operator/malefactor, scandalizer/scandalized relationships. These are relevant, certainly, but the basic issue is always the morality, the justice, of the human acts performed: how well—or how poorly—these acts comport with human reason itself.

48. διὰ δὲ τὸ αὐτὸ τοῦτο καὶ ἀλλότριον ἀγαθὸν δοκεῖ εἶναι ἡ δικαιοσύνη μόνη τῶν ἀρετῶν, ὅτι πρὸς ἕτερόν ἐστιν· ἄλλῳ γὰρ τὰ συμφέροντα πράττει, ἢ ἄρχοντι ἢ κοινωνῷ [*EN* 5.1 1130a3–4; my translation].

CHAPTER 4 FACTORS IN REASON AND JUSTICE: PART I

We saw in chapters 2 and 3 that an important part of Thomas Aquinas's ethical theorizing is the identification of special sins: that is, the identification of acts that serve as central cases, such as allows him to speak of species of sin that might include not just the special sin but also other sins that are called by the same name but are not the special sin. Thus, active and intended scandal is the special sin, although active and unintended scandal is also properly called a sin of scandal.

The language Thomas uses – "special sin," "species of sin," etc. – is borrowed from biology, although he is well aware that the identification of the morally relevant characteristics of human acts is more complicated than the biologist's task of assigning animals to species.[1] Knowing a sin's species allows Thomas to locate it in a general way within the organizational scheme of the moral universe – which is to identify an important factor with respect to the way the act coheres or fails to cohere with reason.[2] Very often, however, as deci-

1. See, for instance, *ST* 1-2.1.3, 18.5c, 18.7 ad 1, and (especially) 18.10.

2. See *ST* 1-2.18.2 & 5.

sive morally as an act's species are its circumstances – which would include who performed the act, where it was performed, by what means, why, how, and when it was performed.[3]

Take the example of a woman the terms of whose employment require her to prepare instruments to be used in an abortion. Although in fulfilling these terms she does not perform an abortion, that she performs the act she does perform (preparing instruments) at that time or in that situation is a circumstance that has a bearing upon her act's reasonability and/or justice. Her act certainly has a connection with the act of the abortionist – and that may in fact be the relevant circumstance – but the connection that that circumstance establishes with reason connects her also to the child killed.[4] The relationship between her act and reason may indeed be one of incompatibility, so that the victim, were he or she able to communicate, could claim to have been done an injustice not only by the abortionist but also by this woman.

We see here, therefore, that the analysis of cooperation must be conducted within a larger context than that of the relationship between the cooperator and the malefactor. Assessing the morality of human acts within this larger context requires us to consider a large number of factors – as many, indeed, as have a bearing upon the reasonability of the acts in question. The purpose of the present chapter and the next is to list some of these factors. Indeed, it is the purpose of the present book to bring to more general attention these factors and to explain how they bear upon the analysis of human action in general and, in particular, upon cases of cooperation.

This is not to say that the moral manualists were unaware of these factors or that the same factors did not occasionally influence their analyses. It is to say, however, that they typically approached issues of

3. On circumstances, see especially chapter 2. The circumstances 'when,' and 'where' are easily associated with cooperation with evil; in section II of chapter 2, it is explained how cooperation can be regarded as a circumstance.

4. As noted in chapter 2, section II, in Thomas says in *Sent.* 4.16.3.1.1 that a circumstance is a proportion or *commensuratio* with respect to reason and (therefore) man's ultimate end (see there note 18).

cooperation with a limited number of tools in their "toolbox" – and that, even when they did employ the appropriate Thomistic tools, they often did so maladroitly, using particular tools to do work better suited to other tools (or combinations of tools). Going at the issues with the fuller toolbox does not make moralists' work easier: it does not allow them – or the proper moral authorities – more easily to formulate rules for avoiding immoral cooperation. But it does provide them with the assurance that they are capable of accurately identifying the factors that are relevant to the evaluation of human acts possibly involving immoral cooperation.

I. Justice and Charity

The first factor to be considered is the way in which any act – including, of course, an act of cooperation – stands in relation to man's ultimate end.[5] This factor was spoken of in chapters 2 and 3, but we must examine it now more closely in connection with an objection that could be raised and that has a particular bearing upon cooperation. Someone might point out that the end for Thomas is twofold:

5. The moral virtues, discussed by Aristotle especially in books 2 through 5 of the *Nicomachean Ethics*, are in a sense subordinate to the intellectual virtue of prudence (in Aristotle, φρόνησις), even though the moral virtues – especially justice – are what determine the structure of the corresponding moral system. According to Aristotle and Thomas, the ends of the virtuous human life depend upon the moral (or "acquired") virtues; prudence makes choices regarding means for attaining these ends and so acquiring the corresponding virtues (see *EN* 6.13 1145a4–6). Charity, which dominates both the realm of acquired and that of theological (or "infused") virtue, works quite differently from prudence since, like a moral virtue, it has its proper end, divine good, and yet it also directs choices with respect to the ends of all the virtues (see *ST* 2-2.23.8). The consequence of all this is that, first, the set of coordinates (the moral system) proper to the human is determined not by prudence but by justice, which Thomas speaks of as a "general virtue"; it is the overarching moral (acquired) virtue (see *ST* 2-2.58.5–6). And, secondly, the set of coordinates or the moral system proper to the theological realm, to which is subordinate the human realm, is determined by charity. Thomas draws the parallel between justice and charity at *ST* 2-2.58.6c: "Just as charity is called a general virtue in as much as it orders the acts of all virtues to the divine good, so also is legal justice in as much as it orders the acts of all virtues to the common good."

one natural and one supernatural, the latter known by man only through grace. Because of this twofold character, there are two sets of coordinates – or systems of moral precepts, etc. – with respect to which human acts can be judged: the system ordered by the theological virtue of charity, which is attainable only through Christ, and the system ordered by the moral – non-supernatural – virtue of justice. How is it then that there can be a single system of ethics with respect to which cooperation is to be analyzed?

A useful passage in this regard is *ST* 2-2.23.7 on "whether true virtue is possible without charity," the first section of whose corpus reads as follows:

> It must be said that, as stated above,[6] virtue is ordered toward the good. Good, however, in the primary sense is an end, for the things that are for an end are not called good except with respect to the end. So, just as 'end' is twofold, one ultimate and the other proximate, so also is good twofold: one, indeed, ultimate and the other proximate and particular.
>
> The ultimate and principal good of man is the enjoyment of God, according to the psalm that says, "for me to adhere to God is good"; and man is ordered to this good by charity. But the good of man that is secondary and, in a sense, particular can be twofold: one which is, indeed, truly good in as much as it can be ordered, with respect to what it is in itself, to the principal good, which is the ultimate end. The other is, however, an apparent and not true good, since it leads away from the final good.

In so far as the secondary good is ordered toward the principal good, it is contained within it. Thomas goes on to say that one might seek "a particular good," which is "a true good, such as the conservation of the city or something of that sort," and that the virtue that is ordered to such a good is "true virtue, although imperfect, unless it is referred to the final and perfect good."[7] So, the virtue of justice,

6. The reference is probably to *ST* 1-2.55.4.

7. "Si vero illud bonum particulare sit verum bonum, puta conservatio civitatis vel aliquid huiusmodi, erit quidem vera virtus, sed imperfecta, nisi referatur ad finale et perfectum bonum" [*ST* 2-2.23.7c].

which, according to Thomas, is ordered toward the particular good of "the just,"[8] is contained within charity in the sense that, even if one knows only to pursue "the just," one is headed toward the higher end, the divine good. The imperfection of the non-believer's justice consists in the fact that it only *heads toward* but does not *pursue* the divine good – pursue it, that is, with that desire that is infused by grace.

In a sense, then, the objection we are considering points to a truth: there are present here two systems of ethics – in as much as justice, in its possibly unrecognized imperfection, can be considered on its own, independently of charity. In another sense, however, there is only one system, since both systems are headed toward the same ultimate good, although one of them also knowingly pursues it. Whether a person knows it or not, when his actions are well ordered with respect to the human good, they are not inconsistent with "the ultimate and principal good." Charity is more comprehensive and will sometimes be more demanding than justice, but following a precept of justice will never contradict charity. The present book, however, has to do primarily with justice, whether recognized as imperfect or not.

II. Voluntary Acts and Choices

In the first few chapters of the third book of *Nicomachean Ethics*, Aristotle sets out the principles of what today would be called his action theory. Fundamental to this theory is his understanding of the voluntary [τὸ ἑκούσιον], discussed in the first chapter, although the type of voluntary act most pertinent to cooperation is that which he introduces only in the second chapter and calls choice or προαίρεσις.[9] Choice, says Aristotle, is the "deliberate desire of things in our own power" [*EN* 3.3 1113a10–11]; it is that which "has been decided on by

8. At *ST* 2-2.57.1, Thomas says that the object of justice is "the just" [iustum] or "the right" [ius].

9. The various translations and editions of the *Nicomachean Ethics* divide the chapters of the work's books in different ways. As mentioned in the introduction, I follow the chapter divisions used in the Revised Oxford Translation; according to that system, chapter 1 finishes at 1111b3; chapter 2 finishes at 1112a17; and chapter 3 finishes at 1113a14.

previous deliberation" [τὸ προβεβουλευμένον]. This latter characteristic, he says, is implied by choice's very name (προ-αίρεσις): it is "what is chosen before other things" [ὂν πρὸ ἑτέρων αἱρετόν].[10]

In a way, what Aristotle actually says in discussing 'choice' is not as central a concern for understanding cooperation as is his understanding of the voluntary. He discusses choice primarily as a way of understanding how individuals orient their lives, by preference, in a certain direction [*EN* 3.2 1111b4–6] — and so, where the choices are bad, the individuals become vicious in that direction. But it is perfectly possible for one who cooperates immorally not to be directing his life, by preference, in the direction of the vicious act (or acts) effected by the malefactor (or malefactors) with whom he cooperates. An act of cooperation might be performed under great pressure, for instance, so that in different circumstances the cooperator would have preferred another course of action. On the other hand, it is true that, for an act of cooperation to be declared immoral, it must meet the criteria specified by Aristotle as characterizing choices: the immoral cooperator must know what he is doing and choose so to cooperate rather than not. That said, however, most of what Aristotle says in *EN* 3 that pertains to cooperation he says not about choice but about the voluntary.

This broader use of the criteria for choice — but also the criteria excluding certain acts identified by Aristotle as voluntary — is reflected in Thomas's action theory. Thomas accepts what Aristotle says about the actions of children and mere animals, that is, that they are voluntary [*EN* 3.1 1111a25–26; 3.2 1111b8–10], by which is meant that children and animals "act on their own initiative" [proprio motu

10. *EN* 3.2 1112a15–17. In saying that choice presupposes a preference for something, Aristotle is referring to the prefix (προ-) of the word translated by means of the term 'choice': προαίρεσις. The latter term could be translated (awkwardly) as "a taking before" or "a taking in preference." The same prefix occurs in the word προβεβουλευμένον: 'that which is pre-deliberated.' The points that Aristotle makes here at the end of chapter 2 are framed as questions, but it becomes clear in chapter 3 that they represent his own position.

sponte agunt] but not "by reason of the will" [ex voluntate].[11] But he is interested primarily in the remaining subclass of the voluntary, which in fact meets the criteria set out for choice. And so, in order to pick out this subclass, he employs the term 'human act' or 'human action'.[12] He also, however, "stretches" the Aristotelian subclass a bit, not denying that it involves deliberation but finding deliberation in actions where it is barely – but sufficiently – present to qualify the corresponding action as morally significant. Thus, as we shall see more clearly below, even some failures to act count as human acts, as do some acts that have become so routine that deliberation is present, at best, implicitly. At *ST* 1-2.74.7 ad 2, Thomas says that the consent required for a sin (a human act) might be simply neglect to "direct human acts according to divine law."[13] It is with good reason, there-

11. "Dicuntur autem voluntarie operari, non quia operentur ex voluntate, sed quia proprio motu sponte agunt, ita quod a nullo exteriori moventur. Hoc enim dicimus esse voluntarium quod quis sponte et proprio motu operatur" [*in EN* 3.4 49–53 (§427)]. (Thomas is commenting here upon *EN* 3.1 1111a25–26, but see also 3.2 1111b9–10.) Thomas goes on then to say that the will is located in the reason ["voluntas autem in ratione est"; *in EN* 3.4 63–64 (§428)], of which children and animals have not the use.

12. See *ST* 1-2.1.1c: "Illae ergo actiones proprie humanae dicuntur, quae ex voluntate deliberata procedunt." See also *Sent.* 2.40.1.5c: "An act is susceptible of moral goodness in so far as it is human: [an act], however, is human in so far as, to some extent, it is derived by reason; this occurs only in those acts which are ordered by the will, which follows upon the deliberation of reason" ["Actus autem susceptibilis est bonitatis moralis, secundum quod humanus est: humanus autem est, secundum quod aliquatenus ratione deducitur: quod contingit in illis actibus tantum qui imperantur a voluntate, quae consequitur deliberationem rationis"]. See also above, chapter 2, notes 59 and 60.

13. The article has to do with the use of higher reason in consenting to sin. (On higher reason, see *ST* 1.79.9; for Thomas, higher reason is just reason.) The second objection argues that it sometimes happens that someone sins without ever thinking about the divine law, and so consent is not present. Thomas responds: "by virtue of the fact that higher reason does not direct human acts according to the divine law and impeding the commission of a sin, it is said to consent, whether it thinks about the divine law or not. For, if it thinks about the law of God, it disdains it; if, however, it does not think about it, it neglects it, as by way of a certain omission" ["ex hoc ipso quod ratio superior non dirigit actus humanos secundum legem divinam, impediens actum peccati, dicitur ipsa consentire; sive cogitet de lege aeterna, sive non. Cum enim cogitat de lege Dei, actu eam contemnit, cum vero non cogitat, eam negligit per modum omissionis cuiusdam"]

fore, that Fr. Stephen Brock says that necessary for human action is that something be "deliberable" – that is to say, not necessarily deliberated but at least "deliberable."[14]

III. The Involuntary by Virtue of Force

An important factor in the analysis of acts of cooperation is force. As noted above, in the first few chapters of the third book of his *Nicomachean Ethics*, Aristotle sets out the principles of his action theory. Beginning with the second sentence of that book – that is, immediately after an opening remark in which he associates virtue with the voluntary – he mentions force (which he calls βία and Latin translations render as *violentia*) and ignorance and their bearing upon the involuntary. He puts off discussing ignorance until later in this first chapter; about force, he remarks as follows:

> [T]hat is forced whose origin is outside and is such that the person who acts or is acted upon contributes nothing: for example, if he should be carried somewhere by a wind or by men who have him in their power.
>
> Such things as are done because of fear of some greater evils or because of something good and honorable – a tyrant, for instance, being in control of one's parents and children, orders one to do some dishonorable thing and performing the action one would rescue them, not performing it they would perish – there is some question whether such acts are involuntary or voluntary. Some such thing occurs also in throwing goods overboard during a storm, for simply speaking no one throws away goods voluntarily; but for the sake of one's own safety and that of others all reasonable people do so. Such actions are, therefore, "mixed," although it would appear rather that they are voluntary, for they are deemed worthy of choice when they are per-

---

[*ST* 1-2.74.7 ad 2]. See also *ST* 1 2.6.3 ad 3 and *ST* 1.49.1 ad 3. See also Brock, *Action and Conduct*, 159–60.

14. Brock, *Action and Conduct*, 39. See also G. E. M. Anscombe, "Action, Intention and 'Double Effect'," in *Human Life, Action and Ethics: Essays by G. E. M. Anscombe*, ed. Mary Geach and Luke Gormally, St. Andrews Studies in Philosophy and Public Affairs (Exeter: Imprint Academic, 2005), 207–26, and her article "Sins of Omission? The Non-Treatment of Controls in Clinical Trials" in the same volume, 285–91.

formed and the end of an action is determined at that deciding moment. And so "voluntary" and "involuntary" are to be declared at the moment when the action is performed. [*EN* 3.1 1110a1–15]

Aristotle's thesis in the first paragraph here appears to be twofold. The case of the person who is carried away "by men who have him in their power" would be one in which the person in question contributes nothing to the overall event: the origin of the entire act is outside of him and resides in the men who carry him away. But the case of the person who is carried away by a wind would be one in which an *aspect* of what the person himself does has its origin outside of him: he contributes nothing to *that aspect*.[15] Aristotle alludes to such acts earlier in this same first paragraph when he says that "that is forced whose origin is outside and is such that the person who *acts* or is acted upon [ὁ πράττων ἢ ὁ πάσχων] contributes nothing." In other words, he acknowledges right from the beginning of this treatise that a forced person might also be acting. It is very likely that, in speaking of being carried away by a wind, he is alluding to the sort of event he describes in his *Metaphysics* where he speaks of a ship's being blown off course and thus forced to enter a port different than the one for which it set out: Aegina instead of, for example, Piraeus.[16] When the ship's pilot brings the ship into Aegina, that act does, in a sense, contain both a voluntary and an involuntary aspect; but the involuntary aspect is isolated from what he does: he presumably gives no consent to it. That particular aspect of the act is like what occurs when a man is carried away "by men who have him in their power" [1110a4–5]. The pilot gives no consent to not going to Piraeus; his bringing the ship into Aegina, on the other hand, is wholly voluntary.

In the subsequent paragraph, Aristotle speaks of a couple of actions that are quite different from the former two. He gives the ex-

15. On the general issue of acts that are voluntary and yet have involuntary aspects, see Flannery, *Action and Character According to Aristotle*, chapter 3.

16. The example of being forced into Aegina occurs at *Metaphysics* 5.30 1025a25–27; see also Flannery, *Action and Character According to Aristotle*, 101–2.

ample of someone who does something base but only because a tyrant holds his parents and children and threatens to kill them unless one performs the base action [1110a5–7]. He also gives the example of someone who jettisons precious goods from a ship in order to keep it afloat [1110a8–9]. All such actions, he says, are "mixed" – that is, partly voluntary and partly involuntary – but, in the end, they must be characterized as voluntary "for they are deemed worthy of choice when they are performed and the end of an action is determined at that deciding moment" [1110a11–14].

That he also regards these two types of act (acts like rescuing family and acts like jettisoning goods) as differing one from the other is indicated in the way he introduces the pair [1110a4–5], saying that "such things" are either done in order to avoid "some greater evils" (which implies that what is done is itself not good) or they are done "because of something good and honorable" [καλόν τι]. The same distinction is suggested by his statement that "*some* such thing happens" [1110a8] with the jettisoning case – that is, some such thing as happens in the hostages case, which is mentioned first. He goes on to say that "all reasonable people" would agree to throw the goods overboard [1110a10–11] and says nothing of the sort about committing the base act, even in order to retrieve the hostages.

So, Aristotle would be saying that mixed actions are different from the former pair (being "carried somewhere by a wind or by men who have him in their power") in so far as, in mixed actions, the agent, at that moment when he chooses his course of action, voluntarily chooses to pursue a particular end (to save the family members or to save the ship). By contrast, the person carried into the other room by men contributes nothing at all to that action; and the pilot who is forced to bring his ship into Aegina never chooses not to go to Piraeus. The pilot needs to bring the ship into a port in any case; the "choice" of ports – or, at least, of not going to Piraeus – is made by the wind.[17]

17. See *EN* 3.1 1110b1–3: ἢ ἁπλῶς μέν, ὁπότ᾽ ἂν ἡ αἰτία ἐν τοῖς ἐκτὸς ᾖ καὶ ὁ πράττων μηδὲν συμβάλληται.

In his commentary on the *Nicomachean Ethics*,[18] Thomas picks up on the distinction that Aristotle makes with the words "who acts or is acted upon" in the statement that "that is forced whose origin is outside and is such that the person who acts or is acted upon contributes nothing" [1110a2–4].[19] His comment reads as follows:

18. Torrell puts the date of this commentary (or *sententia*) at 1271–72 or "contemporaneous with the composition of the *Secunda secundae* [*ST* 2-2], for which it prepares the way" [Torrell, *St. Thomas Aquinas: The Person and His Work*, 343].

19. While writing the fourth book of his commentary on the *Sentences*, Thomas appears not to have appreciated – or, perhaps, not to have read – Aristotle's words at *EN* 3.1 1110a2–3 about one who acts or is acted upon. At *Sent.* 4.29.1.1 obi. 2, we read: "Moreover, the forced, which is the same as the coerced, according to the Philosopher is that 'whose principle is external,' the one suffering the force contributing nothing. But the principle of any consent is internal. Therefore, no consent can be coerced" ["Praeterea, violentum, quod est idem quod coactum, secundum Philosophum, est 'cujus principium est extra,' nil conferente vim passo. Sed consensus omnis principium est intra. Ergo nullus consensus potest esse coactus"]. The idea that is attributed here to Aristotle does not correspond exactly to what he says at *EN* 3.1 1110a1–3, which (in the Latin Thomas used while writing the commentary on *EN*) runs as follows: "The forced is that 'whose principle is external, being [a principle] in which the person who acts or suffers action contributes nothing'" ["Violentum autem est cuius principium extra, tale existens in quo nil confert *operans vel patiens*"]. The objection in the *Sentences* commentary in effect leaves out the words "operans vel." The body of the argument also assumes that this reading of Aristotle is correct. It is likely that in *Sent.* 4.29.1.1 Thomas was following Nemesius (whom he misidentifies as Gregory of Nyssa) rather than Aristotle. In his *De natura hominis*, Nemesius offers a definition of that which is involuntary due to force: ὅρος τοίνυν τοῦ κατὰ βίαν ἀκουσίου ἐστὶν οὗ ἡ ἀρχὴ ἔξωθεν, μηδὲν συμβαλλομένου κατ' οἰκείαν ὁρμὴν τοῦ βιασθέντος [29.5–7] ("the definition of the involuntary due to force is 'that of which the principle is outside, the one forced contributing nothing of his own initiative"). The bit about the one forced contributing nothing is attributed to Gregory at *ST* 1-2.6.6 ad 1: "And so, as Gregory of Nyssa says, in order to exclude things that are done out of fear, in the definition of the forced, stated is not only that the forced is that 'whose principle is external' but added is 'the one suffering the force contributing nothing,' for to that which is done out of fear the will of the one fearing contributes something" ["Et ideo, ut Gregorius Nyssenus dicit, ad excludendum ea quae per metum aguntur, in definitione violenti non solum dicitur quod violentum est cuius principium est extra, sed additur, *nihil conferente vim passo*, quia ad id quod agitur per metum, voluntas timentis aliquid confert"].

And this is what he means when he says that it is fitting that a forced act be one in which a man contributes nothing—that is, through his own appetite—both the man who is said to act, in so far as he *does* something through force, and the man who is said to be acted upon, in as much as he is subject to force. And he proposes an example [of each]: for instance, if "a breath," that is, a wind, through its force drive something to some place, or if men who have dominion and power carry someone away against his will.[20]

With respect to mixed acts, in his commentary, Thomas does not advert to the morally relevant distinction between jettisoning goods and doing something less than good in order to rescue family; he is more interested in Aristotle's argument that all such actions in the end must be judged to be voluntary.[21] He explains that

the aforesaid actions, which come about out of fear, are "mixed," that is, they have something of both: of the involuntary, in as much as, simply speaking, no one wishes to throw his things into the sea; of the voluntary, in as much as any reasonable person wishes this for the safety of his own person and that

20. "Et hoc est quod dicit quod oportet tale esse violentum in quo nil conferat, scilicet per proprium appetitum, homo qui et dicitur operans, in quantum facit aliquid per violentiam, et dicitur patiens, in quantum violentiam patitur. Et ponit exemplum, puta si spiritus, id est ventus, per suam violentiam impulerit rem aliquam ad aliquem locum, vel si homines dominium et potestatem habentes asportaverunt aliquem contra eius voluntatem" [Thomas Aquinas, *in EN* 3.1 96–104 (§387)]. Regarding his use of the term 'appetite' here, Thomas is following Aristotle [*De anima* 2.3 414b2 and 3.9 432b5–7] for whom appetite (ὄρεξις) includes will (*voluntas* or βούλησις), desire (ἐπιθυμία), and passion (θυμός).

21. "And this is what he says in his statement that the aforesaid actions, performed out of fear, are 'voluntary at the moment when they are performed'—that is, all the particular circumstances, which at that moment occur, considered—and that the end and completion of the action is 'according to the particular moment'" ["Et hoc est quod dicit quod praedictae operationes ex timore factae sunt voluntariae tunc quando sunt operatae, idest consideratis omnibus singularibus circumstantiis quae pro tempore illo occurrunt, et secundum hoc singulare tempus est finis et complementum operationis"] — Thomas Aquinas, *in EN* 3.1 145–51 (§390)]. Thomas is commenting here upon EN 3.1 1110a12–14: αἱρεταὶ γάρ εἰσι τότε ὅτε πράττονται, τὸ δὲ τέλος τῆς πράξεως κατὰ τὸν καιρόν ἐστιν ["For they are worthy of choice at the time when they are done, and the end of an action is relative to the occasion"]. The text he was reading was: "Voluntariae enim sunt tunc cum operatae sunt, finis autem operationis secundum tempus est."

of others. But such actions come closer to voluntary than to involuntary actions.[22]

In his commentary on Peter Lombard's *Sentences*, however, Thomas does discuss the distinction between acting out of fear wholly reasonably (as when one jettisons goods in order to save the ship) and acting out of fear unreasonably because immorally. He holds that always the lesser evil or the greater good is to be chosen.[23] "And so," he says,

> the constant man [constans] is constrained through fear of a greater evil to sustain a lesser evil, but he is not constrained toward a greater evil in order to avoid a lesser evil. But the inconstant man [inconstans] is constrained toward the greater evil out of fear for a lesser evil: for instance, toward sin out of fear of bodily pain.[24]

22. "praedictae operationes, quae ex timore fiunt, sunt mixtae, idest habentes aliquid de utroque; de involuntario quidem inquantum nullus vult simpliciter res suas in mare proiicere; de voluntario autem, inquantum quilibet sapiens hoc vult pro salute suae personae et aliorum, sed tamen magis accedunt ad voluntarias operationes quam ad involuntarias" [Thomas Aquinas, *in EN* 3.1 129–36 (§390)]. See also *ST* 1-2.6.6, where Thomas says that mixed acts are involuntary "secundum considerationem tantum," that is, not as actually performed but as considered in the mind.

23. See Kevin L. Flannery, "On Counseling the Lesser Evil," *The Thomist* 75, no. 2 (2011): 245–89.

24. "Semper autem minus malum vel majus bonum eligendum est; et ideo constans ad minus malum sustinendum cogitur metu majoris mali; non autem cogitur ad majus malum ut vitet minus malum. Sed inconstans cogitur ad majus malum propter metum minoris mali; sicut ad peccatum propter metum corporalis poenae" [*Sent.* 4.29.1.2c]. Thomas introduces at this point the other extreme (the one extreme being the inconstant man): this is the *pertinax* who will not throw his goods overboard even in order to save the ship. The *constans* stands between the *inconstans* and the *pertinax*. In the response to the second objection, Thomas says that "sins are the greatest of evils and so in no way can the constant man be constrained toward that; indeed, a man ought rather to die that to sustain such things [that is, sins], as also Aristotle says in the third book of the *Nicomachean Ethics*" ["peccata sunt maxima malorum; et ideo ad hoc nullo modo potest homo constans cogi; immo magis debet homo mori quam talia sustinere, ut etiam Philosophus, in 3 Ethic., dicit"].

Both Aristotle and Thomas acknowledge that, of the mixed acts that are not wholly free of blamable content, many – but not all – reasonably elicit forbearance or lenient judgment. The larger passage in Aristotle reads as follows:

For some such actions, men are sometimes even praised, when they endure something base or painful for the sake of things great and noble; should the opposite be the case, they are blamed, for it is characteristic of the depraved person to endure the most base things for nothing noble or fitting. For some actions, however, praise is not forthcoming but rather forbearance,[25] when, because of pressure which strains human nature to the uttermost and which no one could endure, one does what one ought not to do. But perhaps some things one ought not to allow oneself to be forced to do but ought to die having suffered the most fearful things rather than to do them. For the things that compelled Euripides' Alcmaeon to slay his mother are clearly ludicrous.[26]

It is difficult sometimes to judge what should be chosen instead of what and what should be endured instead of what, and yet more difficult to abide by one's determinations, for as a rule what is expected is painful, and what is compelled is base; and so accordingly praises and blames are conferred on those who have been compelled or not. [*EN* 3.1.1110a19–29][27]

It is difficult to say what Aristotle has in mind when he speaks of enduring "something base or painful [αἰσχρόν τι ἢ λυπηρὸν] for the sake of things great and noble." Thomas interprets the remark as follows:

Sometimes some individuals are praised because they sustain something repulsive – not indeed a sin but some ignominy – or even something sadden-

25. The word employed here, συγγνώμη, might also be translated 'lenient judgment' or 'forgiveness.'

26. Aristotle is referring here to a lost work of Euripides, in which Alcmaeon slays his mother in order to avoid the feared consequences of a curse uttered by his father, Amphiaraos. Amphiaraos utters the oath as he is about to go off to war and fears that, because of the betrayal of Eriphyle, his wife, he will die. Aristotle's point is that certain types of pressure to perform evil acts do not call for συγγνώμη (see previous note).

27. See also Thomas's commentary [Thomas Aquinas, *in EN* 3.2 1–63 (§§392–95)].

ing (that is, something distressing), in order that they might persevere in certain great or good things, for instance, in certain virtuous acts.[28]

Both Aristotle and Thomas also say, however, that some acts one ought never perform even if forced "but one ought rather to perish having suffered the most terrible things" [*EN* 3.1 1110a27].[29] They are also agreed, of course, that performing a bad act for the sake of pleasure is not to suffer coercion. "It is laughable," says Aristotle, "to blame external factors but not oneself who is ensnared by such things: to take credit, that is, for noble deeds and blame pleasurable things for ignoble deeds."[30]

We can draw from all of this a couple of preliminary conclusions regarding the way in which force has a bearing upon the analysis of cases of possibly immoral cooperation with evil. First of all, the appreciation, on the part of both Aristotle and Thomas, of the internal articulation of human acts is extremely important, since a man might perform an act that appears to constitute immoral cooperation but only because of an aspect of his act over which he has no control – or, at least, no control that he is obliged to exert. As we shall see below (especially in chapter 5, sections I and II), that which so isolates a certain aspect of an act might be an established and legitimate structural feature of the society in which the act is performed.

Secondly, Aristotle and Thomas both assert that those "mixed acts" that constitute the performance under pressure of something that is less than noble call sometimes for vituperation and sometimes for pardon. Pertinent to the present argument, however, is not the attitude that one should adopt toward such persons (which should always be merciful) but simply the presupposition that such mixed

28. "[Q]uandoque aliqui laudantur ex eo quod sustinent aliquod turpe, non quidem peccatum sed ignominiam aliquam, vel etiam aliquod triste, id est aliquod afflictivum, propter hoc quod perseverent in aliquibus magnis et bonis, puta in aliquibus virtuosis actibus" [*in EN* 3.2.16–21 (§393)].

29. See above, note 24.

30. *EN* 3.1 1110b13–15; in Thomas, see *in EN* 3.2 142–150 (§403) and *ST* 1-2.6.7.

acts are in the end voluntary and that they not good. In cases of cooperation this is often the situation: that "in a perfect world" the cooperator would not have chosen to do what he does, but he does in fact do it.

IV. Omission (and Consent)

As strange as it may at first seem, for Thomas it is not the case that only actions are voluntary. In *ST* 1-2.71.5, he asks whether in whatever sin there is some act. He acknowledges that there are various opinions regarding this issue, some maintaining that there is always some act, "either interior or exterior," others pointing out that *not doing* that which one is obliged to do is a sin. Thomas acknowledges that both these opinions make sense, but he ultimately sides with the second, without flatly denying the first.[31] He acknowledges that a sinful omission is always going to have some act connected with it, such as deliberately staying up late on Saturday and so not getting to Mass in the morning; but, since the former act is related only per accidens to not getting to Mass (staying up late does not *mean* not getting to Mass) and since "judgment regarding matters [de rebus] is to be given according to that which is per se and not according to that which is per accidens," it is "more true [verius] to say that a sin can be without any act." Thomas's fundamental reason for not connecting sins of omission too closely with acts related per accidens is that this would encroach upon the theory of the way that acts are specified by their objects. As he puts it in concluding the same argument: "Otherwise even circumstantial acts and occasions would pertain to the essence of other actual sins."[32] If things related only per accidens could

31. Aristotle too, at *Metaph.* 5.2 1013b15–16, acknowledges that the absence [στέρησις] of an act can sometimes be an efficient cause. See also Thomas Aquinas, *in Metaph.* 5.2.14 (§776).

32. "Alioquin etiam ad essentiam aliorum peccatorum actualium pertinerent actus et occasiones circumstantes" [*ST* 1-2.71.5c]. By using the expression "actus et occasiones circumstantes" Thomas is deliberately avoiding saying that circumstances (in the

constitute an act of omission itself, then pretty much anything might serve to constitute "the essence of other actual sins."

What then is a culpable omission? The place where Thomas discusses omissions most directly is *ST* 1-2.6.3, where he asks whether there can be voluntariness without any act. He makes a distinction between that which proceeds from the will directly, as when (in the realm of nature) heat proceeds from the action of fire, and that which proceeds indirectly, in which there is no such action. For the latter, switching to the realm of human action, he gives the example of a ship's pilot who "desists" from piloting and the ship goes down. The word used here, *desistit*, must be understood as simply *ceasing* to pilot, and not the simultaneous turning to another activity. What causes the ship to go down is the pilot's *not piloting*. The other activity taking the place of piloting has an intelligibility quite different from not piloting: it is related to it only per accidens.

Understanding this is important for understanding certain cases of cooperation. A hospital administrator who favors certain immoral procedures might turn his attention away from the fact that the hospital does not impede the procedures: he busies himself with other administrative tasks. That is an act and, in a certain sense, a good act: he begins to do things that need to be done. But his will remains – he remains – connected with the immoral procedures by virtue of an absence of action. His situation – his cooperation – is an issue in justice. Strictly speaking, the voluntariness involved here is tied to no act. This itself is indicative of the fact that cooperation is not about – or not necessarily or only about – the relationship between a cooperator's and a malefactor's act, since an instance of cooperation might very well consist in the absence of an act.

Returning though to *ST* 1-2.6.3, one notes that Thomas specifies that something proceeds indirectly from one's will, that is, in the absence of an act, only when the person concerned "can and ought to

technical sense) might not pertain to the essence of a sin. See in appendix 4, Thomas's *De malo* 2.6 [IIIa]; see also chapter 2, sections II and III.

act." "For if," he says, "the pilot [gubernator] cannot steer the ship, or if the piloting of the ship is not commissioned to him, the ship's going down, which occurs through his absence, is not imputed to him."[33] When the pilot is unable to steer the ship – when, for instance, he is swept away from the helm by a wave – although his absence from the helm is the cause of the ship's going down, this is not attributable to his will. It does not register, so to speak, on the grid of justice. The same is the case if it was not his responsibility to be at the helm when the ship went down. Similarly here, his absence from the helm when the ship goes down does not register on "the grid" as an injustice. But if he ought to have been at the helm at that time but was not, the ship's going down can be said to proceed from his will, even in the absence of an act. That circumstance – "the when" of his non-act – establishes a negative relationship between him and justice. Thomas goes on to say that the voluntary can be present in the absence of an exterior act, but with an interior act, "as when someone wills not to act" – wills, for instance, not to go to the helm. Or it can be without even an interior act, as when someone does not so will.[34] The pilot

33. "Sed sciendum quod non semper id quod sequitur ad defectum actionis, reducitur sicut in causam in agens, ex eo quod non agit, sed solum tunc cum potest et debet agere. Si enim gubernator non posset navem dirigere, vel non esset ei commissa gubernatio navis, non imputaretur ei navis submersio, quae per absentiam gubernatoris contingeret" [*ST* 1-2.6.3c]. Thomas probably takes the example of the pilot from Aristotle's *Physics* 2.3 195a13–14: "Thus we ascribe the wreck of a ship to the absence of the pilot whose presence was the cause of its safety" [οἷον τὴν ἀπουσίαν τοῦ κυβερνήτου τῆς τοῦ πλοίου ἀνατροπῆς, οὗ ἦν ἡ παρουσία αἰτία τῆς σωτηρίας]. There is a similar remark at *Metaph.* 5.2 1013b3–15. In his commentary on the latter, Thomas points out (with Aristotle) that either the pilot's absence *or* his presence at the helm can constitute the same type of cause: "For, in the same way that an opposite is the cause of an opposite, this is the cause of that" ["Eodem enim modo oppositum est causa oppositi, quo haec est causa huius"] [Thomas Aquinas, *in Metaph.* 5.2.14 (§776)]. See also David Charles, *Aristotle's Philosophy of Action* (London: Duckworth, 1984), 45. Charles cites *Phys.* 2.3 195b22–24 and 2.4 196b26.

34. "Et sic voluntarium potest esse absque actu, quandoque quidem absque actu exteriori, cum actu interiori, sicut cum vult non agere; aliquando autem et absque actu interiori, sicut cum non vult" [*ST* 1-2.6.3c]. See, however, *ST* 1-2.71.5 (introduced above)

might be enjoying a book in his cabin and never even consider going or not going to the helm.

Before concluding this section, appropriate would be a word about the way in which consent (*consensus*) bears upon omission, for in what we have seen so far it may seem that Thomas is saying that an omission is culpable when the "non-acting agent" is in favor of what occurs as a result of his not acting. In other words, in what we have seen so far it may seem that, for Thomas, the voluntary requires consent in a strong sense. But, in fact, the pilot who, because of his absorption in a book, fails to be at the helm might also regret what happens as a consequence and might say truthfully that, had he known this would happen, he would have set his alarm clock so as to alert himself that he was due at the helm. And so it can hardly be said that in any strong sense he consents to the ship's going down, although (to use the language Thomas uses in *ST* 1-2.6.3) its going down does "proceed from his will."

In *ST* 1-2.15.1 Thomas calls consent an "application of the appetitive power to a thing" and in the subsequent article an "application of appetitive movement to something to be done." Thomas's concluding remark in the body of this article is that properly speaking only a rational creature can consent since only a rational nature "has in its power the appetitive movement and is able to apply it *or not apply it* to this or to that." Connecting this with what he says in *ST* 1-2.6.3, he would be alluding here to the distinction (within the indirectly voluntary) between the case in which there is an interior act, "as when someone wills not to act," and the case in which there is no interior act, "as when someone does not [so] will." This is the difference between a hospital administrator who consciously declines to support another administrator who would impede immoral practices and the administrator who never really thinks about the other administrator's

where Thomas concludes that, with respect to what pertains to them in themselves (per se), some sins of omission can be without any act — although, for an omission to be culpable, there would have to be an act related to it at least per accidens.

proposal (and turns to other tasks). We have been supposing that this latter administrator does favor the immoral practices, but it is conceivable that he does not. In this case, his lack of action would still be culpable.[35]

V. Ignorance and the Voluntary and the Involuntary

We saw at the beginning of section III of the present chapter that, according to Aristotle, not only force but also ignorance can make an action involuntary; so we turn now to this additional factor.[36] It is important to note right from the beginning, however, that, according to both Aristotle and Thomas, in many instances in which ignorance is a factor, the act in question is not involuntary but voluntary. If not knowing or not calling to mind a moral truth is voluntary, this voluntariness spills over into the characterization of the act itself.[37]

Thomas makes a number of distinctions in this regard, all of which are traceable to the third book of the *Nicomachean Ethics* [*EN* 3.1 1110b18–1111a2], although he offers a more explicit explanation than we find in Aristotle of how the various distinctions depend upon

35. On consent, see Brock, *Action and Conduct* 159–60, 178, 220; on omissions, see 223–25. See also above, the very end of section II. Elizabeth Anscombe has a couple of essays on omissions: G. E. M. Anscombe, "Murder and the Morality of Euthanasia," in *Human Life, Action and Ethics: Essays by G. E. M. Anscombe*, ed. Mary Geach and Luke Gormally, St. Andrews Studies in Philosophy and Public Affairs (Exeter: Imprint Academic, 2005), 261–77, and Anscombe, "Sins of Omission? The Non-Treatment of Controls in Clinical Trials." See also Anscombe, "Action, Intention and 'Double Effect'." On the issues discussed in this section generally, see Kevin L. Flannery, "The Field of Moral Action According to Thomas Aquinas," *The Thomist* 69, no. 1 (2005): 1–30.

36. "It appears, therefore, that those things that come about because of force or through ignorance are involuntary" [δοκεῖ δὴ ἀκούσια εἶναι τὰ βίᾳ ἢ δι' ἄγνοιαν γινόμενα—*EN* 3.1 1109b35–1110a1].

37. In commenting on *EN* 3.1 1110b30–33, Thomas says: "And so, if the ignorance itself is considered voluntary as long as a man does not want to avoid it, as he is obliged to do, it follows that neither is that which comes about through such ignorance to be judged involuntary" ["Unde, si ipsa ignorantia reputatur voluntaria dum homo eam non vult vitare sicut tenetur, consequens est quod nec id quod per huiusmodi ignorantiam fit involuntarium iudicetur"] [Thomas Aquinas, *in EN* 3.3.84–87 (§411)].

the manner in which the will causes – or does not cause – the ignorance. For this reason, what Thomas says about ignorance resembles in many ways what he says about omissions, for, just as there (that is, in *ST* 1-2.6.3), so also here he is interested in whether the ignorance "proceeds from the will."[38]

Another parallel with the discourse on omissions is the centrality of the question whether the agent *ought* to be in a certain state or not – in particular, whether he ought to be in the state of knowing something. In the case of the ship's pilot, central was the question whether he *ought* to have been at the helm. Ignorance – which, like an omission, is an absence of something – is culpable only if the person in question ought to have known what he does not know.[39] In fact, Thomas understands the term *ignorantia* in a way that does not correspond precisely to current usage of the term 'ignorance.' He makes a distinction between "nescience," which refers to any absence of knowledge, and *ignorantia*, which refers to the absence of knowledge of things we have a natural aptitude to know. "Some of these," he says,

> anyone is obliged to know, that is, those things without the knowledge of which it is not possible to perform a required act correctly. And so everyone is obliged to know generally those things that are of the Faith and the universal precepts of justice; individuals, however, are obliged to know those things that are related to their particular status or office.[40]

In what follows, we shall be using the terms 'ignorance,' 'ignorant,' etc., in this Thomistic sense. When addressing non-believers within

38. In fact, in *ST* 1-2.6.8, where he introduces the various types of ignorance, he makes reference to *ST* 1-2.6.3 (the article on omission).

39. In *ST* 1-2.76.2c, Thomas speaks of the sin of omitting to know what one is obliged to know.

40. "Horum autem quaedam aliquis scire tenetur, illa scilicet sine quorum scientia non potest debitum actum recte exercere. Unde omnes tenentur scire communiter ea quae sunt fidei, et universalia iuris praecepta, singuli autem ea quae ad eorum statum vel officium spectant" [*ST* 1-2.76.2c]. The "things that are of the Faith" are the so-called articles of the Christian faith. See *ST* 1.2.2 obi. ad 1, also *ST* 2-2.1.5.

a strictly political context, the obligation "to know generally those things that are of the Faith" is not applicable, although a believer is, of course, bound by what he believes in Faith.[41] In the strictly political sphere, the discourse has to do with what Thomas refers to here as "the universal precepts of justice," which all are obliged to know, whether believers or not. These would include such precepts as the prohibition of murder and of sexual activity outside of marriage.

This obligation to know the moral law is indicative of a difference between Thomas's (and, in fact, Aristotle's) understanding of conscience and some contemporary theories of what might be called "personal conscience." As we shall see, Thomas certainly holds that, depending upon the reason for a person's ignorance of that part of the moral law which he ought to know, the voluntariness and culpability of consequent acts might be diminished. But Thomas is also quite confident that the "universal precepts of justice" can be known by anyone who has the use of reason – and that those precepts are binding no matter what the individual's personal attitude toward the precepts (or precept) in question. Far from being an exonerating factor, ignorance of the "universal precepts of justice" is, in almost all cases, both sinful and a cause of sin.[42]

If, for instance, a person does not think that sexual acts outside of marriage are immoral, that is culpable ignorance: something to be corrected and not respected as an exercise of personal conscience.[43]

41. See above, section I. The believer will also maintain in faith some things that are naturally knowable, such as the more axiomatic precepts of the natural law. See *ST* 1-2.94.2.

42. *ST* 1-2.76.1. The exceptions would be cases in which a person, because of some disability, is not responsible for his thought and/or actions.

43. Thomas himself maintains that conscience – even an erroneous conscience – must be followed; but he also says that, if the erroneous character of a person's conscience is that person's fault, the acts he performs in accordance with the erroneous conscience are culpably immoral. On this issue, see *ST* 1-2.19.5–6; see also Kevin L. Flannery, *Christian and Moral Action* (Washington, D.C.: IPS Press, 2012), chapter 6, and Schenk, "*Perplexus supposito quodam*: Notizen zu einem vergessenen Schlüsselbegriff thomanischer Gewissenslehre."

That a person believes that sexual relationships between individuals of the same sex are legitimate or even marital has no bearing upon the morality of his cooperation with such acts, by, for instance, working in support of legislation favoring "gay marriage" – other, that is, than to augment culpability by the addition of a disordered intention. Similarly, a person who regularly assists at abortions cannot argue soundly, on the grounds that he does not believe that abortion is immoral, that his cooperation is not immoral. When a bishops' conference, for instance, calls upon all citizens to avoid immoral cooperation, it is not speaking only to those whose opinions regarding the malefactor's action are consistent with the universal precepts of justice.

Aristotle's discussion of ignorance in *EN* 3 involves a number of divisions and subdivisions. He begins by speaking of that which is done "by reason of ignorance" [δι' ἄγνοιαν], which he eventually distinguishes from that which is done "while ignorant" [ἀγνοῶν]. The latter includes immoral acts that are performed in a state of ignorance that a person has in some way chosen. (We will discuss acts performed "while ignorant" below.) Aristotle also calls that which is done by reason of ignorance "non-voluntary" [οὐχ ἑκούσιον], the non-voluntary including as a subcategory "the involuntary" [τὸ ἀκούσιον]. Because involuntariness constitutes a subcategory, the involuntary agent could, therefore, be called a non-voluntary agent, but Aristotle chooses to reserve the term "the non-voluntary agent" [ὁ οὐχ ἑχών] for one who performs acts outside of the subcategory of the involuntary but within the larger category of the non-voluntary. That is, the non-voluntary agent takes his name from the larger category of the "non-voluntary" but performs acts that would be located outside of the involuntary. An example of such an agent would be an anesthesiologist who assists at an abortion not knowing that the procedure is an abortion but, when he discovers this, he is not at all displeased, since he is strongly in favor of "reproductive rights." His cooperation with the abortion is not voluntary but neither is it *in*voluntary.

Thomas call such ignorance – that is, ignorance which is non-voluntary in Aristotle's limited sense – "concomitant" ignorance, since it just happens to be present along with the action.[44] Besides concomitant ignorance, Thomas recognizes also "antecedent" and "consequent" ignorance. Ignorance that is antecedent – antecedent, that is, to the will to perform some act – is the cause of the involuntary in the fullest sense: it exonerates the agent from culpability for what occurs because of his ignorance. A mark of such involuntary ignorance is regret on the part of the person who has performed the bad act.

When the relevant knowledge is absent by being put out of mind or deliberately not acquired, one goes astray culpably: one commits injustice, either because of the species of the act performed or because of the circumstances in which it is performed. This is the third type of ignorance: consequent ignorance, or ignorance consequent to an act of the will – certainly the most important for present purposes.[45] In *ST* 1-2.6.8, Thomas says that there are two sorts of consequent ig-

44. "Concomitanter quidem, quando ignorantia est de eo quod agitur, tamen, etiam si sciretur, nihilominus ageretur. Tunc enim ignorantia non inducit ad volendum ut hoc fiat, sed accidit simul esse aliquid factum et ignoratum" [*ST* 1-2.6.8]. That the cooperator has a positive reaction to his cooperation with evil, and why his will is so disposed, are separate issues. At *ST* 1-2.76.1, Thomas speaks of such a person as one who "does not sin by reason of ignorance but sins being ignorant" ["non peccat propter ignorantiam, sed peccat ignorans"]. The latter expression ("being ignorant" ["ignorans"]) is a reference to Aristotle's word ἀγνοῶν at *EN* 3.1 1110b27 and to that part of his argument [1110b25–33] in which he discusses agents who, at least in some sense voluntarily, perform immoral actions. Phrases such as "sinning being ignorant" or "acting being ignorant" are awkward in English, so in what follows I will use "sinning while ignorant," "acting while ignorant," etc. The main idea is that acting while ignorant (*ignorans* or ἀγνοῶν) is not acting by reason of ignorance (*propter ignorantiam* or δι᾽ ἄγνοιαν). See Thomas's commentary on the *Nicomachean Ethics*: "He says, therefore, that a person's acting by reason of ignorance appears to be something different from a person's acting while ignorant" ["Dicit ergo quod alterum videtur esse quod aliquis operetur propter ignorantiam ab eo quod aliquis operetur ignorans" [*in EN* 3.3 48–50 (§409)]; "every bad person acts, indeed, not by reason of ignorance but while ignorant of what good things in particular one ought to do and from which bad things one ought to flee" ["omnis malus operatur non quidem propter ignorantiam, sed ignorans in particulari quae bona oporteat facere et a quibus malis oporteat fugere"] [*in EN* 3.3 60–63 (§410)].

45. In *ST* 1-2.6.8, this type is given as the third type.

norance, the distinction corresponding to the distinction he makes between that voluntary which involves an act and that which does not (an omission, that is, of the act of getting to know what one ought to know). The first sort occurs when someone "wants to be ignorant so that he might have an excuse for sin or might not be kept back from sinning."[46] This type of ignorance he calls "desired ignorance" [ignorantia affectata]. In *De malo* 3.8, speaking of the same phenomenon, Thomas says:

> When someone directly wills to be ignorant lest through the knowledge he be kept back from sinning, such ignorance does not excuse the sin either wholly or in part; rather, it augments it, for, on account of a strong love of sinning, it appears to happen that someone wills to suffer loss of knowledge so that he might freely cling to his sin.[47]

Thomas there gives two examples: the person "who directly wills to be ignorant of what we know about salvation, lest he be held back from a sin, which he loves";[48] and the drinker, "who wills to drink wine excessively, because of which he is deprived of the use of reason."[49]

46. "cum aliquis ignorare vult ut excusationem peccati habeat, vel ut non retrahatur a peccando" [*ST* 1-2.6.8c]. Thomas calls this type of ignorance "ignorantia affectata," a phrase sometimes translated "affected ignorance." But that would be an inaccurate translation, since affected ignorance — at least, in contemporary English — is not really ignorance. At *Sent.* 2.22.2.2c, Thomas says that all ignorance that is within the knower's power ("vincible ignorance") is "affectata": "quaedam est in potestate scientis, et haec dicitur ignorantia vincibilis, vel affectata." But later in the same corpus, he recognizes two types of vincible ignorance: vincible "secundum se" and vincible "secundum causam suam." This brings things more into line with *ST* 1-2.6.8.

47. "Cum ergo aliquis directe vult ignorare ut a peccato per scientiam non retrahatur, talis ignorantia non excusat peccatum nec in toto nec in parte, sed magis auget; ex magno enim amore peccandi videtur contingere quod aliquis detrimentum scientiae pati velit ad hoc quod libere peccato inhaereat" [*De malo* 3.8c].

48. "quando aliquis directe vult ignorare scientiam salutis, ne retrahatur a peccato, quod amat" [*De malo* 3.8c].

49. "Directe quidem, sicut apparet in ebrio, qui vult superflue vinum potare, per quod privatur rationis usu" [*De malo* 3.8c]. This second example, Thomas describes as "directe" but also "per accidens," since the ignorance comes *through* the inebriation,

The second sort of consequent ignorance mentioned in *ST* 1-2.6.8 is called, says Thomas, "voluntary ignorance of what one can and ought to know." He mentions two ways in which such ignorance might be present. In the first, a man knows that he ought not to perform a particular act and yet, as he performs it, he diverts his attention from that knowledge and considers the act as that which "is to be done" in this particular situation. In the second, a man does not take care in order to know what he ought to know. Thomas calls this "ignorance of the universals of law" [ignorantia universalium iuris]. Both here in *ST* 1-2.6.8 and in *De malo* 3.8, he associates this ignorance explicitly with negligence.[50] Aristotle speaks in this connection respectively of "ignorance in the choice" [ἡ ἐν τῇ προαιρέσει ἄγνοια] and of "ignorance of the universal" [ἡ καθόλου]. Neither is to man's advantage: the first "makes men wicked"; for the second, men are "blamed."[51]

Attention to the language that Thomas uses in his commentary on *EN* 3.1 1110b24–30 is a help in understanding the sort of acts he has in mind in both these latter cases (that is, of "ignorance in the choice" and of "ignorance of the universal") but also in understanding the relationship between ignorance and human action in general. In that section of the *Nicomachean Ethics*, Aristotle treats of all acts an

---

which is directly willed. He also speaks here of the "per accidens indirecte," in which someone *neglects* to repel passions and so is deprived of the use of reason: — on account of which every bad person is said to be ignorant" ["indirecte autem cum aliquis negligit repellere insurgentes passionis motus, qui percrescentes ligant rationis usum in particulari eligibili, secundum quod dicitur omnis malus ignorans"] [*De malo* 3.8c]. And so it is clear that the drinker "who wills to drink wine excessively, because of which he is deprived of the use of reason," at the very least knows that his drinking will bring about ignorance and proceeds nonetheless.

50. "Secondly, ignorance is called indirectly voluntary because someone does not make the effort to know; and this is ignorance of negligence" ["Secundo ignorantia dicitur voluntaria indirecte quia non adhibet studium ad cognoscendum; et haec est ignorantia negligentiae"] [*De malo* 3.8c].

51. οὐ γὰρ ἡ ἐν τῇ προαιρέσει ἄγνοια αἰτία τοῦ ἀκουσίου ἀλλὰ τῆς μοχθηρίας, οὐδ᾽ ἡ καθόλου (ψέγονται γὰρ διά γε ταύτην) [*EN* 3.1 1110b31–33].

agent might perform "while ignorant" [ἀγνοῶν]. Having first stated that, according to Aristotle, the man who performs a bad act out of anger does not act "by reason of [propter] ignorance but by reason of anger" (and so not involuntarily), Thomas concludes that therefore:

> every wicked man acts not by reason of ignorance but while ignorant in some particular case of those good things it is fitting to do and of those bad things from which it is fitting to flee – in as much, that is, as he estimates that this bad thing is to be done by him now and that this good thing is to be refrained from by him now.[52]

The expressions "to be done" [esse faciendum] and "to be refrained from" [cessandum (ab)], both of Aristotelian extraction, are deliberately open-ended: the reference can be either to that which really should (or should not) be done morally *or* to that which is judged by an individual to be done (or refrained from) by him.[53]

It is tempting here to translate the word *ignorare* (and derivatives) as "to ignore" instead of "to be ignorant" – for that is what such an agent does: he ignores what in some sense he knows. But to translate it thus would be to obscure the point that Thomas is making: that the wicked man is ignorant of the truly advantageous *while* he is pursing that which he desires. Among the cases Thomas has in mind would

52. "omnis malus operatur non quidem propter ignorantiam, sed ignorans in particulari quae bona oporteat facere et a quibus malis oporteat fugere, in quantum scilicet aestimat hoc malum sibi nunc esse faciendum et ab hoc bono sibi nunc esse cessandum" [*in EN* 3.3.60–65 (§410)].

53. Because these expressions can go either way, when Aristotle speaks in this section of what is truly the right thing to do, he speaks of "the things that are advantageous" [τὰ συμφέροντα – *EN* 3.1 1110b31] – of which the wicked man is "ignorant." The words quoted in note 52, "omnis malus operatur . . . ignorans in particulari quae bona oporteat facere et a quibus malis oporteat fugere," have their origin at *EN* 3.1 1110b28–29: ἀγνοεῖ μὲν οὖν πᾶς ὁ μοχθηρὸς ἃ δεῖ πράττειν καὶ ὧν ἀφεκτέον. These same words (in particular, facere and fugere) show up a few lines later in the commentary [*in EN* 3.3 97–100 (§412)] and also at *ST* 1-2.94.2: "Hoc est ergo primum praeceptum legis, quod bonum est faciendum et prosequendum, et malum vitandum" ["This is the first precept of law: that good is to be done and pursued, and evil is to be avoided"]. (Thomas's expression here, "the first precept of law," is a reference to the first precept or principle of the natural law.)

be those in which the agent is genuinely (but culpably) ignorant of what is the right thing to do, but also those in which the agent "in the choice" is ignorant of the right thing to do. Thomas holds that this occurs necessarily, for when a man chooses to perform a wicked act, he does not – indeed, cannot – choose the disorder (the *inordinatio*); he chooses rather the good – the genuinely good – that attracts him to that act.[54] That is all that is within the focus of his attention when he acts. As such, that good is not a problem. The problem (the moral problem) is rather the omission: the fact that the wicked man omits to do what he is obliged to do: to consider the larger picture of reasonability itself and his act's incompatibility with that picture.

Thomas's recognition in this way that even bad acts tap into the genuinely good makes his theory quite different from – even incompatible with – contemporary theories that incorporate the idea of personal conscience. For him, our situation is not one in which we are all attempting to construct an understanding of moral truth, an attempt regarded as forever provisional because of limitations on the very possibility of knowledge, ethical or otherwise. For Thomas, every human being who has the use of reason necessarily acts for genuine goods, the understanding of which is capable of being *expanded* in such a way that the result is a progressively more reasonable and internally consistent way of understanding the moral universe and its obligations.

Not everyone is obliged to expand his moral knowledge in this way to an equal extent. Some persons are, for one reason or another and through no fault of their own, capable of only limited expansion. And some of those who are more obliged to expand that basic knowledge may be obliged to know more than others in that same category. A hospital administrator, for instance, is obliged to work especially

54. See, for instance, *ST* 1-2.72.1c, where Thomas says that the "disorder of an act is related per accidens to the intention of the sinner, for no one acts directing his intention at evil" ["inordinatio actus, per accidens se habet ad intentionem peccantis, nullus enim intendens ad malum operatur"]. In the same place he says that the disorder comes about "through a withdrawal from the law of God" ["per recessum a lege Dei"].

hard in order to understand the moral truth as pertaining to the procedures conducted in the hospital. He can certainly not throw up his hands and say, "There are a lot of theories out there: this one is as good as any," for it is quite likely that his choice will be determined by what is most expedient for him professionally or personally.[55]

Another case would be a philosophy major who neglects to acquire knowledge of the moral truths expressed in the appropriate books because he is busy with other tasks or perhaps because it would take a special effort. It may, for instance, be difficult (but not impossible) to have access to the appropriate books, or he may fear that understanding moral ideas contrary to prevailing ideas will cause him conflict, either internally (that is, psychologically) or externally (with a hiring committee). Nonetheless, he is obliged to make the extra effort not only to read the books but also to arrive, as best he is able, at an expansive grasp of the truth.[56]

In *De malo* 3.8, Thomas speaks of all such cases in which one's bad acts are due to ignorance that is in some sense voluntary. He says:

> such ignorance does not completely cause the act that follows to be involuntary, for the act that follows, because it proceeds from ignorance that is voluntary, is in a sense voluntary. Still, however, the preceding ignorance diminishes the character of the voluntary, for an act that proceeds from such ignorance is less voluntary than if someone knowingly should choose such an act absent all ignorance. And so such ignorance does not entirely excuse the act that follows, although it does do so to some extent.[57]

55. See MacIntyre, "Social Structures and Their Threats to Moral Agency," passim.

56. See *ST* 1-2.76.1–2. See also *EN* 3.1 1110b28–1111a1, *EE* 2.9 (the whole chapter), and Flannery, *Action and Character According to Aristotle*, 113–18.

57. "Quando autem aliquis indirecte vult ignorare quia negligit addiscere, vel etiam quando per accidens ignorantiam vult, dum vult directe vel indirecte aliquid ad quod ignorantia sequitur, talis ignorantia non totaliter causat involuntarium in actu sequenti; quia actus sequens ex hoc ipso quod procedit ex ignorantia, quae est voluntaria, est quodammodo voluntarius; sed tamen ignorantia praecedens diminuit rationem voluntarii; minus enim est voluntarius actus qui ex tali ignorantia procedit, quam si scienter talem actum aliquis eligeret absque omni ignorantia; et ideo talis ignorantia non excusat actum sequentem a toto, sed a tanto" [*De malo* 3.8c].

Acts performed under the influence of such ignorance are not unlike the "mixed acts" discussed by Aristotle in connection with the influence of force.[58] Unlike antecedent ignorance, which might cause a whole act or an entire part of it to be involuntary, here voluntariness permeates the entire act.

VI. Restitution for Cooperation

One of the few passages in which Thomas deals explicitly with cooperation is *ST* 2-2.62.7, which asks whether someone who has not accepted stolen goods but was somehow involved in their theft is obliged to make restitution to the person from whom they were stolen.[59] In the article, he does mention particular ways in which one might cooperate with such evil and so be obliged to make restitution, but here its interest for us lies not so much in these particular cases as in what the article says about cooperation more generally and in the indications Thomas gives as to how one might identify degrees of immoral cooperation.

Impressive in *ST* 2-2.62.7 is the very breadth of the assembly of acts that Thomas is disposed to regard as immoral cooperation. Certainly cases in which, as in the moral manuals, one person helps one other person to steal can be assigned a place in the schema Thomas sets out in this article; but, as we shall see, the swathe of his censure and concern is much broader than that. On the other hand, we must be cautious in applying what Thomas says in *ST* 2-2.62.7 about restitution to cooperation simply speaking. Thomas's primary task in *ST* 2-2.62.7 is to determine when and whether a person is obliged to give

58. See above, section III.

59. In the second objection, cooperation is actually mentioned: "if obliged to make restitution is not only he who accepts but also those who in whatever way cooperate" ["si ad restitutionem teneretur non solum ille qui accepit, sed etiam illi qui qualitercumque cooperantur"]. The latter phrase ("those who in whatever way cooperate") refers to the wide range of types of action to be considered in the article itself. There is also a passage in the commentary on the *Sentences* – *Sent.* 4.15.1.5.3 – where Thomas covers much of the same ground that he covers in *ST* 2-2.62.7.

something, usually money or goods, as restitution to someone who has been unjustly deprived of the same. Cooperation is not just concerned with who must make restitution.

But let us look at *ST* 2-2.62.7 itself. The scope of Thomas's concern is apparent in the first objection and the corresponding response. That objection argues that restitution is a punishment proper to the one who accepts stolen goods, and so one who has not accepted stolen goods is not obliged to make restitution. Thomas's replies that, no, "also one who in any way whatsoever is a cause of the sin" [etiam qui quocumque modo peccati est causa] is obliged to make restitution.[60] The moral issue consists not just in the fact that a thing belonging to another is in the thief's hands but also (indeed, primarily) in the very "injurious accepting" itself. The expression "thing belonging to another" [res aliena] is the expression that Thomas uses when speaking of the object of the exterior act of theft.[61] Because of this object, the act of the man who accepts something belonging to another *is* an act of theft.[62] But other actions, including actions by other persons, might be immoral not because they *are* acts of theft but because of the circumstance of being connected in some way with an act of theft, that is, because of the injustice (or injurious nature) of the accepting itself.

In this connection it should also be mentioned that many of the

60. That the person is a cause of the sin is an important qualification. A man (as in Gn 19:5–8) who is told that his daughters will be raped unless he surrenders to a rabid crowd his innocent guests and who, on moral grounds, refuses to surrender them, in a certain sense causes the rape of his daughters, but he cannot be said to have caused the sin of the rapists. On the causation of cooperation, see below, note 71.

61. *ST* 1-2.18.2c: "ita primum malum in actionibus moralibus est quod est ex obiecto, sicut accipere aliena."

62. See, again, *ST* 1-2.18.2c, where Thomas says that we must understand the phrase *ex genere* ("in its genus") as in effect *ex specie* ("in its species"): "And [such an action] is called evil in its genus, genus understood here as species, employing that manner of speaking by which we call the whole human species the human genus" ["Et dicitur malum ex genere, genere pro specie accepto, eo modo loquendi quo dicimus humanum genus totam humanam speciem."

things that Thomas says in *ST* 2-2.62.7 pertain not only to property unjustly accepted but to unjust injury understood more generally. This section of the *Summa theologiae* (that is, *ST* 2-2.62) is about violations of commutative justice (see especially *ST* 2-2.62.1), and commutative justice takes in a wide range of acts. Aristotle (whom Thomas follows in these regards), in *EN* 5.4, acknowledges that certain "gains" and "losses" – such as the "gain" [ἡ ζημία] accruing to a person who strikes another and the "loss" [τὸ κέρδος] suffered by the person struck – are not easily quantifiable and so a judge must do the best he can in determining just reparation.

> For the term 'gain' is applied in a general way to such cases, even if, applied to certain cases, it is not the opportune word [οἰκεῖον ὄνομα], for instance, when 'gain' is applied to a person who inflicts a wound and 'loss' to the one who suffers it; nonetheless, when the suffering has been measured [μετρηθῇ], the one is called loss and the other gain.[63] [*EN* 5.4 1132a10–14]

63. This approach is of a piece with other remarks Aristotle makes in the same section of the *Nicomachean Ethics*. In a passage that immediately follows an account of corrective justice as establishing "arithmetical proportion" [*EN* 5.4 1132a30], he criticizes the overly mechanical approach of the Pythagoreans, who defined justice as *simply* "requital" or "reciprocity" [τὸ ἀντιπεπονθὸς – *EN* 5.5 1132b21–22]. Aristotle goes on then to say that reestablishing justice after the violent striking of a public authority is different from reestablishing justice when a private individual is struck and that a voluntary act differs much from an involuntary one.

Thomas makes the connection with *EN* 5.4–5 in *ST* 2-2.61.4. In addition, see *ST* 2-2.62.2 ad 1 and 62.5; see also Thomas's comment at *in EN* 5.6.110–125 [§953]. In the commentary on the *Sentences* [*Sent.* 4.15.1.5.1], in speaking about the reparation of injury not quantifiable, Thomas gives some preference to the word *satisfactio* rather than *restitutio*: "For reparation of an inequality existing in things is called 'restitution', reparation, however, of an inequality in actions and sufferings, is called 'satisfaction'; and so sometimes there is satisfaction without any restitution, as when someone, because of certain insults uttered by him, humbles himself before his neighbor" ["Reparatio enim inaequalitatis existentis in rebus, restitutio dicitur; reparatio autem inaequalitatis existentis in actionibus et passionibus, satisfactio nominatur; et ideo quandoque est satisfactio sine restitutione aliqua, ut cum quis se proximo humiliat de aliquibus contumeliis ei dictis"]; but see also *Sent.* 4.15.1.1.2c.

In the corpus of *ST* 2-2.62.7, Thomas goes through the various ways in which an act might be involved somehow in an act that calls for restitution – at least, as we shall see, by someone. The corpus, in its entirely, runs as follows:

Someone is obliged to make restitution not only by reason of a thing belonging to another that he has accepted but also by reason of an injurious accepting. And so whoever is a cause of an unjust accepting is obliged to make restitution. This [unjust accepting] might occur in two ways: either (1) directly or (2) indirectly.

It occurs (1) directly when someone induces another to accept. This itself might occur in three ways: (1a) by moving someone toward the accepting itself – which comes about by ordering, counseling, expressly consenting, and praising someone as fearless for accepting what belongs to another; (1b) with respect to the person himself who accepts: that is, because one receives him or in some other way offers aid; (1c) with respect to the thing accepted, because, that is, one is a participant in a theft or robbery or a sort of confederate in the crime.

It occurs, however, (2) indirectly when someone: (2a) does not impede when he can and ought to impede, or (2b) because he withdraws an order or counsel impeding the theft or robbery, or (2c) because he withdraws aid by means of which he might have hindered it, or (2d) because he conceals after the fact.

All of these are included in the following verses: "Command, counsel, consent, flattery, recourse; participating, being silent, not preventing, not denouncing."[64]

It must be acknowledged, however, that five of the aforesaid always require restitution. First, command: because, that is, he who commands is he who moves principally; and so he is principally bound to make restitution. Secondly, consent – that is to say, in that without which the theft cannot occur. Thirdly, recourse: when, that is, someone is the receiver of thieves and provides them with protection. Fourthly, participation: when, that is, someone participates in the crime of theft and in the spoil. Fifthly, obliged is he

64. The origin of the verses is obscure. They appear also in Albert the Great's commentary on the *Sentences* of Peter Lombard [*Sent.* 4.15.42]. See also Thomas's commentary on the same: *Sent.* 4.15.15.3.

who does not prevent when he is obliged *to* prevent: princes, for instance, who are obliged to protect justice on earth, if through their neglect thieves multiply, are obliged to make restitution, for the compensation they have is a sort of salary established in order that they might protect justice on earth.

In the other enumerated cases, however, one is not always obliged to make restitution. For counsel or flattery or some similar thing is not always an efficacious cause of a theft. Thus only then is a counselor or a flatterer, that is, a praiser, obliged to make restitution, when it is possible to estimate that probably from causes of this sort an unjust acceptance would follow.

We see in the first paragraph here that the obligation to make restitution depends upon someone's being a *cause* of the "injurious accepting" (whether or not he has, or ever had, the goods in his possession). This indicates that the immediate concern of *ST* 2-2.62.7 is a subset of the possible immoral acts in this general area, for, even if someone is not a cooperating cause of someone's *actually* being deprived in some way, his action may be immoral. One sins, for instance, by supporting an attempted but unsuccessful theft. *ST* 2-2.62.7 is not concerned immediately with such cases but with cases in which a cooperator's act has been (in some sense) a cause of a theft.

In his response to the second objection in *ST* 2-2.62.7, Thomas does allude to a case outside the article's proper ambit. The objection argues that justice does not oblige one to increase another's property. As part of this argument, mentioned is the possibility that one might do something with a view to someone's being deprived of some good but (for some reason) the misdeed does not come off. If such a person was obliged to make restitution, the intended victim's property would thereby be increased and not just restored. Thomas replies that in such a case restitution is not required "since restitution is principally ordered toward restoring the thing belonging to the one who has been unjustly injured." It is obvious, however, that cooperation with such an attempted theft is not an upright human act.

A few articles previously, in *ST* 2-2.62.3, Thomas speaks of another such issue. Since he is dealing there with commutative justice, he speaks of inequality, but the example he uses has to do with the "gain" and "loss" pertaining to acts of violence.[65] He acknowledges that, even where there is no inequality, there can be guilt: "for instance, when someone intends to inflict violence but does not prevail."[66] There is a moral issue here, and an issue of justice, even though restitution is not called for: the appropriate remedy is not restitution but rather "punishment, the infliction of which pertains to a judge."[67]

All this said, however, and consistent with what Thomas says in *ST* 2-2.62.7, it does appear that cooperation has to do with causation and not, at least immediately, with these other moral issues. This indeed is implied by the word *cooperari* itself: to cooperate is to do something (*operari*) that somehow contributes to what someone else does (or some others do). Thus, if someone is to be judged guilty of immoral cooperation, he will have to have been involved somehow as a cause in the malefactor's (or malefactors') misdeed. (This is sometimes called "concausality" and the persons so involved "concauses." Those terms will occasionally be used here.) A freshly accredited medical assistant, for instance, who shows up at the abortion clinic where he has just been hired and finds it has been shut down, may be guilty of intending to cooperate in abortions but he has not in fact cooperated. Similarly, if a man counsels his girlfriend to have an abortion and she refuses, he has acted sinfully but he has not cooperated in abortion.

65. See above, at note 63.

66. "Aliud autem est iniustitiae culpa, quae potest esse etiam cum aequalitate rei, puta cum aliquis intendat inferre violentiam sed non praevalet" [*ST* 2-2.62.3c]. See also, for instance, *Quaestiones disputatae de veritate* 24.12 c: "So, on account of a failure of motive power free choice is not impeded from a sin nor from its avoidance, even though occasionally it is impeded from its execution, as when someone wills to kill or to fornicate or to steal but cannot" ["Unde propter defectum virtutis motivae non impeditur liberum arbitrium a peccato vel eius vitatione; quamvis interdum impediatur ab executione, sicut cum quis vult occidere vel fornicari vel furari, nec tamen potest"].

67. "But regarding blame, the remedy is applied through punishment, the infliction of which pertains to a judge" ["Sed quantum ad culpam adhibetur remedium per poenam, cuius inflictio pertinet ad iudicem"] [*ST* 2-2.62.3c].

Let us now look at Thomas's list in *ST* 2-2.62.7 of cooperative behaviors requiring restitution. Among the direct acts or acts of inducement,[68] he lists in (1a) "ordering, counseling, expressly consenting, and praising someone as fearless for accepting what belongs to another." Ordering [praecipiendo] is quite easily recognized as a cause (or a concause). The one thing about it that ought to be noted is that later in the article Thomas describes the one who commands as "he who moves principally."[69] Indeed, in his response to the second objection, he remarks that "principally obliged to make restitution is he who is principal in the act: acting principally is the commander, secondarily is the executor, and the others follow in order."[70] Applying this point to a standard case of cooperation, the judge who orders a public official to issue a "marriage license" to a homosexual couple is (as we might put it) "more principally" the cause of that act than is the public official. Thomas is speaking here about an act's proximity to the evil act of which it is a concause; this is a key issue in the analysis of many cases of cooperation. The proximity at issue here is clearly not physical but intelligible proximity.

Regarding the "counseling" and "praising someone as fearless for accepting what belongs to another" of (1a), it is important to note

68. We will see in chapter 5, section III, that the concept of inducement is important for determining when borrowing from a usurer constitutes immoral cooperation. Thomas also speaks of inducement with respect to per se scandal. Something, he says, can be a cause of sin per se, "when someone by his evil word or deed intends to induce another to sin" ["quando aliquis suo malo verbo vel facto intendit alium ad peccandum inducere" [*ST* 2-2.43.1 ad 4]. He immediately adds: "or, also if he does not so intend, his deed is such that of its nature it is inductive to sin" ["vel, etiam si ipse hoc non intendat, ipsum factum est tale quod de sui ratione habet *ut sit inductivum ad peccandum*"]; but this is not the intentional giving of scandal spoken about either in *ST* 2-2.43.1 or in *ST* 2-2.62.7. For Thomas's discussion of scandal, see chapter 3, section I.

69. "Primo, iussio, quia scilicet ille qui iubet est principaliter movens" [*ST* 2-2.62.7c]. The word *iussio*, which Thomas takes from the verses he quotes, he regards as equivalent to *praecipiendo* (or *praeceptum*).

70. "Ad secundum dicendum quod principaliter tenetur restituere ille qui est principalis in facto, principaliter quidem praecipiens, secundario exequens, et consequenter alii per ordinem" [*ST* 2-2.62.7 ad 2].

that in the last paragraph of the corpus Thomas specifies that the counsel and flattery he has in mind must amount to an "efficacious cause" [efficax causa] and that restitution is due "when it is possible to estimate that probably from causes of this sort an unjust acceptance would follow."[71] Thomas here makes no suggestion – although he could easily have done so if such was his position – that the estimation of probable causality would be done by (or only by) the person praising. Applying this passage, therefore, to cooperation more gen-

71. "quando probabiliter aestimari potest quod ex huiusmodi causis fuerit iniusta acceptio subsecuta" [*ST* 2-2.62.7c]. Thomas has in mind here Aristotle's efficient cause. It is important to bear in mind, however, that Aristotle's understanding of the expression 'efficient cause' is different from the contemporary understanding of the same, which typically reduces causality to a physical relationship. At *Metaph.* 5.2 1013a30–31, the first example that Aristotle gives of an efficient cause is that of "the man who has deliberated" [ὁ βουλεύσας]. Thomas speaks of this latter person as a "counselor" [consiliator] [Thomas Aquinas, *in Metaph.* 5.2.3 (§765)]. This counselor is clearly a cooperator (although not necessarily in evil): "Nam ex consiliatore incipit motus in eo, qui secundum consilium agit ad rei conservationem." Thomas then expounds upon Aristotle's understanding of efficient cause and in doing so draws upon Avicenna, who recognizes four types of efficient cause: "perfecting, dispositive, helping, and counseling" ["perficiens, disponens, adiuvans, et consilians"]. (Thomas gives the same four at Thomas Aquinas, *In octo libros Physicorum Aristotelis expositio*, ed. P. M. Maggiòlo [Turin: Marietti, 1965], 2.5.5 [§180].) The third and fourth of these are especially pertinent to present concerns. Something is called a "helping" cause, Thomas says, "in so far as it operates *for* the principal effect. In this, however, it differs from the principal agent, because the principal agent acts for its own end; that which helps, for another's end" ["Adiuvans autem dicitur causa secundum quod operatur ad principalem effectum. In hoc tamen differt ab agente principali, quia principale agens agit ad finem proprium, adiuvans autem ad finem alienum"] [Thomas Aquinas, *in Metaph.* 5.2.6 (§768)]. A "counseling" efficient cause, says Thomas, "differs from the principal efficient cause in so far as it gives the end and form of acting. And this is the way a primary agent stands by way of intellect with respect to every secondary agent, whether natural or intellectual. For it is a primary intellectual agent that in all cases gives the end and form of acting, for instance, the designer of a ship [gives these] to the ship builder and the first intellect to the whole of nature" ["Consilians autem differt ab efficiente principali, inquantum dat finem et formam agendi. Et haec est habitudo primi agentis per intellectum ad omne agens secundum, sive sit naturale, sive intellectuale. Nam primum agens intellectuale in omnibus dat finem et formam agendi secundo agenti, sicut architector navis navim operanti, et primus intellectus toti naturae"] [Thomas Aquinas, *in Metaph.* 5.2.7 (§769)].

erally, if the words a person uses with another are unlikely to result in a corresponding evil deed (because, for instance, quite unknown to the person, the other finds such deeds repulsive), even if the person believes that his words will help to bring about the evil deed, he has not cooperated in evil. Again, in all likelihood his attempt is sinful, but he has not cooperated.

Regarding consent – or, to be precise, "expressly consenting" [consentiendo expresse] – Thomas specifies that it must be the consent "in that without which the theft cannot take place."[72] Obviously, this is not the consent of one who stands by as someone else gives an order that an unjust act be carried out and who happens to be in agreement with that order: the consent must be manifest to the malefactor and in some way influence his decision to act.

In the above translation, the words "consent – that is to say, in that without which the theft cannot occur" correspond to the Latin "consensus, in eo scilicet sine quo rapina fieri non potest." This is to understand the original as making reference to consent to something without which [*x*] cannot take place. But that is not the only way of construing the construction *in eo sine quo*, and this gave rise to considerable debate in the tradition subsequent to Thomas. Part of the problem lies in the ambiguous referent of the word *eo*, which can conceivably refer to the person who consents. The translation by the English Dominicans, for instance, has: "consent: namely of one without whose consent the robbery cannot take place." As Cajetan (Thomas de Vio) explains, this idea was understood by some learned men (*doctores*) as qualifying the assertion made near the beginning of the corpus of *ST* 2-2.62.7, "whoever is a cause of an unjust accepting is obliged to make restitution," and so as qualifying also whatever Thomas says in the article about causation. The basic idea behind this way of construing the phrase was that, if the person involved in inflicting unjust damage on another was one of several persons who

72. "in eo scilicet sine quo rapina fieri non potest" [*ST* 2-2.62.7c].

might have done so – even though in fact only he performed the act – he was not a true cause of the illicit deed.[73] He was not one without whose consent the robbery could not have taken place.

Cajetan's answer to these learned men is to argue that, "saving their reverence" [salva horum reverentia], even if Thomas does make mention of a causal variant that is present when an unjust act would not have occurred in the absence of a particular agent, more important for him would be the actual causes of the injustice – the actual causes being those identified by Aristotle. "For more prominent is the cause through which something comes about than the cause without which it would not come about, for the latter is not counted among

73. The argument is complicated. According to Cajetan, those who make the argument begin with the principle that, if a man is one of many who might have performed an illicit "accepting," then only the one who actually performed the illicit act is required to make restitution – unless he (the first man) too has obtained something by virtue of the illicit act. They move on from this principle, however, to the idea that, whenever a man is one of several who might perform the illicit act, he cannot be blamed as the cause, even if he did perform the illicit act. "They maintain," says Cajetan, "that what entails the obligation of restitution is a cause without which there would be no accepting; but if the accepting was effected wholly by another, one is not bound to make restitution except on account of something that one obtains. And from this principle is deduced the thesis that particular instrumental causes, whose place could very well be filled by others – for instance, those who assist at usury or lower-ranking military personnel or foot soldiers in a manifestly unjust war – are not obliged unless they have obtained something, for in their place there could have been others who could have done the same" ["Aiuntque quod requiritur ad restitutionis vinculum quod sit causa sine qua non acciperetur: sed si omnino acceptio fuisset per alium facta, non teneri ad restitutionem nisi ratione rei quae ad ipsum devenit. Et ex hoc principio deducitur quod causae instrumentales particulares, loco quarum omnino fuissent aliae, ut ministri ad usuras et inferiores milites et pedites ad bellum manifeste iniustum, non tenentur nisi aliquid ad eos devenerit: quoniam loco eorum alii affuissent qui idem fecissent"] [Thomas Aquinas and Thomas de Vio (Cajetan), *Summa theologiae, cum commentariis Thomae de Vio Caietani Ordinis Praedicatorum*, apud *ST* 2-2.62.7, I (v. 9, 59a)]. As mentioned below, Cajetan goes on then to argue against this thesis that, if someone has several servants, all of whom are capable and prepared to kill, and he gives the command that they should kill a certain man, even if the servant who does the deed is just one of several who might have done so, he (that servant) "is a true cause of the unjust taking of the life" ["vera causa iniustae acceptionis vitae"].

the causes, and the former is truly the cause, as is clear in philosophy."[74] (Cajetan apparently has in mind here Aristotle's *Metaphysics*, book 5, chapter 2.)[75] He goes on say:

And, as everyone understands, if someone has many servants and he gives the order that they kill a certain man – each of them individually being ready and competent to perform the act – if only one of them kills the man, would he not be a true cause of the unjust taking of the life?[76]

It is possible, however, to take a somewhat different approach to the problem while, in effect, making a point similar to Cajetan's. There is no denying that the phrase "consensus, in eo scilicet sine quo rapina fieri non potest," might be translated: "consent – that is to say of one without whose consent the theft cannot take place." That is possible grammatically but it should be noted that nowhere else in his works does Thomas speak of the consent residing *in* a person.[77] Moreover, it is perfectly possible to translate the phrase as we have done above: "consent – that is to say, in that without which the theft cannot occur." Thomas would then be referring to the cause through which the evil comes about and for which the cooperator constitutes

74. "Plus enim in primis est causa per quam fit quam causa sine qua non fieret: quoniam ista inter causas non computatur, illa vere est causa, ut patet in philosophia" [Thomas Aquinas and Thomas de Vio (Cajetan), *Summa theologiae, cum commentariis Thomae de Vio Caietani Ordinis Praedicatorum*, apud *ST* 2-2.62.7, I (v. 9, 59a)].

75. See above, note 71.

76. "Et, ut omnes intelligant, si quis habeat multos famulos, et praecipiat quod occidant talem virum; et, singulis existentibus paratis ad hoc et sufficientibus, si unus eorum solus illum occidat; numquid non est vera causa iniustae acceptionis vitae?" [Thomas Aquinas and Thomas de Vio (Cajetan), *Summa theologiae, cum commentariis Thomae de Vio Caietani Ordinis Praedicatorum*, apud *ST* 2-2.62.7 I (v. 9, 59a)]. No doubt Cajetan uses the word *acceptionis* here because he understands the unjust killing as a violation of commutative justice. See above, note 63. This sort of issue arises in Alphonsus's remarks on cooperation: see appendix 1, section 64.

77. Thomas speaks a number of times of "consensus in delectionem" (see *Sent.* 2.24.3.1 ad 5); in the one place where he uses *in* plus the ablative (*Sent.* 2.24.3.1c), he speaks about consent "in the execution of an act" ["consensus in executione operis"].

a concause in and through his consent.[78] Under this reading, the cooperator is not one of several possible cooperators, all of whom are "ready and competent to perform the act." And preserved here is the idea that a cause without which the evil effect of someone else's action would not have occurred has a special significance.

The remaining behaviors that constitute direct cooperation with theft do not raise any serious problems. The cooperation provided, as in (1b), by one who receives thieves "or in some other way offers aid" is clearly not the principal cause of the theft but a concause. To bring such behavior onto the larger (non-theft specific) stage, an example of this type of concausality would be a supposedly pro-life hospital's providing an operating room to abortionists. Behavior (1c), that of "a participant in a theft or robbery," is the classic example of cooperation with evil.

The list of ways in which one might be an *indirect* cause of a theft (or any evil act) is more intellectually engaging and also very important in the analysis of less obvious cases of cooperation. A person cooperates indirectly when (2a) he "does not impede when he can and ought to impede." In the continuation of *ST* 2-2.62.7c, Thomas specifies that this obligation pertains, for instance, to "princes . . . who are obliged to protect justice on earth." A more contemporary application of this would say that politicians who do not do what they can and should do in order to impede immoral practices are guilty of immoral cooperation with those evils.[79] Such obligations pertain, however, to all who are duty-bound in some way to do something.

The list of ways in which one might cooperate indirectly with theft finishes with a number of even less obvious – but useful for present purposes – reasons why a person might be so blamed. Thom-

78. We come back to this theme in chapter 5, section III.

79. Important here is what Thomas says about its not being reasonable for positive law to prohibit all immoral actions: *ST* 1-2.96.2. On these matters see Flannery, "Voting, Intrinsic Evil, and Commensuration," and Cathleen Kaveny and Kevin Flannery, SJ, "Response and Rejoinder: On Voting, Intrinsic Evil, and Ranking of Political Issues," *American Journal of Jurisprudence* 61, no. 2 (2016): 259–73.

as mentions at (2b) and (2c): "because he withdraws an order or counsel impeding the theft or robbery" and "because he withdraws aid by means of which he might have hindered it." Again, bringing such considerations out onto a less specific stage, an organization – even, for instance, a bishops' conference – that eliminates from a list of practices prohibited in Catholic hospitals sterilizations or the distribution of contraceptives cooperates in the sinful acts that inevitably follow from such an elimination. A similar thing might be said of an organization or agency that withdraws funding from an organization that helps expectant mothers to arrange adoption as an alternative to abortion of the children they carry.

Last mentioned in Thomas's list is (2d) the behavior of one who "conceals [something] after the fact" [quia occultat post factum]. He does not specify whether what is being concealed is a person, the stolen object (or objects), or the fact that a theft has been committed. Given Thomas's condition that cooperation must be a cause, one might be inclined to argue that the condemned behavior would have to involve a prior agreement with the malefactor not to reveal something or other. But certainly a person, all of whose contribution to the crime is "after the fact," is obliged (once his involvement is discovered) to make restitution. Such a person would presumably conceal the thief, the object stolen, or the theft itself in order that the unjust accepting might be successful and go unpunished – and so he would be a "helping" cause.[80] He would also likely be aiding further such crimes. Similar things can be said of cooperation more generally: of a city official, for instance, who seeks to conceal the severe beating of a minor offender by one of his policeman. This can certainly be condemned as cooperation with evil.

Our list of the factors in reason and justice that have a bearing upon cooperation continues in chapter 5.

80. See above, note 71.

CHAPTER 5 FACTORS IN REASON AND JUSTICE: PART II

I. Intention, Paths of Intelligibility, Proportionality

In the previous chapter, especially sections II through V, we took note of a number of ways in which the voluntary might be shaped by factors over which the individuals involved have no – or, at least, no immediate – control. The pilot who is forced to steer his ship into Aegina rather than Piraeus performs what, in itself, is a wholly voluntary act, the essential features of which have, however, been set by the wind. The man whose job does not require him to know a certain area of the law chooses to turn his attention elsewhere; to his action there do not attach the moral implications that attach to another man's failure to acquire that same knowledge, which, in the latter's case, is required by his job. The upright character of the former behavior and blamable character of the latter have nothing necessarily to do with what goes through the mind of either man as he acts or fails to act. The morally relevant societal factors are in place before either man acts or fails to act; these factors are among the circumstances of the acts.[1]

1. In speaking of "societal factors" (or, as below, "the societal factor") I do not mean

In a well-known article in the *secunda secundae* of the *Summa theologiae*, Thomas speaks about these factors, plus a couple of others, together: he speaks, that is, about natural and human law, both of which have a role in establishing the moral contours of society, as well as about intention and an issue not yet mentioned in the present work but which has a bearing upon the theory of cooperation: proportionality. The article is *ST* 2-2.64.7, where Thomas asks whether it is licit to kill in self-defense. It is sometimes considered the place where Thomas formulates the "principle of double effect" – although he does not offer there a principle but simply describes the various factors that need to be considered in determining whether various types of self-defense are moral.[2] Within the manualist tradition, the principle of double effect is often invoked in connection with cooperation. Noldin, for instance, in laying out the conditions under which material cooperation might be licit, says that, "when . . . from some action that is not evil there follows a double effect – one good, the other bad – it is licit to place [i.e., perform] that action, given a proportionately grave reason, although it is foreseen that an evil will follow." The language he uses here tracks fairly closely the language of *ST* 2-2.64.7.[3]

The issue in *ST* 2-2.64.7 is "whether it is licit for someone to kill someone in self-defense." As eventually becomes apparent, he is

---

to exclude the role of natural law. That, for instance, human society prefers monogamy, castigates incest, etc., are societal factors determined by natural law.

2. A translation of *ST* 2-2.64.7 can be found in appendix 5 of the present work.

3. "ubi enim ex aliqua actione non mala sequitur duplex effectus, alter bonus, alter malus, ex causa proportionate gravi licet illam actionem ponere, etsi praevideatur secuturus malus" [H. Noldin and A. Schmitt, *Summa theologiae moralis* (Innsbruck, Leipzig: F. Rauch, 1939–40), 2.118.2b]. In the appended note, Noldin refers to his own section in the previous volume (1.83) (that is, the place where he discusses the principle of double effect). See also Prümmer, *Manuale theologiae moralis secundum principia S. Thomae Aquinatis*, 1.623 (scholion), where Prümmer makes reference to his own treatment of the principles regarding the indirectly voluntary (1.57–60), which is basically an exposition of the principle of double effect.

speaking here about a private individual whose concern is to conserve his own life. Rather unusually for Thomas, he answers the question in the first paragraph of the corpus:

> Nothing prohibits there being two effects of a single act, only one of which is intended, the other being beside the intention. Moral acts, however, take their species with respect to what is intended, not from that which is beside the intention, since this is per accidens, as is made clear above.[4] So, from the act of someone who defends himself there can follow a double effect: one, the conservation of one's own life; the other, killing of the aggressor. Such an act, therefore, in so far as what is intended is the conservation of one's own life, does not have the character of the illicit, for it is natural to whatever thing to conserve itself in being as far as possible.

Clearly Thomas's answer to the question posed involves – even prominently – intention; so, we shall start with that. Having considered Thomas's understanding of intention, we shall then consider the societal factor and also proportionality.

The first two objections of *ST* 2-2.64.7 argue that it is illicit to kill another in self-defense and each cites Augustine, the first a letter to a certain Publicola, the second the first book of *De libero arbitrio*. Thomas gives a quotation from the latter work: "How in view of divine providence 'are they free from sin who, for these things [pro his rebus] which one ought to despise, are defiled by human bloodshed?'"[5] The second objection goes on then to explain that "these

4. Modern editions of the *Summa theologiae* direct readers to *ST* 1-2.72.1 and 2-2.43.3. On these two articles and their relationship with *ST* 2-2.64.7, see Kevin L. Flannery, "Thomas Aquinas and the New Natural Law Theory on the Object of the Human Act," *National Catholic Bioethics Quarterly* 13, no. 1 (2013): 85–92.

5. "[Q]uomodo apud divinam providentiam a peccato liberi sunt qui pro his rebus quas contemni oportet, humana caede polluti sunt?" [*ST* 2-2.64.7 ad 2]. Approximately this wording is found at *De libero arbitrio* 1.5.13: "Quomodo enim apud eam [i.e., divine providence] sunt isti peccato liberi, qui pro his rebus quas contemni oportet, humana caede polluti sint?" See also *De libero arbitrio* 1.5.12: "Therefore, they are free to kill no one for those things which unwilling they can lose and for this reason ought not to love" ["Liberum eis itaque est neminem necare pro his rebus quas inviti possunt amittere, et ob hoc amare non debent"].

things which one ought to despise" are, according to the argument of *De libero arbitrio*, those things that might be taken away from someone unwillingly, such as life in the body, as contrasted with those things that cannot, such as one's own virtue. And so, both objections conclude, killing in self-defense is illicit.

Thomas responds to the two objections together, paying special attention to Augustine's precise wording in the *De libero arbitrio* quotation. His response runs as follows:

> The authority of Augustine is to be understood as applying to that case in which someone *intends* to kill a man in order to free himself from death. It is with respect to this case also that the authority, introduced from *De libero arbitrio*, is understood. And so, significantly, it is said, "for these things [pro his rebus]," by which is designated intention. And with this the response to the second objection is obvious.[6]

What is objectionable for Augustine (and for Thomas) is killing *for* [pro] the conservation of one's life; the word *pro* signals that the *killing* is intended and not just the conservation of one's life.

What is the mark of such "doing something for [pro] something else"? Thomas answers this crucial question in his response to the fourth objection. The objection itself argues that killing is a more serious sin than either fornication or adultery, and yet it is clearly forbidden to commit fornication or adultery "for [pro] the preservation of one's life"; and so it is also forbidden to kill in order to [ut] preserve one's life.[7] Thomas responds that "an act of fornication or adultery

6. "Ad primum ergo dicendum quod auctoritas Augustini intelligenda est in eo casu quo quis intendit occidere hominem ut seipsum a morte liberet. In quo etiam casu intelligitur auctoritas inducta ex libro De libero arbitrio. Unde signanter dicitur, pro his rebus, in quo designatur intentio. Et per hoc patet responsio ad secundum" [*ST* 2-2.64.7 ad 1/2].

7. "Praeterea, homicidium est gravius peccatum quam simplex fornicatio vel adulterium. Sed nulli licet committere simplicem fornicationem vel adulterium, vel quodcumque aliud peccatum mortale, pro conservatione propriae vitae, quia vita spiritualis praeferenda est corporali. Ergo nulli licet, defendendo seipsum, alium occidere ut propriam vitam conservet" [*ST* 2-2.64.7 obi. 4].

is not ordered toward the conservation of one's own life from necessity, as is an act from which a killing sometimes follows."[8]

In order to understand this response, it is necessary to know something about Thomas's fairly intricate use of the term 'intention' (and related terms). Intention is primarily for an end. It is with this sense in mind that Thomas says at the beginning of the corpus of *ST* 2-2.64.7 that someone who defends himself might intend only the conservation of his life and not the killing of the aggressor, which is "beside the intention" [praeter intentionem]. But intention is for the end *as* understood within a certain context: the context of doing something in order to arrive at that intended end. As Thomas puts it at *ST* 1-2.12.1 ad 4, the act of the will that is intention is that act which

> considers the end as the terminus of something that is ordered toward it. We are not said to intend health simply because we *will* it but because we will to arrive at it through something else.[9]

Most people will to be healthy; they intend to be healthy only when they take steps aimed at improving or at maintaining their health – going to the gym, for instance. What is intended is health, although, in a secondary sense, so is going to the gym.

In the same article, Thomas is careful to point out that the ordering of the thing toward the terminus is the work of the intellect.[10]

8. "Ad quartum dicendum quod actus fornicationis vel adulterii non ordinatur ad conservationem propriae vitae ex necessitate, sicut actus ex quo quandoque sequitur homicidium" [*ST* 2-2.64.7 ad 4].

9. "Ad quartum dicendum quod intentio est actus voluntatis respectu finis. Sed voluntas respicit finem tripliciter.... Tertio modo consideratur finis secundum quod est terminus alicuius quod in ipsum ordinatur, et sic intentio respicit finem. Non enim solum ex hoc intendere dicimur sanitatem, quia volumus eam, sed quia volumus ad eam per aliquid aliud pervenire" [*ST* 1-2.12.1 ad 4].

10. See *ST* 1-2.12.1 ad 3: "this word 'intention' picks out an act of the will, presupposing an ordering on the part of reason which orders something to an end" ["hoc nomen intentio nominat actum voluntatis, praesupposita ordinatione rationis ordinantis aliquid in finem"]. Given what we have learned in previous chapters of the present work about the relationship between reason and justice, it will be apparent that it is here – in the ordering of things toward the end – that the primary moral issues will be located.

Because intention necessarily occurs within such a context, we can sometimes say that that through which the intended terminus is to be reached is also intended. Thomas makes this point in his *Quaestiones disputatae de veritate* 22.13:

> Since it is proper to reason to put things in order and to compare them, whenever there appears in an act of the will some comparison or ordering, such an act will be of the will not absolutely but in connection with reason. It is in this way that to intend is an act of the will, since to intend appears to be nothing other than, from that which someone wills, to tend toward something else as toward an end.[11]

In other words, when reason is put to work ordering and comparing, the intending is directed not just at the end but at that "something else" that goes toward the end and that reason has elaborated and/or discovered. The term 'intention' (and related terms) can, therefore, be used of such tending toward something else "*as* toward an end."

This tending toward something else as toward an end is what Thomas is speaking about when he speaks in *ST* 2-2.64.7 ad 1 of things done "for these things [pro his rebus]" and in obi./ad 4 of committing fornication or adultery "for [pro] the conservation of one's life." If committing fornication or adultery is somehow going to save someone's life, it has to be part of some scheme (some effort to "put things in order and to compare them"), for neither is "ordered toward the conservation of one's own life from necessity." By contrast, "an act from which a killing sometimes follows" (and performed while one is being attacked) is presumably part of no such scheme.[12] Considered

11. "Cum enim proprium rationis sit ordinare et conferre, quandocumque in actu voluntatis apparet aliqua collatio vel ordinatio, talis actus erit voluntatis non absolute, sed in ordine ad rationem: et hoc modo intendere est actus voluntatis; cum intendere nihil aliud esse videatur quam ex eo quod quis vult, in aliud tendere sicut in finem" [*Quaestiones disputatae de veritate* 22.13c]. See also *ST* 1-2.4 and, for the interpretation of the latter, Brock, *Action and Conduct: Thomas Aquinas and the Theory of Action*, 186 n. 123.

12. Later in *ST* 2-2.64.7, Thomas speaks of a public official's intending to kill in order to protect himself—so having the intention of protecting oneself does not entail that one does not intend to kill.

in itself, defending oneself with such an action *is* to conserve one's life – or, at least, to attempt to do so; the two, that is, acting thus and conserving of one's life, are of a piece. There is intention also here, of course: one does something in order to conserve one's life. (That is Thomas's point in the opening sentences of the corpus of *ST* 2-2.64.7: "in so far as what is intended is the conservation of one's own life.") But what one effects on the *way* to that terminus is, according to the language employed in those initial sentences, not *that which* is intended – although that which is done in order to arrive at that terminus is, in a wider sense of that term, intended.[13]

Up until this point, our focus has been upon Thomas's understanding of intention. But in explaining how he uses the terms 'intention,' 'intended,' etc., the second factor has begun to emerge from the background: what was referred to above as the "societal factor."[14] Its character as societal is not yet apparent: at the moment, all that has emerged is the idea that intention has to do not just with the end but with the way to that end (which sometimes involves intending to do some distinct thing in order to arrive at that end). But when what Thomas says about intention at the beginning of *ST* 2-2.64.7c is compared to what he says later, the societal character of the remarks about intention becomes apparent. It may seem that, in saying that

13. This last point calls perhaps for yet further explanation. Within the context of a particular description of an act, intention looks to the end – not necessarily the ultimate end – for which one does something, even though under another description that which one does in order to achieve that end might also be called the intention for which one does something. Let us say that the agent spoken of at the beginning of *ST* 2-2.64.7 picks up a club in order to defend himself. In order to do that he takes steps toward the club – so it is apparent that under this description the agent intends to pick up the club: that is the reason why he takes the steps. But that is not the "piece" of the action upon which Thomas focuses in *ST* 2-2.64.7. There he is interested in identifying the sort of action that goes straight toward the conservation of life, and so he speaks of the reason why the agent has (for instance) struck out with a club. Under this description, the intention to pick up the club moves into the subsidiary position occupied previously by the taking steps toward the club. (On intention, see *ST* 1-2.12, especially articles 1 – mentioned above – and 2.)

14. See above, note 1.

an individual's act of self-defense is licit provided there is no intended killing, Thomas's point is that intending to kill is always immoral; but he counteracts that impression in what he goes on to say. It is illicit, he goes on to say, "for a man to intend to kill a man in order to defend himself, *except* for one who has public authority, who, *intending to kill a man* in self-defense,[15] refers this to the public good." Whether an act of intentionally killing in self-defense is moral or not depends upon whether the person defending himself is acting in a public capacity or not. Thomas mentions as examples of the latter, "the soldier fighting against foes and of the minister of a judge fighting against a thief."

Thomas's wider position is, therefore, that the morality of killing in self-defense depends upon (among other things) the societal factor. This factor manifests itself in what we might speak of as "paths of intelligibility." In *ST* 2-2.64.7, two such paths play a role: one determined by natural law, the other by human law (human law presumably not inconsistent with natural law).[16] In speaking in the early section of *ST* 2-2.64.7c of self-defense by a private individual, Thomas indicates the natural law basis of that position: "Such an act, therefore, in so far as what is intended is the conservation of one's own life, does not have the character of the illicit, for it is natural to whatever thing to conserve itself in being as far as possible."[17] In speaking subsequently of self-defense by a public official, he does not indicate a basis for his position, but his adherence in *ST* 2-2.64.7 to the ideas set out in Augustine's *De libero arbitrio* suggest what this basis might be.[18] *De libero arbitrio* is a dialogue between two literary characters,

15. Even when speaking about the acts of those acting with public authority, Thomas continues (as here) to speak of acts of self defense. The reason for this is that this article is *about* self-defense: that fact depends upon the schema Thomas sets out in the prologue to *ST* 2-2.64.

16. See *ST* 1-2.91.2–3, 95.2.

17. See *ST* 1-2.94.2.

18. In specifying that intended self-defense is illicit "unless by public authority for the common good," he says, "as was made clear above." He is referring to *ST* 2-2.64.2

one called Augustine, the other Evodius. As he discusses killing in self-defense with Evodius, the position of Augustine shifts occasionally; but one thesis remains firm in his mind. It is expressed in the following:

> So, is not the law just which gives to a traveller the power to kill a highwayman lest he be killed by him – or [which gives] to any man or woman [the power] to kill, if possible, a violently onrushing rapist before being raped? For a soldier is even *ordered* by law to kill an enemy and, if he declines to effect this bloodshed [caede], a penalty is levied by the emperor. Are we to be so bold as to say that these laws are unjust – or, indeed, null and void?[19]

Augustine – the character and evidently also the author – regards this as basic. Throughout *ST* 2-2.64.7 (and elsewhere), it is evident that Thomas, like Augustine, simply presupposes that certain principles of ethics can be discerned in established human law, such as is found in Gregory IX's *Decretals*, cited in *ST* 2-2.64.7 with regard to personal self-defense.

Both natural and established human law (human law, that is, which is consistent with both natural and eternal law), establish paths of intelligibility in the sense that remaining within certain lines of action – aspects of the voluntary, whether actions or not, whether intended or not, going toward intended ends – an agent does something that is intelligible: reasonable. These paths are set by either

("Whether it is licit to kill sinners") and *ST* 2-2.64.3 ("Whether it is licit for a private person to kill a man who is a sinner"). In the latter he says: "it is licit to kill a malefactor in as much as it is ordered to the welfare of the whole community; and so this belongs to him alone to whom is committed the task of conserving the community's welfare."

19. "Non ergo lex iusta est, quae dat potestatem vel viatori ut latronem, ne ab eo ipse occidatur, occidat; vel cuipiam viro aut feminae ut violenter sibi stupratorem irruentem ante illatum stuprum, si possit, interimat. Nam militi etiam iubetur lege, ut hostem necet: a qua caede si temperaverit, ab imperatore poenas luit. Num istas leges iniustas, vel potius nullas dicere audebimus?" [*De libero arbitrio* 1.5.11]. The very next sentence reads: "For it seems to me that a law which will not have been just is no law at all" ["Nam mihi lex esse non videtur, quae iusta non fuerit"]. This remark is one of Augustine's most famous – or, among legal positivists, infamous. (See below, chapter 6, note 17.)

natural or sound human law, that is, human law in accordance with natural law.[20]

An action in accordance with natural law can often be identified by looking to the compactness (the tightness and simplicity) of the relationship between an exterior act and its own object. A person uses something that is his own. There is something "pure" about that act: using things one's own is what things one's own are *for*. When one uses (or takes) something not one's own (an *alienum*), that is, when one steals, although no one intends the disorder of that (or any) act, there is disorder or lack of intelligibility in the act.[21] We see the same thing in regard to truth-telling and lying. Communicating is *for* telling the truth, not for lying. There is a lack of order or intelligibility in a lie. This is not to say that every act of using something one's own or telling the truth is morally upright but only that that basic pathway, the relationship between the act itself and its object, is good because reasonable. We see a similar thing in an act of personal self-defense in which the killing of the attacker is not intended. This is a simple act in the way that using something one's own or telling the truth is simple: reacting to an attack with an act "from which a killing sometimes follows" is natural and good. As Thomas says in *ST* 2-2.64.7, "it is natural to whatever thing to conserve itself in being as far as possible."

None of this is to say, however, that only acts that have such simple structures can be good. A person might dance a jig in order to raise money to fund experiments to cure cancer: there is no necessary connection between dancing jigs and curing cancer, and yet the complex action (as described) is good.

Thomas also says in *ST* 2-2.64.7 that a soldier battling against foes quite likely intends to kill them. The intended killings are a means to

20. An obligation in a particular country to drive on the right (not the left) side of the road is not set by natural law but by human law, but setting such a law is in accordance with natural law.

21. For Thomas's analysis of stealing, see *ST* 1-2.18.2 and *De malo* 2.4 and 2.6 (Ia). On not intending disorder, see *ST* 1-2.72.1c.

conserving his life and, as Thomas says, they are referred to "the public good." This too is a complex of actions, involving intended means along the way – intended means that would make a private individual's similar actions immoral – and yet what the soldier does is moral. In this case, the justifying path of intelligibility is set by law: human law, presumably consistent with natural and eternal law.[22] The intended killings do not make the soldier's behavior immoral. To quote once again the crucial remark by Augustine: "a soldier is even *ordered* by law to kill an enemy and, if he declines to effect this bloodshed, a penalty is levied by the emperor." By contrast, even if a private citizen refers his intended act of killing to the public good, it is still immoral: such an act stands outside the path of intelligibility that makes "beside the intention" [praeter intentionem] killing for the conservation of one's own life moral.[23]

The analysis of such actions is, however, further complicated by the third factor mentioned above and in *ST* 2-2.64.7: proportionality. Thomas employs this concept in connection with personal self-defense, although the same concept is at work in what he says about self-defense by the soldier or the minister of a judge. Regarding the first, immediately after saying that "it is natural to whatever thing to conserve itself in being as far as possible," he adds: "It is possible,

22. See chapter 5 ("Intelligibility and the per se") of Flannery, *Action and Character According to Aristotle*. In the introduction to that book, I characterize the argument of that chapter in these words: "[F]or Aristotle, the per se / per accidens distinction is a tool he uses in order to point to relationships of various types. His use of the expression 'per se,' for example, indicates only that he sees some type of intelligible relationship between two or more things. It may be a type of relationship which, in another context or with respect to something else, he declares to be lacking in intelligibility (and to be, therefore, per accidens)" [Flannery, *Action and Character According to Aristotle*, xxi].

23. Thomas, following ideas in Aristotle's *Rhetoric*, would allow that, given changed circumstances, human law that is consistent with eternal and natural law in one epoch might not be so consistent in another. See Kevin L. Flannery, "Moral Taxonomy and Moral Absolutes," in *Wisdom's Apprentice: Thomistic Essays in Honor of Lawrence Dewan, O.P.*, ed. Peter A. Kwasniewski (Washington, D.C.: The Catholic University of America Press, 2007), 237–59, and Kevin L. Flannery, "Capital Punishment and the Law," *Ave Maria Law Review* 5, no. 2 (2008): 399–427.

however, for some act proceeding from a good intention to be rendered illicit, if it is not proportionate to the end. So, if someone in defending his own life uses more force than is called for, the act will be illicit."[24] Since what made personal self-defense at least in some cases moral was the straight, clean path tending toward ("in-tending") the conservation of one's life, we can assume that what goes wrong when disproportionate force is used is that that path has grown (at best) wavering or ambivalent. It is now not so clear that only the conservation of one's life is intended; and this is for that path to stray – or, at least, to begin to stray – from the path of natural law and reasonability.

Regarding publicly sanctioned self-defense, at the very end of the corpus, having stated that the "soldier fighting against foes" and "the minister of a judge fighting against a thief" do so morally, he adds very briefly: "although even these sin if they are moved by private passion [si privata libidine moveantur]." One wishes that Thomas had been more expansive on this point, saying, for instance, whether in the case he has in mind "private passion" results in the use of unnecessarily violent means. In any case, we can assume that actions so moved would lack proportionality, although the situation would be subject to a different sort of analysis than would be employed when a person without public authority (possibly also moved by private passion) uses more force than necessary in order to protect his own life. Presumably, a private passion, as such, would not, for instance, pull a soldier's lethal action outside of that path of intelligibility in such a way that his action, qua public action, would be illicit. But, even if disproportionately violent means are not used, there would be in the soul of the man seized by that private passion, a departure from the

24. This concept itself finds its basis in law, for he goes on to say: "If, however, he should repel a force moderately, the defense will be lawful, for, according to law, it is licit 'to repel force by force,' provided it is 'with the moderation of blameless self-protection.'" Thomas is referring to Gregory IX's *Decretals*, the canon entitled *Significasti* [Aemilius Ludovicus Richter and Aemilius Friedberg, eds., *Decretalium Collectiones*, vol. 2, *Corpus Iuris Canonici* (Leipzig: B. Tauchnitz, 1881), Decretal. Gregor. 9.5.12.18 (coll. 800–801)].

straight path of reason – and this can certainly be described as a lack of proportionality.[25]

How does all this pertain to cooperation with evil? In a passage, most of which we saw in chapter 2, section II, Thomas says:

> Our acts are called moral as they are ordered by reason toward the end of the will: from this they have the character of good and evil. But everything that is ordered toward an end must be proportionate to the end. And so reason, which orders our act toward the end, considers the act's proportion toward those things that might occur together with [concurrere] the act; and this correspondence [commensuratio] is called a circumstance.[26]

The answer to the question posed can be drawn out of that last quoted word: 'circumstance.' Immoral cooperation is a circumstance – and circumstances can make an act as bad as any object or end can do. Whether and how one has strayed from the straight path will sometimes depend on one's role in society. A priest whose refusal to testify regarding something heard in the confessional may, by that refusal, help a dangerous criminal to go free: he has not cooperated immorally in whatever evil acts follow, however inevitably. Sometimes, however, behaving morally will simply be a matter of behaving naturally (in a strong sense, as when someone reacts as his nature prompts him and defends his own life). A scrupulously honest man might blurt out a truth that helps a criminal enterprise in which he has no part: he

25. We have not found a place where Thomas discusses this issue, but one imagines that he would agree that, if private passion should move a soldier to adopt means prohibited by laws pertaining to the proper conduct of war, those particular means will have departed from the path of intelligibility which renders other actions by soldiers licit.

26. "Respondeo dicendum ad primam quaestionem, quod actus nostri dicuntur morales secundum quod a ratione ordinantur in finem voluntatis; ex hoc enim habent rationem boni vel mali. Omne autem quod ordinatur ad finem, oportet esse proportionatum fini; et ideo ratio quae actum nostrum in finem ordinat, attendit proportionem actus ad ea quae ad actum concurrere possunt, et ista commensuratio circumstantia dicitur" [*Sent.* 4.16.3.1.1]. It is interesting – and relevant to the argument of the present section – that Thomas does not speak in this passage of intended means for an end but simply of "those things that might occur together with the act" ["ea quae ad actum concurrere possunt"].

does not cooperate immorally, as does another man who utters the same truth, intending that it aid the criminal enterprise. The scrupulously honest man proceeds along a good and honest path.

II. The Judge and the Physician

Studying, as we have, *ST* 2-2.64.7, we have acquired some insight into the possible role of paths of intelligibility in the analysis of cooperation, even though the cases discussed there are not, strictly speaking, cases of cooperation. But there are a couple of places where Thomas actually speaks of such paths, and fairly extensively, in connection with what either appear to be or could be cases of cooperation. The first (to be discussed in this section) involves a judge, the second (the subject of section III) a person seeking a loan from a usurer. An examination of what Thomas says in these places sheds further light upon these issues – but also adds to the complications.

In *ST* 2-2.64.6, Thomas asks whether it is ever licit to kill the innocent. The third objection argues that it can be licit since occasionally someone is constrained [cogitur] by the very order of justice to kill an innocent person. A judge, for instance, who is obliged to issue judgments based upon the evidence presented in court, might be constrained by the testimony of false witnesses to condemn to death a person he knows privately to be innocent. Thomas's response to this argument is that, in such cases, it is actually the false witnesses who kill the innocent person; they do so, of course, illicitly. He says that the judge must be extra diligent in questioning the false witnesses so that, if possible, he might expose their unreliability and thereby free the innocent person. If he is not successful in this, he must, if possible, remand the case to a superior authority. "But, if also this is not possible, he does not sin in issuing a sentence consistent with the evidence because it is not he who kills the innocent but those who assert that he is not innocent."[27]

27. "Ad tertium dicendum quod iudex, si scit aliquem esse innocentem qui falsis testibus convincitur, debet diligentius examinare testes, ut inveniat occasionem liberandi

ST 2-2.67.2 makes more explicit the theory behind Thomas's position. The *sed contra* quotes Ambrose on Psalm 118: "a good judge does nothing from his own choice but pronounces according to the laws and rights."[28] Thomas probably has at the back of his mind also Aristotle's various pronouncements about lawmakers and the law, such as the following:

Yet surely the ruler cannot dispense with the general principle which exists in law; and that is a better ruler which is free from passion than that in which it is innate. Whereas the law is passionless, passion must always sway the heart of man.[29]

---

innoxium. . . . Si autem hoc non potest, debet eum ad superiorem remittere iudicandum. Si autem nec hoc potest, non peccat secundum allegata sententiam ferens, quia non ipse occidit innocentem, sed illi qui eum asserunt nocentem" [*ST* 2-2.64.6 ad 3]. Some manuscripts have *superiori relinquere* ("leave [the case] to a superior") rather than *ad superiorem remittere* ("remand [the case] to a superior"). (The Ottawa edition of the *Summa theologiae* gives the former.) This has a bearing upon Cajetan's interpretation of the passage (to be considered below), for he argues, against those who say that to remit the case would be to expose the innocent person to a sentence of death, that Thomas does not speak of 'remitting to' but of 'leaving to' [Thomas Aquinas and Thomas de Vio (Cajetan), *Summa theologiae, cum commentariis Thomae de Vio Caietani Ordinis Praedicatorum*, apud *ST* 2-2.67.2 (v. 6 99b–100a)]. I am assured, incidentally, by John Finnis (in private conversation) that in contemporary legal systems (at least in the West), a judge placed in these circumstances will always have the option of recusing himself.

28. Thomas mistakenly attributes the remark to Augustine. "Sed contra est quod Augustinus dicit, super Psalt., bonus iudex nihil ex arbitrio suo facit, sed secundum leges et iura pronuntiat" [*ST* 2-2.67.2 *sed contra*]. The corresponding text in Ambrose runs: "For a good judge does nothing from his own choice and from private purpose but pronounces according to the laws and rights; he is compliant with the ordinances of law; he does not indulge his own will; he puts forward nothing prepared and meditated at home but, according to what he hears, so he judges; and, as the nature of the case stands, so he decides" ["Bonus enim iudex nihil ex arbitrio suo facit, et domesticae proposito voluntatis, sed juxta leges et jura pronuntiat, scitis juris obtemperat, non indulget propriae voluntati, nihil paratum et meditatum domo defert, sed sicut audit, ita judicat, et sicut se habet negotii natura, decernit"] [*Expositio in Psalmum CXVIII*, sermon 20, §36, PL15 1494].

29. *Pol.* 3.15 1286a16–20 (Revised Oxford Translation). A chapter later, he remarks similarly: "The law is reason unaffected by desire" [*Pol.* 3.16 1287a32]. See also *EN* 5.6 1134a35–b1: "This is why we do not allow a man to rule, but law, because a man behaves

ST 2-2.67.2 says that "in judging, a judge must be informed not according to that which he knows as a private person but according to that which becomes known to him as a public person."[30] Qua judge, a judge's job is defined in terms of the law; and, since the law specifies the way in which evidence can enter into a judgment, the judge may not introduce information obtained by any another route. Thomas says in *ST* 2-2.64.6 ad 3 that a judge may make use of his private knowledge in framing his questioning of the witnesses; but any information entering into the judgment itself must do so as is allowed by law, that is, by way of the legal proceedings.

Cajetan (Thomas de Vio) interprets *ST* 2-2.64.6 ad 3 (and *ST* 2-2.67.2) as making an argument parallel to the central argument of *ST* 2-2.64.7. He has good reason for this: *ST* 2-2.64.6 ad 3 comes immediately before *ST* 2-2.64.7: the last words of Thomas's response are followed by the title of *ST* 2-2.64.7: "Whether it is permissible to kill someone in self-defense."

Cajetan considers a number of arguments against Thomas's position, including an especially strong one that runs as follows:

> An end and a means [medium] ordered to an end are related in such a way that, if means [media] lead to the contrary of the end, they are not means [media] to the end, nor by the wise man are they to be commanded to be executed, as is clear in the case of health and medicines: for if he [a wise physician] verifies that the medicines induce infirmity contrary to the health intended, according to the standards [canones] of all physicians he would be foolish to use them.
>
> But proofs in a judgment are like means ordered both toward the end of the truth to be made known and toward the justice to be rendered to each, since it is for this reason that witnesses and other documents are produced regarding the event in question, as is clear. If, therefore, he [a wise judge] ver-

---

thus in his own interests and becomes a tyrant." The Revised Oxford Translation reads νόμον for λόγον in line 1134a35.

30. "Et ideo informari debet in iudicando non secundum id quod ipse novit tanquam privata persona, sed secundum id quod sibi innotescit tanquam personae publicae" [*ST* 2-2.67.2c].

ifies that such means lead to the contrary of truth and of the right of the man in question, it becomes incumbent upon the wise judge not to pursue such means in opposition to the end. So doing, issuing a judgment in this case according to the allegations and proofs, he acts foolishly and thus does ill.

And this is confirmed: for, just as equity [epieikeia] must incline a judge in certain cases toward judging not according to the written laws, even so it must in this case incline him toward not following the written laws, according to which judgment is to be made according to the allegations and proofs: for this is in favor of innocence and is the end of justice itself.[31]

It would appear that in formulating this argument (with which ultimately he disagrees), Cajetan has in mind Thomas's argument in *ST* 1-2.21.1, that any act issuing from a natural power is correct when "the middle does not pull away from the extremes, that is, the act from the *order* of the active principle toward the end."[32] The same ap-

31. "Finis et medium ordinatum ad finem sic se habent quod, si media ducunt ad contrarium finis, non sunt media ad finem, nec a sapiente executioni mandantur, ut patet in sanitate et medicinis: si enim medicinas inducere constat infirmitatem contrariam sanitati intentae, fatuus esset prosequens illas propter canones omnium medicorum. Sed probationes in iudicio sunt ut media ordinata ad finem veritatis innotescendae et ius suum unicuique reddendi: quoniam idcirco afferuntur testes et alia documenta facti in iudicio, ut patet. Si ergo constat quod huiusmodi media ducunt ad contrarium veritatis et iuris istius hominis, consequens est ut ad sapientem iudicem spectet non prosequi talia media contra finem. Et sic fatue, ac per hoc male facit, iudicando in hoc casu secundum allegata et probata. — Et confirmatur. Quia sicut epieikeia debet iudicem inclinare, in casibus, ad iudicandum non secundum leges scriptas; ita debet in hoc casu inclinare ad non sequendum leges scriptas secundum quas est secundum allegata et probata iudicandum: quoniam hoc est in favorem innocentiae, et finis ipsius iuris" [Thomas Aquinas and Thomas de Vio (Cajetan), *Summa Theologiae, Cum Commentariis Thomae de Vio Caietani Ordinis Praedicatorum*, apud *ST* 2-2.67.2 (v. 6 99a–b)].

32. "When, therefore, an act proceeds from a natural power according to a natural inclination to an end, then there is preserved correctness in the act, for 'the middle does not pull away from the extremes,' that is, the act from the order of the active principle toward the end. When, however, from such correctness some act does recede, then the character of sin edges in" ["Quando ergo actus procedit a virtute naturali secundum naturalem inclinationem in finem, tunc servatur rectitudo in actu, quia medium non exit ab extremis, scilicet actus ab ordine activi principii ad finem. Quando autem a rectitudine tali actus aliquis recedit, tunc incidit ratio peccati"] [*ST* 1-2.21.1]. The word *medium* in "medium non exit ab extremis" might also be translated 'mean' instead of 'middle.'

plies also to an act issuing from the will, says Thomas, although here that which defines staying within the extremes is human reason and the eternal law. "When, therefore, the act of a man proceeds toward an end according to the order of reason and the eternal law, then the act is correct; when, however, it should twist aside [obliquatur] from this rectitude, then it is said to be a sin."[33]

In Thomas, in addition to *ST* 1-2.21.1, the definition of 'correct' (*rectum*) as that "whose middle does not pull away from the extremes" appears in his commentary on the Book of Job:

> In prowling about, the craftiness of Satan is displayed, in seeking out those whom he can deceive. Thus, in 1 Peter 5,8 we read: "Your adversary the devil prowls around like a lion seeking someone to devour." "Prowling about" fittingly corresponds to his craftiness, just as "direct" corresponds to simple justice. For the direct is that "whose middle does not pull away from the extremes." Because, therefore, the action of the just does not diverge from its principle, which is the will, and its intended end, "directness" [or "rectitude"] is fittingly ascribed to the just.[34]

33. "Quando ergo actus procedit a virtute naturali secundum naturalem inclinationem in finem, tunc servatur rectitudo in actu, quia medium non exit ab extremis, scilicet actus ab ordine activi principii ad finem. . . . Quando ergo actus hominis procedit in finem secundum ordinem rationis et legis aeternae, tunc actus est rectus, quando autem ab hac rectitudine obliquatur, tunc dicitur esse peccatum" [*ST* 1-2.21.1c]. Stephen Brock has pointed out to me that the phrase "Rectum enim est cuius medium non exit ab extremis" is found also in Bonaventure. See the prooemium to his *in II Sent.* [Bonaventure, *Opera Omnia* (Quaracchi: Collegium S. Bonaventurae, 1882–1902), v. 2 p. 4]: "Rectum enim est cuius medium non exit ab extremis." See also Bonaventure's "De reductione artium ad theologiam" [Bonaventure, *Opera omnia*, v. 5 p. 325], where the phrase also appears. The editors, in explanation of the *in II Sent.* text, give as a reference Plato's *Parmenides* 137e3–4 and even include the Greek text: Καὶ μὴν εὐθύ γε, οὗ ἂν τὸ μέσον ἀμφοῖν τοῖν ἐσχάτοιν ἐπίπροσθεν ᾖ, for which they offer the following translation (also found in the Stephanus edition of Plato): "Rectum vero illud, cuius medium extremis utrisque e regione est." Sir Thomas Heath renders Plato's definition of the straight line as "'that of which the middle covers the ends' (relatively, that is, to an eye placed at either end and looking along the straight line)" and then as "straight is whatever has its middle in front of (i.e., so placed as to obstruct the view of) both its ends" [Thomas L. Heath, *Euclid, the Thirteen Books of the Elements: Translated with Introduction and Commentary* (New York: Dover, 1956), 1.165–66].

34. "Per circuitum autem Satan calliditas eius ostenditur ad explorandum quos

In other words, if we suppose that there is a straight path from the will to its end such as defines acting correctly, the devil's prowling is equivalent to straying from this path. In the devil's case, the middle – the *medium* or the means leading to the end – does "pull away from the extremes."

According to the objection formulated by Cajetan, then, the problem with judging the innocent man by means of the evidence presented in court is that this middle (or means) does "pull away from the extremes" and so from the order to the end, which is justice. And this would be for the judge to stray from the fixed path of the moral law. Just as in *ST* 2-2.64.7 the man who, in order to defend himself, strays from the path of intelligibility requiring the use of moderate force, so also the judge who rules against the innocent man strays from the path leading to the end of justice for all. This all sounds very solidly Thomistic.

Cajetan certainly accepts Thomas's general approach to moral analysis as found (among other places) in *ST* 1-2.21.1 with its talk of the middle not pulling away from the extremes. But he maintains that the flaw in the objection's argument lies in its misidentification of the end of the activity of judging. The objection, he maintains, fails to appreciate the nature – the public nature – of judging itself. "The end of human public justice is not the truth of the matter as known absolutely but the public truth of the matter as known to a man."[35] He

decipere possit, secundum illud I Petri [5.8]: 'adversarius vester diabolus tamquam leo rugiens circuit, quaerens quem devoret.' Convenienter autem per circuitum calliditas designatur, sicut per rectum simplex iustitia, nam rectum est cuius medium non exit ab extremis: quia igitur actio iusti a suo principio quod est voluntas et fine intento non discrepat, convenienter iustis ascribitur rectitudo" [Thomas Aquinas, *Expositio Super Iob Ad Litteram*, vol. 28, *Opera omnia* (Rome: Commissio Leonina, 1965), 1.365–75].

35. "Ad sextum dicitur quod finis iustitiae publicae humanae non est veritas facti absolute, sed veritas facti publica homini" [Thomas Aquinas and Thomas de Vio (Cajetan), *Summa Theologiae, Cum Commentariis Thomae de Vio Caietani Ordinis Praedicatorum*, apud *ST* 2-2.67.2 (v. 6 100b)]. The contrast here is between "the truth of the matter as known absolutely" [veritas facti absolute] and the truth of the matter as known to a judge. Cajetan acknowledges in this same argument that legal procedures do and should

who judges according to the allegations and proofs — as it is a judge's role qua "public man" to do — judges not according to the truth simply speaking but according to public truth.

And it is said similarly that, although the end of justice is to render to each what is truly his right, the end of human public justice is to render to each his right not simply speaking [simpliciter] but as far as public authority and knowledge can extend themselves: for no more is demanded of a man.[36]

Now, with reason one objects to Cajetan's interpretation here — in particular, to his distinction between the truth known absolutely and "the public truth." Does it make any sense to call the basis of the judge's sentence "public *truth*" when the facts contradict it? And do we really want to say that the *end* of human public justice is this "public truth" which is not really truth at all? It is better to say simply that morality itself entails that a judge follow legal procedures. For justice is *about* procedures, which apply to all equally. Even false witnesses have a right not to have their testimony undermined by means not acceptable within the judicial system. And, taking the larger view, a society rightly expects higher court judges to apply the law rather than to impose their wills.[37]

Is there, then, a better solution to this problem, a solution based upon Thomistic principles? There is. Key in Thomas's philosophy is the idea that the various human disciplines are defined with respect to their objects. The object of biology, for instance, is animals. But any such object presupposes an intelligible context within which it serves

---

seek to make the whole truth of the matter public but also that this is sometimes not possible.

36. "Et simili modo dicitur quod licet finis iustitiae sit reddere unicuique ius vere suum, finis tamen iustitiae publicae humanae est reddere unicuique ius suum non simpliciter, sed quantum potestas et scientia publica se extendere possunt: neque enim plus exigendum ab homine est" [Thomas Aquinas and Thomas de Vio (Cajetan), *Summa Theologiae, Cum Commentariis Thomae de Vio Caietani Ordinis Praedicatorum*, apud *ST* 2-2.67.2 (v. 6 100b)].

37. See above, note 29.

as an object.[38] Domesticating (or animal training) has as its object animals, but animals considered differently from how they are considered in biology. This dependence upon context holds also of both medicine and judging, the two disciplines mentioned in the objection reported by Cajetan.

Medicine's defining object is human bodies, but human bodies as treated medically (or within medicine). The "standards" [canones] of medicine themselves say that, if certain medicines will harm the health of a patient, a physician (as Cajetan puts it) "would be foolish to use them." That is essential to medicine itself. If it should happen that *all* the standard medical remedies will cause harm to the patient's health, the physician is obliged to refrain from using any of them. But judicial procedure does not work like that. No canon of public justice says that, when the standard means of arriving at justice go in an undesirable direction, a judge is free to set aside those means and continue as he sees fit. On the contrary, the canons of public justice exclude such recourse, since all individuals subject to that judicial system – again, including possibly false witnesses – have the right to be treated as the law dictates.

And so we are back to talking about paths of intelligibility: both the physician and the judge are obliged to proceed according to reason; neither should ever "twist aside from this rectitude."[39] But we

38. See above, chapter 2, sections I through III. See also Flannery, *Action and Character According to Aristotle*, 131–34.

39. Cajetan does also say this: "And, as in the question above about killing [*ST* 2-2.64.7], for that reason for which it is concluded that the person defending himself is not obliged to omit an act defending himself on the grounds that it is seen that from it follows the death of the other who is also impenitent – because, that is, his responsibility toward himself is more incumbent upon him than his responsibility toward his neighbor – it could just as easily be concluded that, because incumbent upon the person of the judge is his responsibility to exercise public office and not his responsibility toward his neighbor except by virtue of his public office, so therefore he is not obliged to abstain from exercising his public office because of the consequent harm to his neighbor" ["Et quemadmodum superius in quaestione de homicidio per hanc rationem conclusum est quod defendens se non tenetur omittere actum defensionis propriae per hoc quod videtur

must now also acknowledge that not all paths are alike. Medicine is more "open-ended" than a judicial procedure. There are, of course, rules of medicine, the primary one being "do no harm to the patient";[40] but medicine must at every moment be open to a possible change of direction, looking always toward likely outcome. A patient hopes to find in a doctor not one who will stick strictly to the procedures but one who knows the procedures and sticks to them as long as they promise the best results for his health. The moment a doctor sees that a procedure is not going in this direction, he must alter the procedure or (if possible) find another. But a person appearing in court does hope to find – indeed, has a right to find – a judge who will follow the law, even punctiliously. This is not to deny that a judge must sometimes employ equity, for the latter is included within proper legal procedure. Equity comes into play where the legal procedures do leave room for judicial discretion.[41]

How does what Thomas says about such matters – and, in particular, about the judge – bear upon cases of cooperation with evil? In the first place, it must be acknowledged that in some cases, the role that a person fills insulates him from immoral cooperation. This is especially the case when the role is integral to a legal system, as in the case of the judge which we have been considering. The reason why

ex ipso sequi mortem alterius etiam impoenitentis, quia scilicet sibi magis incumbit cura sui quam proximi; eadem efficacia potest hic concludi quod quia personae iudicis incumbit cura ut utatur publico officio, et non cura proximi nisi ratione publici officii, ideo non tenetur abstinere ab usu publici officii propter damnum consequens proximi"] [Thomas Aquinas and Thomas de Vio (Cajetan), *Summa theologiae, Cum commentariis Thomae de Vio Caietani Ordinis Praedicatorum*, apud *ST* 2-2.67.2 (v. 6 100a)]. On one's duty in charity to love oneself more than one's neighbor, see *ST* 2-2.26.4.

40. Patients would include fetuses, subject to doctors' actions.

41. On equity (in Greek ἐπιείκεια or τὸ ἐπιεικές), see Aristotle's *EN* 5.10.1173a31–1138a3 and *Rhetoric* 1.13.1374a25-b24. See also Thomas's *ST* 1-2.94.4. See also Kevin L. Flannery, "Determinacy in Natural Law," *Nova et Vetera (English)* 9, no. 3 (2011): 763–73, and Thomas V. Berg and Kevin L. Flannery, "*Amoris Laetitia*, Pastoral Discernment, and Thomas Aquinas," *Nova et Vetera (English)* 16, no. 1 (2018): 95–101. When equity is invoked in the application of a law, what is invoked is the so-called "mind of the legislator."

such roles must be singled out is that morality has so much to do with justice – which itself is closely bound up with what is legal and what not. The role of a lawyer too insulates its occupant from some immoral cooperation. A Catholic lawyer might, for instance, provide legal advice to an indigent person whom he knows has committed a crime, simply in order to ensure that his legal rights are fully respected.

But there are limits to what either a judge or a lawyer may morally do, even granting that their roles place them into a special category. We have already seen that, according to Thomas, the judge he discusses must be diligent in questioning the false witnesses and that he must do what he can to remand the case to a superior authority. If the judge fails to do his utmost with respect to either of these responsibilities, his role does not insulate him from involvement (cooperation) with the evil to be effected by the false witnesses. In contemporary Western legal systems, a judge can in most instances recuse himself from a case. If a judge does not consider and then exercise this legal option when it is possible and proper to do so, he too is not insulated from the immoral cooperation inherent in the relevant case. As Thomas puts it in *ST* 1-2.21.1, his actions will likely "pull away from the extremes" – stray from the path of intelligibility proper to his office – and so be immoral.[42]

Such insulation is a factor also in other professions. We have already spoken of the way in which the medical profession differs from the legal, arguing that a medical doctor has fewer opportunities to claim validly, "I was only doing what my role calls for." But also the medical doctor, if he exercises due diligence in choosing a procedure, can often claim validly that he was acting qua doctor and so properly, even if a procedure proves damaging to the health of a patient. On

42. For a good treatment of such issues within the context of contemporary jurisprudence, see John H. Garvey and Amy V. Coney, "Catholic Judges in Capital Cases," *Marquette Law Review* 81 (Winter 1998): 303–50. Pages 317 to 350 deal explicitly with cooperation with evil. See also Albert L. Schlitzer, "Catholic Lawyer and Divorce Cases," *Notre Dame Law Review* 29, no. 1 (1953): 37–48, and John J. Coughlin, "Divorce and the Catholic Lawyer," *Jurist* 61, no. 1–2 (2001): 209–310.

the other hand, as Alasdair MacIntyre points out, the claim that 'I was only acting qua *x*' or 'qua *y*' is often indicative of nothing other than a failure to organize one's life and commitments in a way that is fully – coherently and courageously – rational.[43]

III. Usury

One final place in which Thomas actually discusses cases of cooperation is *ST* 2-2.78.4, where he asks whether it is licit to accept money under usurious conditions ("sub usura").[44] His position is that, in certain circumstances, it is licit. The first two objections argue that it is never licit, since this would be to consent to the usurer's sin and to give active scandal (presenting, that is, the occasion of sin) to the usurer. The third objection argues that, since it is "wholly [omnino] illicit" to deposit money with a usurer for safekeeping, and since placing a deposit can be just as necessary as taking a loan, taking money from a usurer is just as illicit as depositing it. The primary issue in this latter objection (and response) is not so much whether one might take a loan under usurious conditions but rather whether one might deposit money that will subsequently be used by a usurer in order to make usurious loans.

Thomas's answer to the overall question is that, if the affair involves inducing the usurer to give a loan, then it is illicit; if it does not involve inducement, then it can be licit, since even God uses [utitur] evil in order to elicit good. In fact, citing Augustine's *Enchiridion de fide, spe et caritate*, Thomas notes that from *any* evil God elicits some good.[45] He

43. Writes MacIntyre: "the powers of moral agency can only be exercised by those who understand themselves as moral agents, and, that is to say, by those who understand their moral identity as to some degree distinct from and independent of their social roles" [MacIntyre, "Social Structures and Their Threats to Moral Agency," 195].

44. One finds related remarks also at *Sent.* 3.37.6 ad 6 and at *Quaestiones disputatae de malo* 13.4, especially ad 18 & 19 (these latter two to be discussed below). I discuss *ST* 2-2.78.4 and also Cajetan's commentary on the same at Flannery, "On Counseling the Lesser Evil," 252–58.

45. "For neither would God, who is omnipotent – which even the infidels confess:

then quotes Augustine's letter to Publicola – which, as we have seen in section I above, he cites also in *ST* 2-2.64.7 – as follows: "he who uses the good faith [qui utitur fide] of a man who swears by false gods, not for ill but for good, does not associate himself with the sin by which he swears by demons but with the good pact, with respect to which he has maintained good faith [fidem]." Clearly Thomas holds that in such a case one can segregate the good from the bad and go only toward the good. As long as one is not inducing the person and thus including the bad aspect of his act in one's own act, one can take advantage of the good in his act without moral scruple.[46]

We have encountered above the adage attributed to pseudo-Dionysius: "any singular defect causes evil, but good is caused by a wholly sound cause."[47] This means that, if just one aspect of one's action is bad – even just a circumstance – the whole act is bad. One cannot identify within one's own act what is good and declare that that aspect is what counts and that the bad aspect does not. But one *can* do that when the act is someone else's. As long as one is not inducing the other into performing a bad act, which would cause its bad aspect to come into one's own act as a circumstance, one can (so to speak) isolate and *use* the good aspect of the other's person's bad act – "even God uses evil in order to elicit good."

'Of all things, he has supreme power' (since he is the highest good) – in any way permit anything evil in his works, unless he might be omnipotent and good by bringing good even from evil" ["Neque enim Deus omnipotens quod etiam infideles fatentur: Rerum cui summa potestas cum summe bonus sit, ullo modo sineret mali esse aliquid in operibus suis nisi usque adeo esset omnipotens et bonus ut bene faceret et de malo"] [Augustine, *Enchiridion ad Laurentium de fide et spe et caritate*, ed. E. Evans, Corpus Christianorum, Series Latina, v. 46 (Turnhout [Belgium]: Brepols, 1969), 1.3.11 (p. 53)]. The phrase quoted from Virgil (*Aeneid* 10,100) is actually "rerum cui prima potestas."

46. Using somewhat different language, Cajetan at one point speaks of the inducement that Thomas rejects as inducing toward the "whole," as contrasted with inducing toward the part: the idea is that the whole act is bad but a part of it is good [Cajetan (Thomas de Vio), "Tractatus 31: Responsiones," in *Opuscula omnia Thomae de Vio Caietani Cardinalis* (Lyon: Haeredes Iacobi Iuntae, 1562), 133. See Flannery, "On Counseling the Lesser Evil," 263].

47. See above, chapter 2, section V (toward the end, especially).

Thomas goes on in the corpus of *ST* 2-2.78.4 to talk about how one might distinguish inducing from merely using the good in another's act. He says: "from one who is prepared to effect usury and is in that business [usuras exercet], it is licit to accept a usurious loan for the sake of some good, which in this case is relief from one's own need or that of another."[48] So, one indication that a person is not inducing would be the other person's occupation – or, at least, what he's given to doing. Regarding the case at hand, one must know that the person is a usurer and so is given to practicing usury in any case.

The fact, however, that the other person "is prepared to effect usury and is in that business" is not sufficient to ensure that asking him for a loan is not inducement, for Thomas also specifies that the borrower accepts the usurious loan "for the sake of some good, which in this case is relief from one's own need or that of another." Although the word here translated 'need' is *necessitas*, we need not suppose that Thomas is saying that the borrower's action is necessitated in the way that one might be carried away by force or even in the way that a pilot might be forced to bring his ship into a port for which he did not set out (see chapter 4, section III). In *De malo* 13.4 ad 19, with reference to the same sort of situation, Thomas speaks simply of avoiding what is troublesome or inconvenient ("pro aliquo incommodo vitando").[49]

48. "[L]icet tamen ab eo qui hoc paratus est facere et usuras exercet, mutuum accipere sub usuris, propter aliquod bonum, quod est subventio suae necessitatis vel alterius" [*ST* 2-2.78.4c].

49. The one place which would seem to go against this less strong understanding of necessity is (the early) *Sent.* 3.37.6 ad 6. In the corresponding objection it is argued that anyone who accepts a usurious loan participates in the sin of the usurer: "ille qui dat usuras accipiens mutuum, communicat ei qui accipit usuras dans mutuum." Thomas responds that "he who pays usurious interest and accepts a loan out of necessity does not sin, nor does he participate in the usury by so acting, for he does not pay usurious interest voluntarily but as if coerced by necessity" ["ille qui usuras dat et mutuum accipit in necessitate, non peccat, nec usurario communicat inquantum hujusmodi: quia non voluntarius usuram dat, sed quasi coactus necessitate"] [*Sent.* 3.37.6 ad 6]. The contrast between this passage and (especially) *De malo* 13.4 ad 19 amounts to evidence that Thomas eventually softened his position. (One notices, however, that even in *Sent.* 3.37.6 ad 6 he says that the act of paying the usurious interest is "*as if* coerced by necessity.")

Thomas concludes the argument of the corpus with another example, this one drawn from Scripture. "It is also licit," he says,

> for one who has fallen in among thieves to indicate [manifestare] the goods that he has, in seizing which the thieves would sin, in order that he might not be killed, as did, for example, the ten men who said to Ismahel, 'Do not kill us for we have treasure in the field' – as is recounted in Jeremiah 41.[50]

Here obviously the ten men are in grave need: of means to save their lives. Whether those among whom they have fallen are "professionals" or not seems irrelevant: it is clear to the ten what the others are prepared and ready to do. So, although the thieves would not have committed theft without this help, again, this would not constitute inducement.

But how does all this relate to what we have encountered in Thomas's writings regarding consent to evil, scandal, and intention? The answers to these questions come out in his responses to the three objections. The first response is fairly straightforward. Citing Scripture (Romans 1.32), the objection had argued that those who merely consent to sins are as bad as those who commit them; one borrowing from a usurer consents to his sin; therefore, also taking the loan is sinful. Thomas responds: "he who accepts a usurious loan does not consent to [non consentit in] the sin of usury but uses it." Even consent – which might in any case involve the will very minimally (see chapter 4, section IV) – can be selective: it need not pertain to the whole of the malefactor's act (that is, his sin).[51] This is obviously im-

50. "Jeremiah 41 recounts the crimes of Ishmael, son of Nethaniah, a bandit chieftain. First Ishmael kills Gedaliah, governor of Judah at the time, in the city of Mizpah, where he ruled. When the next day eighty pilgrims arrive, Ishmael first seduces them into the city, saying to them, 'Come in to Gedaliah' (Jer. 48,6), then slays them as well – with the exception of ten who say to Ishmael, 'Do not kill us for we have stores of wheat, barley, oil, and honey hidden in the fields' [Jer. 41,8 (RSV)]. The presumption is that the ten will not tell Ishmael where the stores are hidden unless he spares their lives – which he apparently does" [Flannery, "On Counseling the Lesser Evil," 246].

51. On consent, besides chapter 4, section IV, see chapter 4, section VI (on restitution).

portant for the analysis of cooperation: mere involvement in bad acts is not necessarily consenting to them – and so not necessarily immoral – but might be simply using something in them, as God uses any ill for good. Thomas adds that it does not "please" the borrower that the usurer accepts the usurious interest, but it does please him that he now has the loan, which is a good.

Although scandal is alluded to in the first objection, Thomas addresses that issue not in the first response but in the second.[52] Genuine inducement having been declared immoral in the corpus of the article, Thomas's argument in the second response is that asking a dedicated usurer for a loan is not to present "the occasion of sinning" and so it is not immoral scandal.[53] In borrowing that is not inducement to usury, says Thomas, "there is passive scandal on the part of [the usurer] but not active scandal on the part of the one requesting the loan."[54] He also specifies that the passive scandal so identified is not the scandal of the weak or of the ignorant – either of which would still require the person to desist at least for a time from the act that occasions the passive scandal.[55]

In effect, Thomas's argument here is similar to what we saw in the corpus: that the occasion offered to the usurer by the borrower is not the occasion of profiting by usury but the occasion of making a loan. Understood here (again) is that this is possible in so far as the borrower has need and the usurer is in that business anyhow. In a manner

52. The inclusion of the topic of scandal in *ST* 2-2.78.4, itself suggests that the insistence by some recent scholars that scandal must be distinguished from cooperation ought to be met with reservation by those interested in interpreting Thomas. See chapter 3, introductory section, note 1. When borrowing does amount to inducement, it is clearly both giving to another the occasion of sin and immoral cooperation in the evil of usury. In *ST* 2-2.78.4 ad 3 Thomas uses the phrase "particeps culpae": "participant in his guilt."

53. At least for the *borrower* it is not immoral scandal; we shall see shortly that there is immoral scandal here, but caused entirely by the usurer.

54. See *ST* 2-2.43.6 ad 2, another place where Thomas recognizes that it is possible for there to be passive scandal without active scandal on the part of another person.

55. On these two types of scandal, see *ST* 2-2.43.7; see also chapter 3, section I.

not unlike what we saw happening in *ST* 2-2.64.7, this set of circumstances determines that the borrower's intention is directed not at the bad effect of the usurer's sinning but at the good effect of relieving the need. There is present here an occasion of sinning, but that aspect or part of it – the sin-related part – issues not from the borrower but from the malice in the heart of the usurer ("ex malitia cordis sui").[56] The borrower has nothing to do with that and so, in the analysis of his action, it can be ignored.

The fact that the borrower does not sin cannot be explained, however, simply in terms of his not *intending* to provide the occasion of sin. As we saw in chapter 3, section I, while considering Thomas's remarks on scandal in *ST* 2-2.43, it is quite possible to commit scandal without intending to do so. It is even possible to do so "beside the intention of the agent *and* beside the condition of the thing done" [*ST* 2-2.43.1 ad 4]. In the same place, Thomas gives as an example of the latter the person who allows it to be known that he has certain goods, thus causing another, who is "ill disposed [male dispositus]," to desire them.[57] To all appearances this is identical to the example of the ten men and Ismahel mentioned in the corpus of *ST* 2-2.78.4 – except that Thomas's reason for mentioning the latter is that the ten men do *not* act immorally in pointing to their goods. The crucial difference between the person who sinfully lets it be known that he has certain goods and (on the other hand) the ten men is that the latter do not

56. See *ST* 2-2.43.6 ad 1: "passive scandal is always caused by some active scandal but not always by some active scandal of another but of the very person who is scandalized, because, that is, he scandalizes himself" ["scandalum passivum semper ab aliquo activo causatur, sed non semper ab aliquo scandalo activo alterius, sed eiusdem qui scandalizatur; quia scilicet ipse seipsum scandalizat"].

57. " Per accidens, however, some word or deed of one person can be a cause of sinning for another when, even beside the agent's intention and beside the condition of the act, on account of such an act, someone who is ill-disposed is induced to sinning – for instance, when someone covets the goods of another" ["Per accidens autem aliquod verbum vel factum unius est alteri causa peccandi, quando etiam praeter intentionem operantis, et praeter conditionem operis, aliquis male dispositus ex huiusmodi opere inducitur ad peccandum, puta cum aliquis invidet bonis aliorum"] [*ST* 2-2.43.1 ad 4].

induce the theft — and this depends upon the overall situation. The ten men, like the borrower, are trying to escape from a bad situation, the badness of which they can reduce by presenting goods to those whose behavior indicates that, without that occasion, they would do greater evil. The negligently inadvertent tempter, by contrast, causes the scandalized person to do what he would otherwise not do.

There is this difference between the borrower and the ten men of Jeremiah 41: regarding the former, no reduction of evil is effected through the borrower's act of taking out a loan. Like the ten men, however, the borrower is isolated from responsibility for the evil that does occur. The factor making the difference between inducement and non-inducement — which is the key idea in *ST* 2-2.78.4c — is causation. In the latter (non-inducement), one does something that does not qualify as a cause of the eventual bad act, such as is the case when someone, even inadvertently, provides the occasion of another's performing an evil that — notwithstanding his ill-disposition or character — he would not have performed otherwise. Thus, in the case of the borrower, no such even indirect causation is present.

As we saw in chapter 4, section VI, Thomas says in *ST* 2-2.62.7 ad 1, that "one who in any way whatsoever is a cause of the sin" is obliged to make restitution. But he also says in that article that, of the types of behavior that might require restitution, only five do so always: (1) commanding that a theft take place; (2) consent "in that without which the theft cannot occur"; (3) recourse (receiving thieves or providing them protection); (4) participation "in the crime of theft and in the spoil"; and (5) not preventing when one is obliged to prevent, as are, for example, princes. Of the other behaviors mentioned in the article, including counsel and not preventing when one is not obliged to prevent, they do not necessarily call for restitution, Thomas says there, since they do not necessarily constitute "an efficacious cause [efficax causa] of a theft."

That brings us finally to the third response, which (as we shall see below) is useful in connection with other things that have been mentioned thus far in the present book, such as the significance of *ST* 2-2.64.7 (as a generally applicable principle of double effect) and the terminology employed by Alphonsus and others (in particular, 'formal cooperation' and 'material cooperation').

The third objection in *ST* 2-2.78.4 reads as follows:

> The necessity involved when someone deposits his money with a usurer does not appear to be less than when he accepts from him a loan. But to deposit money with a usurer appears to be altogether illicit, just as it is illicit to leave a sword with a madman or to entrust a maiden to a lecher, or food to a glutton. And so neither is it licit to accept a loan from a usurer.[58]

The objection presumes that the basis of any argument to the effect that borrowing from a usurer is moral would be that the borrower needs the money. But, it maintains, there might be no less need [necessitas] present when one deposits money with a usurer for safekeeping. (In medieval times, the major reason for depositing money in a bank or its equivalent was to avoid being robbed.) But so doing is (for instance) like leaving a sword with a madman, who is likely to use it to kill someone.[59] And so, since the need of the depositer who wants to protect his money does not excuse providing the occasion of sin to the usurer, neither does the need of a borrower excuse doing the same.

Thomas responds as follows:

> If someone should entrust his money to a usurer who would not otherwise be able to engage in usury, or should entrust it with the intention of making

58. "Non minor videtur esse necessitas quandoque deponendi pecuniam suam apud usurarium quam mutuum accipiendi ab ipso. Sed deponere pecuniam apud usurarium videtur esse omnino illicitum, sicut illicitum esset deponere gladium apud furiosum, vel virginem committere luxurioso, seu cibum guloso. Ergo neque licitum est accipere mutuum ab usurario" [*ST* 2-2.78.4 obi. 1].

59. This example is a classical one: see, for instance, Plato's *Republic* 1.331 c1–d3; Thomas uses the example at *ST* 1-2.94.4c (where he discusses, among other things, the practice of depositing things with others). On *ST* 1-2.94.4, see Berg and Flannery, "*Amoris Laetitia*, Pastoral Discernment, and Thomas Aquinas," 94–101. See also Flannery, "Determinacy in Natural Law."

more money as a consequence of usury, he would give material for sinning. He would thus also be a party to the guilt. If, however, someone entrusts his money for safekeeping to a usurer who is otherwise able to engage in usury, he does not sin but uses the man, the sinner, for good.[60]

In this response, Thomas is obviously focused not so much on the morality of usury as on the morality of depositing money with a usurer (the basis of the objection's argument). He acknowledges that sometimes depositing money with a usurer is immoral but argues that it is not always such. It is immoral, he says, when the usurer would otherwise not have the means of engaging in subsequent acts of usury. This he calls furnishing "material for sinning" – which is to come quite close, at least linguistically, to calling it material cooperation.

In arguing that, if the usurer would otherwise not be able to commit usury, making the deposit with him is immoral, he is in effect identifying another objective mark of inducement. If without the deposit the usurer could not engage in usury, the depositer would be inducing the usurer to sin. Whether or not the depositer has need of the usurer's custodial services – and, we might add, would perhaps even prefer not to give the deposit to the usurer – makes no difference. To deposit the money for safe-keeping would be illicit.

The depositer is also conceived of as possibly entrusting money to the usurer "with the intention of making more money as a consequence of usury," that is, with the expectation that the usurer will

60. "Ad tertium dicendum quod si quis committeret pecuniam suam usurario non habenti alias unde usuras exerceret, vel hac intentione committeret ut inde copiosius per usuram lucraretur, daret materiam peccandi. Unde et ipse esset particeps culpae. Si autem aliquis usurario alias habenti unde usuras exerceat, pecuniam suam committat ut tutius servetur, non peccat, sed utitur homine peccatore ad bonum" [*ST* 2-2.78.4 ad 3]. This text is taken from the Ottawa edition of the *Summa theologiae* (which follows the edition made under Pius V, the so-called *editio Piana*); it has "would give material for sinning" ["daret materiam peccandi"] where the Leonine edition has "would give material to the sinner" [daret materiam peccanti"]. As we shall see below, *De malo* 13.4 ad 18 speaks of offering to the usurer "materiam peccandi" – which provides some confirmation for the Ottawa reading.

use that money as part of a usurious transaction and then pay him for the use of the deposit. But, although Thomas explicitly uses the word *intentio* in this context, it is not absolutely clear here whether he would also use it regarding simply making a deposit with a usurer not otherwise able to engage in usury – although it would appear that he would not, since he uses it only when speaking of the person who hopes to profit.

A comparison with what Thomas says in *De malo* 13.4 ad 18 confirms this understanding – and also tells us something about how Thomas understands intention and consent in connection with cooperation. The eighteenth objection of *De malo* 13.4 argues that anyone who provides assistance [subministrat] to one sinning mortally sins also himself, just as one sins who lends arms to a madman or to one who intends to kill. The first part of Thomas's response runs as follows:

> If someone entrusts money to some usurer with the intention of obtaining therefrom usurious profit, without doubt he sins just as if [tamquam] consenting to the sin. And it appears that one ought to say the same thing of one who knowingly yields [concedit] his money to one whom he believes would use it for usurious profit – that which otherwise he would not be able to do.[61]

The juxtaposition of these two sentences – the fact that Thomas regards the two cases as distinct – suggests that "the same thing" that one ought to say of the second case is that the person involved (like the person in the first case) sins but that only the person in the first case has an intention with respect to usury. The word *concedit* ("yields") used of the person in the second case suggests the same thing: the action of the person in the first case cannot really be called a *yielding* of his money.

The rest of *De malo* 13.4 ad 18 reads as follows:

61. "Ad decimumoctavum dicendum, quod si quis ea intentione pecuniam alicui usurario committeret, ut exinde lucrum usurarium quaereret, absque dubio peccaret tamquam consentiens in peccatum. Et idem videtur dicendum de eo qui concedit pecuniam suam scienter ei de quo credit quod utatur ea ad usurarium lucrum, quod alias exercere non posset" [*De malo* 13.4 ad 18].

If, however, someone gives money to a usurer who could otherwise practice usury, not in order that he [ille] might make a profit but on account of his own need [necessitatem], he more uses his malice than consents to his sin or gives him the material of sinning; and so he can do this without sin.[62]

In this case the depositer—who is more clearly described in *ST* 2-2.78.4 ad 3 as entrusting his money to the usurer "for safekeeping"—neither intends that the usurer profit nor even gives his consent to the sin. He acts completely morally. Note also that Thomas says here that the depositer does not provide the "material of sinning." He is presuming that the depositer does, however, provide the material for loans (which will inevitably be usurious), for in the very next response he says that a man who in need borrows from a usurer "can licitly use his malice, or not withdraw the material from him, but provide it."[63] The material here is not material of sinning but simply the money to be used in the transaction. So, Thomas's position in *ST* 2-2.78.4, as well as here in *De malo* 13.4, is that, given certain circumstances—namely, that the borrower is in need and does not induce the lender who is a dedicated usurer—it is licit to ask for a usurious loan.

As mentioned above, ideas found in *ST* 2-2.78.4—and so in the closely related *De malo* 13.4 ad 18—are useful in considering ideas mentioned earlier in the present book, such as the significance of *ST* 2-2.64.7 (the article on self-defense) and the use of the terms 'formal cooperation' and 'material cooperation.'

62. "Si vero aliquis pecuniam suam usurario tradat alias usuras exercenti, non ut ille lucretur, sed propter suam necessitatem, magis utitur malitia eius, quam in peccatum ipsius consentiat vel materiam peccandi ei tradat; et ideo hoc absque peccato fieri potest" [*De malo* 13.4 ad 18]. The translations that I have consulted all understand the word *ille* as referring to the usurer. But Thomas is indicating a contrast with the case mentioned in the first sentence where the *depositer* expects to profit from the usurer's profit—that, presumably, being why he makes the deposit with the usurer. It is in that respect that that depositer's intention is bound up with the usurious profit.

63. "pro aliquo incommodo vitando potest homo licite uti malitia alterius, vel materiam ei non subtrahere, sed praebere" [*De malo* 13.4 ad 19].

To begin with *ST* 2-2.64.7, in analyzing *ST* 2-2.78.4 ad 3 and *De malo* 13.4 ad 18, we have seen that Thomas draws a distinction between intending that an evil come about and merely giving material for sinning. The man who hopes that a consequence of his giving money to the otherwise hard up usurer will be more money for himself, intends the evil; the man, however, who merely wants a safe place to leave his money and so gives it to the same usurer, does not intend the evil. But this does not mean that the latter is without fault, for Thomas holds that both men in effect consent to the sin. On the other hand, if the usurer is not hard up – if he would engage in usury independently of any particular person's deposit – then leaving a deposit with him simply for safekeeping would not be immoral.[64]

We see here what we saw above in analyzing *ST* 2-2.64.7 (chapter 5, section I): that a good intention itself does not make a human action good – and also that what someone can plausibly be said to intend or not to intend often depends on the particular situation in which an act occurs (or would occur). In *ST* 2-2.64.7 – at least at the beginning of the corpus – the idea is that, in as much as a man intends only to save his life and not to bring about the death of the attacker, he avoids the evil of murder. We saw in our analysis of the text that turning this idea into a general principle to the effect that intention of good (or ill) is the decisive factor in the analysis of human action, is, among other difficulties, incompatible with how Thomas understands scandal – which might not be intended but is immoral nonetheless.

So, we now have confirmation of this interpretation in *ST* 2-2.78.4 ad 3 and *De malo* 13.4 ad 18. But we see in these places something more: that constriction or force is not necessarily the decisive factor either. The fact that a man is attacked by another is what allows his act to be an act of personal self-defense in which his intention is sole-

64. Thomas never actually says this, but presumably a man who hopes to profit from his relationship with a non-hard-up usurer would intend – as well as consent to – the evil to be perpetrated by the usurer.

ly to preserve his life and so a licit act; but the man who is forced to leave a deposit with a hard-up usurer still does not act morally.

What then about the terminology, 'formal cooperation' and 'material cooperation'? First of all, it is quite likely that *ST* 2-2.78.4 ad 3, together perhaps with *De malo* 13.4 ad 18, is the original source of this terminology. This thesis grows in plausibility if we read in *ST* 2-2.78.4 ad 3 "daret materiam peccandi" ("give material for sinning") rather than "daret materiam peccanti" ("give material to the sinner").[65] For, when Alphonsus, for instance, speaks of material cooperation, he says that it is cooperating "in the bad action of the other" – that action being the sin.[66] Thomas, in both places, also distinguishes such giving material for sinning from doing so with the intention of profiting therefrom. He does not use the term 'formal,' although he could very well have done; he associates intention with form elsewhere: in *ST* 1-2.18.6, for instance. A cooperator who intends that another's sin be committed does give material for sinning, and so Thomas, if pressed by an insistent manualist, would probably have to say that one who cooperates formally also cooperates materially. But that is a defensible thesis in any case.

The advantage, however, of using Thomas's analyses of such matters rather than those of Alphonsus and similar others (discussed earlier in the present book) is that he gives us the means of accurately identifying the factors that have a bearing upon the morality of acts connected in some way with the evil acts of others. We saw just above that he recognizes that, in the analysis of a person's acting together with someone else who is doing evil, one can identify parts or aspects of the malefactor's act that enter into (or do not enter into) the other person's act. Such aspects are always there. This is connected with Thomas's denial that there exist individual indifferent acts. Human acts have in them, as constituents, everything needed in order to assess their morality – and these constituents are discernible once the

65. See above, note 60.

66. *Theologia moralis* 2, §63.

analyst knows what to look for and also the details of the situation within which a person is acting. Although intention is certainly one of these constituents – and an important one – such an analyst is never left with *just* intention as the determinative factor, as are those who recognize indifferent acts whose morality (and non-indifference) depend then upon the possible cooperator's intention. For Thomas, even when intention is a determinative factor, it is not independent of other factors.

CHAPTER 6 CONCLUDING IDEAS: COOPERATION AND JUSTICE

Thus far it has been argued that the ethical analysis of cooperation regarding evil, as found in the Catholic manualist tradition, in certain regards lacks coherence. It has also been argued that the core of the problem is the presence in this tradition of what Elizabeth Anscombe refers to as a strain of "Cartesian psychology," which, in the analysis of the moral act, looks primarily to "an interior act of the mind which could be produced at will."[1] Rather, then, than attempting to identify and parse such interior acts of the mind, it has been suggested that a more promising approach would be to consider the ways in which acts of cooperation are situated within the reality of justice itself.

In section I of this final chapter, we consider the way in which Aristotle and Thomas emphasize the objective and yet personal nature of justice. Then, in the remainder of the chapter, some concluding ideas are offered about the advantages, but also the challenges, of adopting this Thomistic approach to the general issue of cooperation

1. Anscombe, "War and Murder," 58–59. See also the introduction to the present work, section I, at notes 3 through 5; see also chapter 2, section IV.

with evil: in section II the reader is asked to imagine an ideal legislature responsible for passing laws regarding cooperation with evil; section III is a discussion of how Thomas's moral theory—including his understanding of justice—helps individuals and corporate entities to determine whether or not their actions constitute immoral cooperation with evil.

I. Justice

Following Aristotle, Thomas Aquinas draws a distinction between the intellectual and the moral virtues. The primary intellectual virtue is wisdom (σοφία in Aristotle's Greek, *sapientia* in Thomas's Latin), which is the virtue possessed by one who has mastered a theoretical discipline, especially metaphysics. Also counting as an intellectual virtue is practical wisdom (φρόνησις in Aristotle's Greek, *prudentia* in Thomas's Latin), which is concerned not so much with theory as with the practical life: human action. It is classified as intellectual because, unlike the moral virtues, whose defining objects are *ends* such as are determinative of moral character, to have practical wisdom is to have an *understanding* of what is conducive to and in accordance with those ends.

Practical wisdom is responsible for choices conducive to and in accordance with the moral virtues; the moral virtues determine the ends with respect to which practical wisdom chooses—in the sense that, if one has the virtue, one's character is oriented toward the end corresponding to that particular virtue. The moral virtues aim at (or desire) the mean between two extremes. Temperance, for instance, aims at eating and drinking not too little and not too much but, given the physical characteristics of the person concerned, the proper quantity: the mean. But this latter is "determined by reason and in the way in which the man of practical wisdom [ὁ φρόνιμος] would determine it" [*EN* 2.6 1106b36–1107a2].

One cannot be practically wise without being morally virtuous; but neither can one become morally virtuous without the help of practical wisdom. This reciprocal relationship between practical wisdom and the moral virtues would be viciously circular were it not for the fact that one becomes practically wise initially not by making practically wise choices *in the way* that truly practically wise persons make them (that is, wisely) but by doing what truly practically wise persons – in homes and in more public contexts – discipline or teach one to do.[2] By performing virtuous acts, a maturing person develops the moral virtues, which in turn, as character traits, provide the ends with respect to which eventually what we might call 'practical wisdom in progress' makes further choices. Practical reason itself is capable of determining what is the proper mean between extremes in so far as morally virtuous persons understand where, according to reason, the mean is located. Such determinations may have been made in the past and set down in laws or customs, or they may be occasioned by circumstances newly encountered.

When Aristotle speaks of practical wisdom in the sixth book of the *Nicomachean Ethics*, he associates it first of all with those who are involved in some way in political life – the life of the πόλις – and whom we might refer to as "politicians."[3] Aristotle affirms that practically wise politicians know not only what is good in general but also what is good "for themselves" [*EN* 6.5 1140b7–11]; clearly, however, it is their political wisdom, as manifested in their ability to make just decisions and to frame just laws, that primarily characterizes such individuals as practically wise. When Aristotle speaks of politicians recognizing both the good in general and the good for themselves, he is not promoting self-centeredness among politicians; he is in effect alluding to his earlier statement that the good of individuals is the same as the common good, although, as he says, the latter is more noble

2. On performing actions in the way that virtuous persons perform them, see *EN* 2.4 1105b7–9.

3. The term "politician" will be used here to refer to anyone involved somehow in the running of society, including those who are usually called politicians but also judges and non-elected authorities such as kings.

and divine [*EN* 1.2 1094b7–10]. Non-politicians too can, therefore, be practically wise, which is to say that they can acquire the intellectual habit that enables them to make good choices regarding what is good for themselves as human beings – which good is (in a sense) not distinct from the common good.[4]

The virtue of justice is a singular – even peculiar – virtue. Whereas the other moral virtues, such as courage and temperance, have primarily to do with the virtuous person himself and his affective bearing with respect to the ends of those virtues, justice has primarily to do with "the other."[5] As we have seen, temperance has as its end the mean between, for instance, consuming too much and consuming too little food or drink; courage has as its end the mean between cowardice and rashness. We do not hesitate to say that temperance exists in the temperate person or that courage exists in the courageous person. But, although it is not incorrect to say that a person is just and that therefore justice exists *in* that person, justice has to do primarily with a person's relationship with others – with individual others but also with others in general: with society.

Thomas discusses the meaning (or meanings) of the term *jus* – the root of the word *justitia* – in the very first article of his very long treatise on justice (*ST* 2-2.57–79). Justice is unusual among the moral virtues, he says, in as much as the other moral virtues "perfect a man solely in those things that benefit him with respect to himself." Thus, "the fitting" [rectum] for the other virtues, which serves as their proper object, is not to be understood "except in relation to the agent." In the case of justice, however, the fitting, "even independently of its relation to the agent, is constituted in relation to the other." "And so," Thomas concludes, "in a way special to justice, as distinct from the other virtues, its object – which object is called 'the just' [iustum] –

4. See Kevin L. Flannery, "The Common Good in Aristotle and Thomas Aquinas," in *Self-Transcendence and Virtue: Perspectives from Philosophy, Psychology, and Theology*, ed. Jennifer A. Frey and Candace Vogler (London: Routledge, 2018), 154–72.

5. See *ST* 2-2.57.1; also *in EN* 5.1 15–29 (§§885–86).

is determined according to itself. And this indeed is 'the right' [jus]" [*ST* 2-2.57.1].[6]

Moreover, whereas the other moral virtues bear upon what we might call the "lower affective appetites" — the temperate person, for instance, is one who does not even *feel* within himself that base desire to eat too much — justice is a virtue of the will, which has its place in the rational part of the human soul, as contrasted with the non-rational part where reside desire and passion.[7] The term that Aristotle uses for this faculty is βoύλησις; Thomas calls it *voluntas*. Both speak of it as an appetite; but the will is an appetite that is — in as much as it is qualified by the moral virtue of justice — pointed outwards, toward the good of others. Thomas explains that the will is *naturally* inclined toward that which is good for the individual to whom it belongs: that is to say, it does not have to be habituated ("morally") in order to tend toward this. Even as such (that is, as natural) it moves the lower appetites — the appetite to eat, for instance, or to defend oneself — and so brings about good for that individual himself. But in order to be directed toward that which is beyond the self, the will needs something that it does not have naturally. In the realm of human relations, this is the moral virtue of justice.[8]

6. In saying that justice's object is "determined with respect to itself," Thomas is contrasting this object with "the fitting" (that is to say, the objects of the other moral virtues) which "is not understood except in relation to the agent" ["non accipitur nisi per comparationem ad agentem"] [*ST* 2-2.57.1c].

7. See *De an.* 3.9 432b5–6 and 3.10 433a23–25.

8. In the *sed contra* of *ST* 1-2.56.6, Thomas does say that, qua mover of the lower appetites, the will more requires a virtue than do those lower appetites (which do, however, also require their respective virtues). This would seem to suggest that the will requires the virtue of justice so that it (the will) might bring order to the lower appetites. But that which is required would not be justice, since justice is toward the other. If, then, we are to assume that the *sed contra* expresses Thomas's opinion (and that is not always the case with a *sed contra*), we would have to say that there he has in mind the will's ordering the lower appetites in order that it (the will) might bring about good not just for the individual whose will it is but also (and primarily) with respect to some "other." Or, alternatively, we might say that Thomas has in mind what Aristotle says near the beginning of his treatise on justice (*EN* 5), where he says that justice (in a certain sense) is "excellence

Of course, a person's will might be inclined toward that which is not good either (ultimately) for himself or for others; but even still he would be pursuing characteristically that good *as* good. Aristotle calls this "good" the apparent good; but he also suggests that, in pursuing the (or an) apparent good, one is pursuing the genuine good even while misunderstanding what it is (*EN* 3.4 1113a15–b2). But when the will has the moral virtue proper to it, that is, when it has the moral virtue of justice, it has as its object "the right." As we have seen, practical wisdom has as its end the acts that, with habituation, bring about the moral virtues, including justice; justice, because its end is the just, is what makes politicians good politicians. In other words, it brings it about that politicians have a will (that is to say, that particular appetite) for the right – or, as one might put it, for "the right thing to do" in whatever particular situation. But it also brings it about that the wills of private individuals are oriented toward the right, with respect to other individuals or others in general.

Those who pursue characteristically an apparent good very often do so for reasons having to do primarily with themselves; as Aristotle says, in most cases of pursuing the apparent good, the cause is pleasure [*EN* 3.4 1113a33–b2]. In so far as this is the case, the will clearly has not the virtue of justice. But it is also possible, in the realm of human relations, to pursue that which is not just, but not in order to attain pleasure for oneself. This too would be to pursue an apparent good, and such a person also – in this particular regard – would not have the virtue of justice.

This all points to that very important feature of justice: its objectivity. This is the antidote to the "Cartesian psychology" that (as

---

entire" (that is, "virtue entire" [ὅλη ἀρετή]). The two, he says, "are the same but being them is not the same; what, as a relation to others, is justice is, as a certain kind of state without qualification, excellence [ἀρετή]" [*EN* 5.1 1130a8–13]. In the sentence to which this note is attached, we have specified that *in the realm of human relations* the (human) moral virtue of justice is required. A person, says Thomas, has need rather of theological virtue in order for his affections to be ordered toward "the other" known as God. See the last remark in the body of *ST* 1-2.56.6, and also ad 2.

we have seen) Elizabeth Anscombe maintains infects the manualists' analysis of cooperation.[9] This objectivity is already apparent in the fact that justice is not about having well-ordered lower appetites; but it becomes yet more apparent when we consider the difference between its object, "the right," and what, in contemporary parlance, are termed "rights." In most contemporary western languages – certainly, in English – the word 'right,' as in 'we have a right to (this or that)' signifies something that morally cannot be denied a person in any situation whatsoever.[10] Sometimes the term is quite appropriate, as when reference is made to innocent persons' right to life. But sometimes so-called "rights" are morally incompatible with other persons' "rights," or even with the same person's genuine obligations and duties, and so can – or even must – be denied. In the contemporary public square, this problem persists but is also characteristically ignored. Advocates of various causes include in their rhetoric talk of rights, by which they mean things that morally cannot be denied one, fully aware, however, that such rights cannot be granted without failing to respect other rights or duties. Such rhetoric – which can be found not only in mouths of political activists but also in ecclesial documents – amounts in effect to complicity in incoherence.[11]

The Thomistic concept of the right is not subject to this problem, for "the right" (*jus*) signifies simply and solely 'that which is in accordance with justice.' As its object, the right gives justice its "species": its nature or its definition. If something cannot in justice be done, it cannot be the right, for the right is what justice, by definition, does.

9. See just above, note 1.

10. See Mary Ann Glendon, *Rights Talk: The Impoverishment of Political Discourse* (New York: Free Press, 1991), passim. See also John Finnis, "Absolute Rights: Some Problems Illustrated," *American Journal of Jurisprudence* 61, no. 2 (2016): 195–215, and John Finnis, *Natural Law and Natural Rights*, 2nd ed. (Oxford: Oxford University Press, 2011), 206–7.

11. See Kevin L. Flannery, "The Moral Principles Governing the Immigration Policies of Polities," in *Catholic Social Teaching: A Volume of Scholarly Essays*, ed. Christian Brugger and Gerard V. Bradley (Cambridge: Cambridge University Press, forthcoming).

What has caused the problem in contemporary rhetoric is that "the right" has moved from being about justice as existing outside the self — that is, from being about one's relationship in justice with others — to being a personal possession of individuals, where it no longer need conform to the objective norms of justice.[12] A sound system of justice excludes contradiction; rights rhetoric very often simply ignores it.

But what is "the right" that thus serves as the defining object of justice? We have seen that Thomas, in *ST* 2-2.57.1, says that the object of justice "is called 'the just' [iustum]" and that 'the just' is equivalent to 'the right' (or *jus*). He is, in effect, linking the legal language of his day with the vocabulary of Aristotle, who speaks of 'the just'.[13] And Aristotle, near the beginning of his treatise on justice, declares: "The just is therefore the lawful and the equal; the unjust the unlawful and the unequal" [*EN* 5.1 1129a34-b1]. So, we can say that the right is the equal, as established in law.

Thomas is well aware that a large portion of the Aristotelian treatise that follows the remark about the lawful and the equal is devoted to a quasi-mathematical analysis of justice, which speaks of restoring equality between two parties, one of whom has unjustly acquired property rightfully belonging to the other, or of establishing a just distribution of goods among people of unequal merit. But he (with Aristotle) is also aware that establishing or reestablishing justice often does not admit of a strictly quantitative approach. When a man has struck another with a plank, for instance, justice must take into consideration not only the days the other was not able to work and the *denarii* he has lost as a consequence, but also such factors as the pain and humiliation he has suffered and the neglect or malice with which

12. See Finnis, *Natural Law and Natural Rights*, 206–7.

13. See Thomas's commentary on the *Nicomachean Ethics* [*in EN* 5.12 15–16 (§1016)], where he says that the jurists "call 'the right' what Aristotle calls 'the just'" ["idem enim nominant illi ius quod Aristotiles iustum"]. (Aristotle's Greek term is τὸ δίκαιον.) Thomas then cites for this equivalence Isidore of Seville, who is also mentioned in *ST* 2-2.57.1.

the person who caused the injury acted. These and other extenuating factors, such as the duress under which the one person acted, are extremely difficult – if not impossible – to measure in a strictly mathematical way. They can also play a part in rectifying acts of immoral cooperation.

Moreover, neither Aristotle nor Thomas held that a quantification – in such a literal sense – is always to be attempted or is even appropriate. As Thomas suggests, re-establishing "equality" is more a matter of adjusting ("ad-just-ing") things.[14] Establishing the right in particular situations is more a matter of establishing what Augustine of Hippo calls "the tranquillity of order."

It is worth quoting at some length what Augustine says regarding these things:

> The peace of the body, therefore, lies in the balanced ordering of its parts; the peace of the irrational soul lies in the rightly ordered disposition of the appetites; the peace of the rational soul lies in the rightly ordered relationship of cognition and action; the peace of body and soul lies in the rightly ordered life and health of a living creature; peace between mortal man and God is an ordered obedience, in faith, under an eternal law; and peace between men is an ordered agreement of mind with mind. The peace of a household is an ordered concord, with respect to command and obedience, of those who dwell together; the peace of a city is an ordered concord, with respect to command and obedience, of the citizens; and the peace of the Heavenly City is a perfectly ordered and perfectly harmonious fellowship in the enjoyment of God, and of one another in God. The peace of all things lies in the tranquillity of order; and order is the disposition of equal and unequal things in such a way as to give to each its proper place.[15]

14. See *ST* 2-2.57.1, where Thomas says that the term *jus* suggests "a sort of equality"; in common parlance, he says, "those things that have been equalized are said to be adjusted" ["Importat enim aequalitatem quandam, ut ipsum nomen demonstrat, dicuntur enim vulgariter ea quae adaequantur iustari"]. The verb *iustare* does not show up in most Latin dictionaries, but it make an appearance in Charles du Fresne du Cange, *Glossarium Mediae et Infimae Latinitatis* (Paris: Librairie des Sciences et des Arts, 1937–38).

15. See *City of God* 19.13.1 (translation from Augustine, *The City of God against the Pagans*, ed. and trans. R. W. Dyson, Cambridge Texts in the History of Political Thought

Thomas refers to Augustine's *tranquillitas ordinis* frequently, on one occasion connecting it explicitly with the classical definition of justice as giving to each what is his.[16] This too is justice understood as a species of equality.

II. Advantages—and Challenges—of an Ideal Legislature

Given then that cooperation with evil is most reasonably considered an issue in justice and is not simply – or even primarily – about the relationship of a cooperator with a malefactor, a good way to approach cases of cooperation would be to imagine a legislature that must establish laws that prohibit certain ways of cooperating with evil. This legislature, however, does not establish laws that govern a particular polity, for many of the laws will have to do with situations in which certain individuals or entities are, within a particular polity, performing evil acts that are perfectly legal. This legislature stands above particular polities, and the laws it passes pertain to those within those polities who choose not to cooperate with such legally sanctioned evil. In other words, this legislature must determine what constitutes cooperation that comes so close to the certain bad acts as to be immoral cooperation. Determining that certain acts of cooperation are too close to the bad acts and so impermissible is not a question of the relationship of cooperator (or cooperators) to malefactor (malefactors) but

---

[Cambridge: Cambridge University Press, 1998], 938). The Latin of the last translated sentence is as follows: "pax omnium rerum tranquillitas ordinis. Ordo est parium dispariumque rerum sua cuique loca tribuens dispositio." See George Weigel, Tranquillitas Ordinis: *The Present Failure and Future Promise of American Catholic Thought on War and Peace* (Oxford: Oxford University Press, 1987), 26–32.

16. "In the same way neither can union of souls through charity endure unless it is bound together; but a true binding of this sort is the peace, which, according to Augustine, is tranquillity of measure, form, and order – when, that is, each person has what is his" ["Eodem modo nec coniunctio animorum per charitatem stare potest, nisi ligetur; huiusmodi autem verum ligamen est pax, quae est, secundum Augustinum, tranquillitas modi, speciei et ordinis, quando scilicet unusquisque habet quod suum est"] [Thomas Aquinas, "Super Epistolam ad Ephesios lectura," in *Super Epistolas S. Pauli lectura, II*, 8th ed., ed. R. Cai (Turin: Marietti, 1953), 4.1 §194]. That definition of justice appears in the first book of Plato's *Republic* (331e3–4) and also at Aristotle's *EN* 5.5 1133b30–1134a16.

rather of the nature of the situation in which the various parties find themselves. This "nature of the situation" depends upon the factors discussed above, especially in chapters 4 and 5 (or any other factors that might be deemed relevant and necessary for maintaining justice).

This legislature presupposes a system of moral principles in accordance with reason. The wellspring of the precepts it establishes is, therefore, not ideology or self-interest but rather that *tranquillitas ordinis* itself that all men, because of inclinations proper to their nature, are capable of recognizing but only just men truly know and desire. The factors discussed in chapters 4 and 5 are factors pertinent to the identification of types of behavior that establish and preserve this tranquil order, within individual souls and among individuals and within entities that consider themselves to be governed by this legislature, for their own happiness.

Sometimes formulating a law in accordance with this system of moral principles is a fairly straightforward matter. A person who furnishes to a malefactor something necessary for committing an injustice cooperates immorally. A person, for instance, who purchases a pistol for a convicted criminal who cannot purchase a firearm legally on his own, is an accomplice to the killing that the criminal goes on to commit with the pistol. And a hospital that grants access to a surgeon who performs there abortions is an accomplice (a corporate accomplice) to the taking of an innocent life. A law that says that any such cooperation is immoral is clearly a law in accordance with justice.

Sometimes, however, the correct assessment of a moral situation is not so obvious or simple. This is often the case when, for instance, the pertinent Thomistic factor is the office occupied or the role being played by the cooperator (or supposed cooperator). Does the fact that one is a credentialed attorney and so a functioning part of the legal system allow one to represent *any* defendant, even a defendant whom one knows to be guilty? Does playing that role allow one to formulate *any* sort of defense, even one arguing that the culprit could not have committed the evil? And then there is the factor of "force" – or the pressure to which a person may be subject to go along with some evil.[17] As we have seen in considering usury (chapter 5, section III), it can sometimes happen that one who has need of a loan can avail himself of a usurer's services without incurring any guilt as a cooperator in the evil of usury. Can the factor or factors involved in that determination be applied in similar cases?

Questions of this sort come increasingly into play as the relevant situations become more concrete or particular. The ancient Greeks, including both Plato and Aristotle, made a distinction between νόμοι (laws) and ψηφίσματα (often translated "decrees").[18] Although Aristotle insists that, in a just polity, law must always be the supreme guiding force, he acknowledges too that sometimes all a judge can do is – so to speak – *plunk* for a particular course of action. This colloquialism is strikingly appropriate as a description of what Aristotle had in mind. The root of the word ψηφίσματα (or ψήφισμα) is ψῆφος – which refers to a pebble that a person casts in draughts or in voting. Determining whether an instance of cooperation is culpable cooperation and so to be declared illegal is an inexact science but one governed by reason and the principles of justice. Such determinations (plunkings) are necessary in order to provide needed – and wanted – guidance to those who desire to know what is permissible and what not.

The central claim of the present book is not that adopting a Thomistic approach – as contrasted with the the moral manualists' approach – to cooperation with evil will allow moral authorities (represented here by our ideal legislature) more easily to formulate rules regarding such cooperation; nor does the book claim that adopting a Thomistic approach will make the analysis of particular cases less conditioned by – or attentive to – variable particulars. The truth is that both approaches (the Thomistic and the manualist) involve a certain amount of imprecision and require prudential judgment, the amount

17. See chapter 4, section III.

18. In Aristotle see, for instance, *EN* 5.10 1137b13–32 but also *Pol.* 4.4 1292a32–37; in Plato, *Theaetetus* 173d2–4.

depending, of course, upon the issue. As we have seen, Alphonsus's conclusions regarding cooperation are typically not that a particular type of act is definitely immoral but that, of the various probable positions put forward by reputable authors, a particular position is (in his opinion) more probable than the others.[19] Thomas Aquinas does not speak in such terms, although, as we have seen, his way of analyzing such complex ethical issues as the liceity of self-defense is to consider cases discussed by other authorities of sound judgment (such as Augustine or the various contributors to Roman law) and to identify the factors that inform their judgments. With respect to self-defense, he is able to formulate precepts that are quite precise, although even these are qualified by talk of proportionality and avoidance of vindictiveness. It is this prudentially attentive approach – attentive, that is, to the practical wisdom of his predecessors but also to the complexity of human life in the concrete – that allows these same factors to be applied to other cases not explicitly considered by him.

The primary advantage of a genuinely Thomistic approach to cooperation with evil – besides, for instance, the avoidance of confusion regarding act indifference and the resulting emphasis on intention, understood in a particular way – is that, when the approach is adopted by those tasked with determining what is immoral cooperation and what is not, they know what they are doing. They have the proper tools for their particular task. Strong evidence that these are the proper tools consists in the fact that these tools – the factors that pertain to the analysis of cooperation – are the very tools that Thomas uses in the analysis of all human action. A person who, reading through the early questions of the *prima secundae* of the *Summa theologiae* (up to and including question 21), disagrees with Thomas's ultimate conclusions regarding what are good and what are bad human acts – even such a one will have trouble not acknowledging that the factors Thomas identifies as bearing upon the morality of human acts are *there*, and are pertinent to the moral character of those acts.

19. See Cummings, *The Servant and the Ladder*, 189–215.

APPENDIX 1 ALPHONSUS LIGUORI, *THEOLOGIA MORALIS*, BOOK 2, §§59–67 (ON COOPERATION)

Article III: Whether it is licit to cooperate materially with the sin of another.

59. When is it licit to cooperate materially with the sin of a neighbor? — 60. Whether it is licit to marry a man who is in a state of mortal sin or

In the translations from Alphonsus that make up this and the next two appendixes, words that he takes over from Busenbaum's *Medulla theologiae moralis* are given (as in this paragraph) in all caps. (On Alphonsus's use of Busenbaum, see chapter 1, sections I and II.) Such passages correspond to those which the Gaudé edition indicates with the repeated symbol « to the left of all Busenbaum text. Also, in these appendixes Alphonsus makes reference to a huge number of other authors. A list of their dates and works cited can be found in volume four of the Gaudé edition of the *Theologia moralis*, pp. 785–817. For summaries of the main positions of many of these other authors, see chapters 2 and 3 of Cummings, *The Servant and the Ladder*.

In what comes later (but is not included in this translation), the issue is whether a person can request sacraments from a priest who has been excommunicated. In the second paragraph of the number referred to (§79), it is stated that some authors say that it is licit, "if there is present necessity or notable utility." The question is then raised whether requesting sacraments is licit when the utility is not great "even if the priest is prepared sacrilegiously to administer [the sacrament]" ["etiamsi sacerdos paratus ad sacrilege ministrandum"]. Reference is made to various authors who discuss this question.

impeded by a vow of chastity? — 61. Whether it is licit to render to him "the debt"? — 62. Whether it is licit to give communion to a concealed sinner? — 63. What is licit for servants? And what is material and what formal cooperation? — 64. Whether it is licit to assist a master as he goes to a brothel, etc.? Whether it is licit to assist a concubine as she goes to one's master? — 65. Whether it is licit to carry gifts to a prostitute? — 66. Whether it is licit to open the gate to a prostitute? Whether it is licit to carry a ladder so that a master might ascend it and go to a woman? — 67. Whether it is licit to write amorous letters? — 68. Whether it is licit to serve meat [on a day when it is prohibited]? — 69. Whether it is licit for innkeepers to give wine to drunkards or meat on a day when it is prohibited? (See other issues in Busenbaum.) — 70. Whether it is licit to rent a house to a prostitute or to usurers? — 71. Whether it is licit to sell dice, swords, poisons, etc.? — 72. Whether it is licit to sell a lamb to a Jew? — 73. Whether it is licit for captive Christians to row, etc. — 74. Whether it is licit to aid a tyrant? — 75. Whether it is licit to convey provisions to heretics? Whether it is licit for drivers to convey a prostitute? — 76. Whether it is licit to accept gifts from a lover? Whether it is licit to return a sword to one who will kill? — 77. Whether it is licit to request an oath from one who will perjure himself? Whether it is licit, without a weighty reason, to request a loan from a usurer? — 78. Whether it is licit to help a usurer? Whether it is licit to give a loan to someone who will ill use it? — 79. Whether it is licit to request the sacraments from one who has been excommunicated or from a sinner — and from one so prepared?[2] — 80. Whether it is licit to give prohibited foods?

◆

59. I RESPOND THAT IT IS LICIT TO COOPERATE ONLY MATERIALLY, FURNISHING ONLY THE MATERIAL AND MEANS OF SINNING, OR EXHIBITING THE OBJECT, IF THE FOLLOWING CONDITIONS ARE PRESENT. 1ST. IF YOUR ACT OR COOPERATION IS IN ITSELF GOOD OR AT LEAST INDIFFERENT. 2ND. IF IT COMES ABOUT WITH A GOOD INTENTION AND FOR A REASONABLE CAUSE AND NOT IN ORDER TO HELP THE OTHER TO SIN. 3RD. IF YOU CANNOT IMPEDE THE SIN OF THE OTHER OR AT LEAST, BECAUSE OF A REASONABLE CAUSE, ARE NOT OBLIGED TO DO SO. REGARDING WHICH CAUSE, SÁNCHEZ AND LAYMANN NOTE THAT, ALTHOUGH ITS GRAVITY CANNOT BE DEFINED BY MEANS OF A FIXED RULE, IT IS HOWEVER TO BE MEASURED WITH RESPECT TO THE JUDGMENT OF THE PRUDENT MAN. A MORE

GRAVE CAUSE IS REQUIRED: 1ST, TO THE EXTENT THAT THE SIN, TO WHICH OCCASION IS GIVEN, IS MORE GRAVE; 2ND, TO THE EXTENT THAT IT IS MORE PROBABLE, SHOULD YOU NOT COOPERATE, THE OTHER WILL NOT SIN, OR TO THE EXTENT THAT THE DISPOSITION TO SIN IS MORE CERTAIN; 3RD, TO THE EXTENT THAT YOUR COOPERATION APPROACHES MORE CLOSELY TO THE SIN; 4TH, TO THE EXTENT THAT YOU HAVE LESS RIGHT TO SUCH AN ACT;[1] 5TH AND FINALLY, TO THE EXTENT THAT THE SIN CLASHES WITH JUSTICE, IN PARTICULAR WITH RESPECT TO THE HARM INCURRED BY A THIRD PARTY. — LAYMANN.

St. Antoninus, Gabriel, Sylvester, etc., according to Sánchez,[2] appear to think that in no case is it licit to cooperate with the sin of another: but the learned generally permit this if the required conditions are present. See Tamburini.[3] Also Sánchez judges the authors cited to have spoken of the case in which there is absent a just excusing cause, or when the cooperation is intrinsically evil. That action is always intrinsically evil which, of itself, is determined toward sin, as would be seeking out a concubine for a master, manufacturing idols, and anything similar. The situation is different if the action can be performed without sin, for instance, waiting on table, opening a door, etc. — In this regard, i.e., licitly cooperating with the sin of another, see the conditions required by Busenbaum, as just above.

HOW TO RESOLVE THESE CASES:

60. 1ST. IN THIS WAY, A WOMAN LICITLY COOPERATES MATERIALLY MARRYING A MAN WHOM SHE KNOWS RECEIVES THE SACRAMENT IN MORTAL SIN. KNOWING HIM, HOWEVER, TO HAVE A VOW OF CHASTITY, SHE SINS CONTRACTING MARRIAGE WITH HIM SINCE SHE COOPERATES IN AN ILLICIT CONTRACT. LAYMANN AND SÁNCHEZ.[4]

1. At this point, the editors of the Gaudé edition mention that, contrary to Alphonsus's suggestion, Laymann and Sánchez do not include this condition [Alphonsus Maria de Ligorio, *Theologia moralis*, v. 1 p. 356 n. 59a].

2. Sanchez [Sánchez], *Opus morale in praecepta decalogi*, lb. 1 c. 7 §4.

3. Thomas Tamburini, *Decal.* l. 5. c. 1. §. 4.

4. On the second case, Laymann says: "However, a woman would sin if, knowing of a man's vow of chastity she contracts with him, for such a betrothal, in which by accepting the promise the woman actively concurs, is injurious to God" ["Attamen peccavat mulier, si sciens viri votum castitatis, cum eo contraxit; quia talis desponsatio, ad quam

61. 2ND. A WIFE ALSO LICITLY, AFTER A CONTRACTED MARRIAGE, MATERIALLY COOPERATES IF SHE RENDERS "THE DEBT" TO A HUSBAND BOUND BY A VOW OF CHASTITY;[5] OR, MORE CORRECTLY, SHE IS OBLIGED IN JUSTICE IF, UPON HIS INSISTING, SHE CANNOT DISSUADE HIM FROM THAT PURPOSE. [And this is the most general and more probable position, as in Suárez, Lugo, Laymann, Bonacina, Palaus, Sánchez, Concina, Holzmann, Bossio, etc. Although the opposite position,[6] maintained by Pontio, Lacroix, Comitolo, Silvester, etc., is also probable. See below, book VI, §994].

62. 3RD. SIMILARLY A PASTOR CAN LICITLY AND MUST ADMINISTER THE EUCHARIST TO A SINNER—BOTH ONE WHO IS EXCOMMUNICATED AND THE SECRET HERETIC—IF HE REQUESTS IT PUBLICLY; INDEED, A CONFESSOR MUST OBLIGE ONE WHO MAKES THE REQUEST EVEN PRIVATELY, IF ONLY BY WAY OF CONFESSION HE KNOWS OF HIS SIN. [According to the most general position, this is obligatory, as in Sporer, etc., against Petrocorensis.[7] See below, book VI, §658.]

63. 4TH. SERVANTS ARE EXEMPT FROM SIN IF BY REASON OF THEIR SERVITUDE THEY CONTRIBUTE CERTAIN SERVICES WHICH THEY COULD NOT DENY WITHOUT GRAVE INCONVENIENCE—SHOULD THEY, FOR EXAMPLE, DRESS THEIR MASTER, SADDLE HIS HORSE, ACCOMPANY HIM TO A BROTHEL, BEAR GIFTS TO A PROSTITUTE, OPEN THE DOOR TO THE LATTER WHEN SHE ARRIVES: FOR THESE ACTS ARE ONLY REMOTELY RELATED TO THE SIN AND WITHOUT THEM[8] THE SIN

---

mulier active concurrit promissionem acceptando, Deo injuriosa est"] [Laymann, *Theologia moralis: In V libros distributa*, lb. 2 tract. 3 ch. 12 §4].

The reference to Sánchez is: Thomas Sanchez [Tomás Sánchez], *Tomus secundus disputationum de sancto matrimonii sacramento*, in *De sancto matrimonii sacramento* (Antwerp: M. Nutii [Nuyts], 1620), lb. 7 disp. 11 §11.

5. Reference here is to the so-called marital or conjugal debt to have intercourse with one's spouse.

6. At this point, the editors of the Gaudé edition clarify: "That is, they maintain that in this case the one spouse is not obliged in justice to render the debt" [Alphonsus Maria de Ligorio, *Theologia moralis*, v. 1 p. 356 n. 61a].

7. By means of the word "Petrocorensis," Alphonsus is making reference to a multivolume manual of moral theology used at the seminary at Périgord, France. The remarks referred to can be found at *Theologia moralis, ad usum seminarii Petrocorensis, tomus IV* (Padua: J. Manfrè, 1752), lb. 2 tract. 1 (*De poenit.*) cap. 4 q. 6 resp. 2 §2 (p. 95). The Gaudé edition of Alphonsus, referring to an edition of this manual appearing in 1735, notes that this work contains six books in twelve volumes.

8. I.e., the services.

MIGHT COME ABOUT. WHENCE, HOWEVER, IT DOES NOT FOLLOW THAT IT IS LICIT TO CONTRIBUTE SUCH SERVICES TO ANYONE ELSE WHOMSOEVER. BONACINA, AZOR, LAYMANN, SÁNCHEZ. [But see the next section, §64.]

In distinguishing, however, when cooperation is material and when formal, others – such as de Cardenas and Master Milante – say that cooperation is material when it per accidens and remotely leads to the sin of the other, but formal when per se or on account of some adjoined circumstance it leads proximately to the performance of the sin, even if per se it might be indifferent.

But it is better with others to say that that cooperation is formal which cooperates in the will of another and cannot be without sin, but material that which cooperates only in the bad action of the other, beside the intention of the one who cooperates. This, however, is licit when the action is per se good or indifferent, and when there is present a cause which is just and proportionate to the gravity of the sin of the other and to the proximity of the cooperation which is contributed to the execution of the sin. The reason for this is that, when you contribute an indifferent action without a vicious intention, if the other wishes to ill use it in the execution of his own sin, you are not bound, except out of charity, to impede that. And, because charity does not oblige in the event of grave inconvenience, in making available with a just cause your cooperation, you do not sin, for then the sin of that person does not issue from your cooperation but from the wickedness of him who ill uses your action. Nor does it do to say that your action, although indifferent, conjoined with the circumstance of the wicked intention of the other, ends up bad, for in fact your action is not conjoined with the bad will of that other but that other conjoins his bad will with your action,[9] so that your action will not then be the cause per se flowing into the sin but only the occasion, which is ill used in order to sin. See below, book III, §571, the second "Respectu."[10]

9. The Latin of the Gaudé edition reads as follows: "actio tua non est per se conjuncta cum mala voluntate illius, sed *illud* conjungit suam malam voluntatem cum actione tua." Earlier editions have "ille" instead of "illud." The earlier editions are probably right, although it is just possible that Alphonsus deliberately switches to referring to the malefactor ("that other") by means of a neuter pronoun in order to emphasize the distance between the role of the malefactor and that of the cooperator.

10. Alphonsus is referring here to his later treatment of restitution, in which at one

64. It is asked 1st: *Whether a servant, by virtue of his servitude, might accompany his master to a brothel or saddle his horse?*

Busenbaum says yes here, along with Navarrus,[11] Manuel Rodriguez, etc., according to Sánchez.

— But it is more probable that the mere fact of servitude would not constitute a sufficient reason for this, even if without the assistance of the servant the master would proceed; at the very least is required grave fear of injury. So maintain Sánchez, Viva, and the Salmanticenses, who correctly call attention to the fact that this is never licit if the master would be rendered more animated by virtue of the accompaniment.

Whether however *it would be licit for a servant to escort a concubine to the house of his master?* Sánchez, along with Navarrus and Manuel Rodriguez, says that if there was already an agreement between the master and the concubine, in this case the servant is excused solely by virtue of his servitude, since the master also without the servant would equally commit the sin; otherwise he is not excused, unless because of grave fear of injury, as maintains Sánchez. — And he says the same of a servant who conveys a concubine in a carriage or coach. But with good reason de Cardenas, Milante, and Father Concina do not allow this. — Even more to be disallowed would be the case of a servant who calls a concubine to the house of his master: but Azor opposes this. — And I say the same of drivers and sailors conveying a prostitute to a lover, such as can only be excused because of grave fear of injury. See n. 75 at the words "An autem."

65. It is asked 2nd: *Whether it is licit for a servant, on account of his servitude, to bear gifts to a prostitute?*

Speaking only of edibles and other small presents, Busenbaum, Sánchez, Sporer, and Palaus, together with Navarrus and Azor say yes. — But Father Concina contends more truly that this is intrinsically evil since in fact the gifts per se foster obscene love.

---

point he says that he will consider the effects of cooperation, first, "with respect to the owner who is to suffer the harm [respectu domini damnum passuri]"; second, "with respect to the injury that the thief inflicts [respectu furis damnum inferentis]" [Alphonsus Maria de Ligorio, *Theologia moralis*, 3 §571 (p. 67)]. What he says now has to do with the "second respect."

11. That is, Martin Aspilcueta (or Azpilcoeta), often called Doctor Navarrus.

66. It is asked 3rd: *Whether it is licit for a servant to open the door to a prostitute?*

Lacroix says no. But saying yes with Busenbaum are the Salmanticenses, Laymann, Tamburini, along with Sánchez, Diana, Azor, Sà, Manuel Rodriguez, etc. — Nor does Innocent XI's [condemned] proposition 51 block this, which reads as follows: *A servant who in lowering his shoulders knowingly assists his master to ascend through windows in order to debauch a virgin and many times serves the same master by carrying the ladder, by opening a door, or by cooperating with regard to something similar, does not sin mortally if he does it out of fear of notable detriment, for example, lest he be ill treated by the master, lest he subject to piercing stares, lest he be expelled from the house.* For, from the context itself, the expression "opening a door" is understood to refer to an act of opening by force, as Roncaglia and the Salmanticenses correctly say. Provided (they maintain) that, should he [the servant] not open it, there is present some other who would.[12]

12. At this point the Gaudé edition appends a note reading as follows: "This condition is not in reference to the [condemned] proposition of Innocent XI but to the principal question at issue. And, according to Roncaglia, a servant could open a house to a concubine herself, 'provided especially [he does not say "only"] that, when [the servant] not does not actually open it, yet there would be someone who would open it.' The Salmanticenses, however, say simply, 'when it comes about according to the order of the master.'" ["Haec conditio, non quidem ad propositionem Innocentii XI, sed ad principale quaesitum referenda est: et juxta Roncaglia, famulus posset ipsi concubinae domum aperire, 'maxime (non dicit "modo") dum etiam eo non aperiente, adhuc esset qui aperiret.' Salmanticenses vero absolute dicunt licere, 'quando jussu domini fit.'"] In other words, in the sentence to which the note is appended, Alphonsus is speaking not about the phrase in the condemned proposition but about Roncaglia's position that the servant's opening the door to the master's house would be licit, especially if someone else could do the same instead of the servant. The Gaudé edition points out an inaccuracy in Alphonsus's reportage: Roncaglia does not say "provided only [modo]" but rather "provided especially [maxime]." That is, Roncaglia wrote: "maxime dum etiam eo non aperiente, adhuc esset qui aperiret": "provided especially that, when [the servant] not does not actually open it, yet there would be someone who would open it." The Salmanticenses (with reason) say that the condemned proposition is not talking about opening the door to the concubine when she comes to the master's house but about opening a door (to get into the virgin's house) either by means of a key or by force. Roncaglia makes the same point, although he speaks only of forcing the door. Roncaglia also talks not just about debauching a virgin but about sex with any woman.

It is asked 4th: *Whether, out of fear of death or grave injury, it is licit for a servant to lower his shoulders, or to carry a ladder so that his master might ascend and fornicate, or to open the door – and similar things?*

Saying no are Viva and Milante, Father Concina, the Salmanticenses, Lacroix, and others. For, as they say, such actions are never licit in as much as they are intrinsically evil. But contradicting them are Busenbaum (see below, §68), Sánchez, and Lessius, whose position, considering the reason provided, appears to me the more probable. The reason is, as we said just above,[13] when you contribute an action per se indifferent – that is, which can be both good and evil – you are not obliged except in charity to abstain from it lest another misuse it in order to sin but, when you fear grave injury otherwise, you can licitly permit the sin of the other. For, on the one hand, charity does not oblige you with grave injury to avert his sin, while, on the other hand, the other's wickedness cannot alter the nature of your action in such a way that from an indifferent action it becomes intrinsically evil. The learned authority who continued the work of Tournély, agrees with me, saying: *I am not obliged to suffer grave harm so that I might avert the sin of another; he himself would reasonably impute his own wickedness to himself.*[14]

Nor will it do to say that the aforesaid actions are per se evil because they cooperate with the sin of debauching: this can be proved from the condemned proposition itself where it says, "or by cooperating with regard to something similar." For it is responded that "by cooperating" is not to be understood as referring to formal but rather to material cooperation, since the authors of the proposition spoke of that and it was clearly in that sense that the proposition was proscribed. But included in the words "if he does it out of fear of notable detriment" is not fear of death, for there it is declared what sort of fear does not excuse: "for example,

13. That is, in §63.

14. The reference here is to Peter Collet, who "continued" the lectures in moral theology of Honoré Tournély (*Praelectiones theologicae: Cursus theologicus scholastico-dogmaticus*); the anonymous work that Collet produced is entitled *Prælectionum theologicarum Honorati Tournely continuatio sive universae theologiae moralis tractatus*. The passage cited here ("De restitutione in genere," cap. 2 a. 6 sect. 3 concl. 3) is in the first volume: Anonymous [Peter Collet], *Praelectionum theologicarum Honorati Tournely continuatio* (Venice: N. Pezzana, 1746).

lest he be ill treated by the master, lest he subject to piercing stares, lest he be expelled from the house" – which evils certainly do not include the injury of death.[15]

Because, however, the aforesaid types of cooperation truly cooperate in the injury of debauching, although they cooperate only materially in the sin of the debaucher, I believe that no other fear excuses the cooperator except that of death. For otherwise it would be licit to cooperate in the loss of honor of a young woman to be deflowered provided only that one fears forfeiting one's means or fears disgrace.[16] See below, book III, §571, where we say in like manner that it is not licit for you to hand over a ladder or keys to a thief otherwise than because of a fear of death or of disgrace – agreeing thus with Tournély.[17] But handing over a sword to one who is prepared to kill is never licit, for it is not licit to kill the innocent so that you might avoid death – as Concina and [the one who continued] Tournély very correctly teach. See below, book III, §571, at the words, "Secus etiam."[18]

67. It is asked 5th: *Whether it is licit for a servant because of grave fear to write or to carry amorous letters to the concubine of his master?*[19]

15. Alphonsus is here objecting to Milante's assumption that, when in the condemned proposition mention is made of "fear of notable detriment," meant is fear of death. See Pius-Thomas Milante, *Exercitationes Dogmatico-Morales in Propositiones Proscriptas a SS. Innocentio XI* (Naples: Ex typographia Januarii, et Vincentii Mutio, 1739), ex.28 301 (in the paragraph beginning "Quid insuper").

16. The Latin here is either corrupt or very awkwardly phrased: "Nam alias, ob solum metum jacturae facultatum vel infamiae, non licet concurrere ad dehonorationem puellae deflorandae."

17. The Gaudé edition appends a note at this point saying that Collet (to use Alphonsus's expression, the "continuator" of Tournley) denies that it is licit to do these things except out of fear of "grave harm" ["De restitutione in genere," cap. 2 a. 6 sect. 3 concl. 3].

18. In the translation of III, §571, these words are rendered, "Furthermore, otherwise." In a note appended to the final sentence in book II, §66, the Gaudé edition calls attention to a number of places, including III, §571, where Alphonsus qualifies what he says here about handing over a sword to one who is prepared to kill; that is, he says that one must not hand over the sword if one can so refuse "without danger of death or an equally grave harm" ["sine periculo mortis aut aequalis gravis damni"].

19. It is not immediately apparent what is meant by "writing" amorous letters to the concubine; but, in the first source that Alphonsus cites in this regard, the question

Whatever others say, I believe, with the Salmanticenses, Sánchez, Viva, Laymann, Bonacina, Tamburini, etc., along with Lacroix, that these things are never licit since they cooperate formally in the sin of the master, fostering his obscene love. — And, along with Sánchez and the Salmanticenses (against Castropalaus[20] and Rebellus, according to Tamburini), I judge that this is to be maintained even when there is a doubt whether the contents of the letters are amorous, for, given that the obscene love is known,[21] it is believed morally that the contents are indecent. — If, however, they contain only polite greetings,[22] even so, required in order to excuse the servant is a just cause beyond the mere deference of servitude — as say the Salmanticenses, Sánchez, and Tamburini.

---

is framed in the following manner: "Whether servants can licitly convey amorous letters to a concubine or write them upon the order of a master" ["An servi licite possint deferre litteras amatorias concubinae aut eas iussu domini scribere"] [*Collegii Salmanticensis Fratrum Discalceatorum Beatae Mariae de Monte Carmeli primitivae observatiae cursus theologiae moralis*, vol. 5 tract. 21 cap. 8 n. 67].

20. Alphonsus also refers to this Spanish Jesuit, Ferdinand Castropalaus (1581–1633), as "Palaus."

21. Tamburini stipulates that the servant "is certain of the indecent character of the master's love — or the persons between whom these writings run are extremely suspect" ["est certus de turpitudine amoris domini, vel personae, inter quas intercurrunt illa scripta, sunt valde suspectae"] [lb. 5 cap. 1 IV §18].

22. The Latin is "sola signa urbanitatis," which corresponds to Tamburini's "internuncia solius urbanitatis" [lb. 5 cap. 1 IV §18].

APPENDIX 2 *ALPHONSUS LIGUORI, THEOLOGIA MORALIS, BOOK 3, §571 (ON RESTITUTION)*

571. 6th. LIKEWISE [OBLIGED TO MAKE RESTITUTION] IS ONE PARTICIPATING IN SPOILS OR IN WHATEVER WAY COOPERATING, SUCH AS KEEPING A WATCH, PLACING A LADDER, PREPARING INSTRUMENTS, COMPOSING LETTERS, ETC.; IN AN UNJUST WAR, CONVEYING MISSILES, ETC. — BUT EXCUSED (PROVIDED THAT THE ACTION IS NOT PER SE EVIL) ARE THOSE WHO DO THESE THINGS NOT ON THEIR OWN INITIATIVE BUT CONSTRAINED BY REASONABLE FEAR, AS WHEN, FOR

In this general section (lb. III, tract. V, cap. 2, dub. 2), Busenbaum considers types of activity possibly requiring restitution. He considers them as – and in the order in which – they are listed in the verses repeated by Thomas Aquinas at *ST* 2-2.62.7: "Command, counsel, consent, flattery, recourse, / participating, being silent, not preventing, not denouncing" [Iussio, consilium, consensus, palpo, recursus, / participans, mutus, non obstans, non manifestans]. At the beginning of §571, Alphonsus quotes what Busenbaum says of the sixth of these, "participating," and then, at some length, comments upon it. (Because Busenbaum and Alphonsus understand participating in an action and partaking of spoils as species of that to which the Latin word 'participatio' refers, and also exploit this linguistic connection in presenting their theory, in what follows I translate 'participans,' 'participantes,' 'participatio,' etc., in such a way that this connection is maintained. For instance, I speak of "participating in spoils," even though standard English would speak of partaking of spoils.)

EXAMPLE, A THEFT HAVING BEEN COMMITTED BY SOLDIERS, COUNTRY DWELLERS ARE FORCED TO CONVEY THE SPOILS OR TO LEAD AWAY CATTLE. — LESSIUS.

Participants can be understood in two ways, namely: as participating in a thing stolen or in the action of theft. Participants *in a thing stolen* are indeed obliged to give back as much of it as came to them. As for participants *in the action of theft*, however, it needs to be ascertained whether they cooperate in the whole of the injury or in part – according to what is said below in §579.

But, if the participation is in the action of theft, the question is: *Whether those who cooperate in some way in the infliction of the injury would be excused from restitution on account of grave fear of harm?*

[I] The *first* position – which among more recent authors is the most common and is maintained by the Salmanticenses, Sporer, Holzmann, and Viva, together with Lessius and Bonacina – makes a distinction. If the actions of the cooperator remotely cooperate in the theft, as would be holding a ladder for a thief who ascends it, handing over keys or instruments in order to open a strong-box, bearing away spoils already lifted, and similar actions, then the one who cooperates because of fear of death or some other grave injury is excused both from restitution and from fault since these actions are per se indifferent, nor do they harm the owner except as issuing from the wickedness of the thief. – On the other hand, if the actions are proximately flowing into the theft,[1] as would be breaking open gates, setting fire to a house, manufacturing false keys, tossing stolen things from a window, leading cattle away from their sta-

1. I resist the temptation to translate "influentes in furtum" as "influencing the theft" or "having an influence upon the theft" since the idea behind the Latin word is much more specific than that. A person who holds a ladder for a thief has an influence upon the theft (as we would say in English) but his action does not "flow into" the theft. It is true that here Alphonsus specifies that the "influxio" is proximate (so that also material cooperation might be an "influxio" but not a proximate one); in other passages, however, where he is clearly speaking of formal cooperation, he does not make this specification. In his *Homo Apostolicus*, for instance, Alphonsus says that formal cooperation is that cooperation "which comes about when one directly cooperates in a sin (as in him who fornicates), or else when it flows into the bad will of one's neighbor who wills to sin" ["quae evenit cum directe cooperatur ad peccatum (ut est in eo, qui fornicatur): aut cum influit in pravam voluntatem proximi volentis peccare"] [Alphonsus Maria de Ligorio, *Homo Apostolicus*, tract. 4 punct. 5 §31 (v. 1 p. 121)].

ble, and similar actions, then the one who cooperates is excused neither from restitution nor from fault. The reason is, as they say, that these actions, in as much as they are intrinsically evil, cannot be excused on account of whatever fear. — So maintain the authors cited.

(Indeed, the Salmanticenses, reversing themselves, say that even actions of the first type, referred to in the first location, are equally intrinsically evil.[2] The reason, they assert, is that these actions flow proximately into the sin of injustice which the thief intends to commit; and so they turn out to be intrinsically evil and formally unjust, even if performed in order to avoid death.)[3]

And although, in the face of such a degree of danger it is licit secretly to take away or to destroy goods belonging to another (for in this case the owner would be irrationally unwilling if he – you being in a situation of extreme necessity – should not be willing to consent to your receiving or destroying his goods in order that you might save your life), you cannot, however, in the face of any fear whatsoever cooperate proximately in an unjust act of theft, for then you would formally cooperate in his sin and you would offend justice. And so, if you do this, you sin and are obliged to make restitution. — To this extent Viva and Roncaglia excuse you: if the evil that threatens is great and the inconvenience that the owner is to suffer is light, or if the harm would be inflicted all the same, even if you do not help – to which consents also Laymann, together with St. Antoninus, de Palude, Molina, Pedro de Navarra, Adrianus, and Sylvester, as was said in §563, at the words "Et sic."

[II] The *second* position, however, which Busenbaum (see book II, §68, at the end) Sánchez, and Lessius hold, judges that such participants

2. The "first location" is volume 3 of the *Cursus theologiæ moralis* [Salmanticenses (Collegium Fratrum Discalceatorum Beatae Mariae de Monte Carmeli primitivae observantiae) (Venice: N. Pezzana, 1750), tract. 13 cap. 1 §129]; the Salmanticenses reverse themselves in volume 5 of the same work, tract. 21 cap. 8 §75.

3. I depart here from the Gaudé edition's format. They do not put this paragraph in parentheses and do not mark a paragraph change at the words, "Et quamvis . . ." ("And although . . ."). But since after the latter words, Alphonsus returns to the "first position," which recognizes a distinction between remote and proximate cooperation in the relevant regards, setting off the Salmanticenses late change-of-heart in this way helps one to grasp the structure of the argument.

do not sin if they contribute the aforesaid actions because of fear of great harm.[4]

With regard to this problem, in the manner in which I put forward my opinion – submitting it to the wise as one who is less wise, no one preceding me – so I speak. This sin of a cooperator can be considered either with respect to the owner who is to suffer the harm or with respect to the thief inflicting the harm.

1st. *With respect to* the owner, I say, that if you fear only the loss of your means, you cannot without sin cooperate in someone else's loss in order that you might preserve yourself from loss regarding your own goods – unless you do this with the intention of compensating [the other], as assert Bonacina, Viva and Lessius, along with Navarrus.[5] If, however, you fear an evil of a superior order than the order of the goods, namely death or mutilation of a bodily member, or grave infamy, then you could without sin – if you do so beside your intention [praeter intentionem] – cooperate in the harm of another, as says the author who continued the work of Tournély.[6] For then the owner is obliged to consent, even with the loss if his own goods, to your looking to your life or honor; otherwise he would be irrationally unwilling.[7]

2nd. *With respect*, however, *to the sin of the thief*, I advise the second, more probable position.[8] The reason is that all of the aforementioned

4. With the phrase "such participants" ["eiusmodi participantes"], Alphonsus is referring to those who cooperate proximately. Alphonsus favors this position, which allows that even proximate cooperation can be licit, given certain dire circumstances. (As John DeJak has pointed out to me, the word translated here 'harm' – that is, *nocumentum* – might also be translated 'nuisance.')

5. The Gaudé edition notes that Navarrus, although agreed with the other authors mentioned on all other points, says nothing about an "intention of compensating."

6. See above, appendix 1, note 14.

7. The Gaudé edition appends a note here indicating that Alphonsus qualified this teaching in the sixth edition of his *Istruztione e prattica* (Naples, 1765), cap.10, §56: "In my *Theologia moralis*, I made this point in another manner, saying that the action of the cooperator must be considered differently than the sin of the thief. Regarding the harm, I said that no one can cooperate in harm to another in order to avoid harm to oneself, when the harm is of the same order. This, however, holds when the cooperation is, in itself, cause of the harm but not when it is material, for then I am not obliged, with equal harm to myself, to avoid harm to another."

8. He advises, that is, II (the second position).

actions, whether of the first or the second type,[9] are in truth indifferent, since, according to the end for which they come about, they can be either licit or illicit. For if you contribute them with the vicious end of harming the master, certainly they will be for you illicit. If, however, you contribute them in order to prevent harm to yourself, whether to your life or to your honor, then they will be licit for you – and the thief's ill using them, in order to effect his corrupt will, is related per accidens: you would then cooperate with his sin only materially, which for a just cause you permit licitly. Nor is it true that you formally run up to the sin of theft, for this would be the case if you positively brought your influence into his bad will. When, however, you contribute only those actions that the thief afterwards ill uses in order to inflict damage, your action will not be the cause of the damage but only the malice of the thief will be (according to what we have said at more length in book II, §63, at the words, "Sed melius").[10] And that these actions would not be formally flowing into the sin of the thief nor intrinsically evil (as the adversaries affirm) to me appears indubitable. For otherwise, if a thief should force you to break open your own strong-box in order to hand over to him the money there contained, you would not be able to do this without sin, for you would formally cooperate in his sin. Who, however, of sound mind would be so audacious as to assert that?

Expressly lending me support is the teaching of Father Molina, who teaches as follows: *Subject to fear of death or loss of limb, it is permissible for such captives to inflict damage upon Christians with respect to their external goods, upon the order of infidels destroying them, seizing them....*[11] *For in that*

9. Alphonsus is referring here to the two types of action he has identified under the "first position": that is (1) to the type, introduced with the words, "If the actions of the cooperator remotely cooperate in the theft ..." ["Si actiones cooperantis remote concurrant ad furtum ..."], and (2) to the second type, introduced with the words, "On the other hand, if the actions are proximately flowing into the theft ..." ["Secus, si actiones sint proxime influentes in furtum ..."] [*Theologia moralis*, lb. 3 n. 571 p. 66ab].

10. In the translation of II, §63, these words are rendered, "But it is better."

11. The passage in Molina which Alphonsus is quoting [*De iustitia et iure*, tract. 2 disp. 115 concl. 5] is actually about cooperating during an unjust war; he considers, for instance, the cooperation engaged in by captives who are required to row the boats of infidels, etc. The words eliminated after the word "capiendi" ["seizing them"] are "& ad triremes asportando" ["and carrying [the goods] away to triremes"]. The text

event they are in extreme need of those goods for the conservation of their own life. Therefore, to the extent that it is permissible for someone in extreme need to take from among the goods of another in order to save his own life, to that extent will it also be permissible for such captives to inflict harm with respect to external goods in order to protect their own life. So says Molina. — The author who continued the work of Tournély upholds with me the same position in the place where he says the following: *For I am not obliged to suffer great damage so that I might avert the sin of another; he himself (namely, the thief) would reasonably impute his own wickedness to himself. This would be imputed to me incorrectly since this only I intend: to look to my own things and protect them from harm.*[12] — And this is expressly confirmed by St. Thomas who says: *It is licit for him who falls among thieves to show goods which he has, which the thieves sin in seizing, in order not to be killed; an example would be the ten men who say to Ishmael:* Do not kill us for we have treasures hidden in the field (Jer 41:8).[13]

There is a greater problem: *Whether such a cooperator is obliged to make restitution?* All of the authors cited in favor of the first position say yes, as we said above. But, considering the intrinsic sense of the matter, it seems to me, along with Father Milante, that it is more probable that the cooperator neither sins nor is obliged to make restitution.

This question appears to depend upon another (discussed in book III, quaer. 5, §520: see the words "Sic igitur"); that is, the question, Whether he who in extreme necessity takes away secretly the goods of another, the necessity having ceased, is obliged to make restitution? There we said that the position is true that says that he is obliged if in hope he was not a pauper; the answer would be otherwise if he was a pauper both in fact and in hope. — And this appears to be what ought to be said in the present case; that is, that, if out of fear of death or of grave infamy the participant cooperates in harm to another, he is considered dispensed from restitution only if at the time of the cooperation he was absolutely a pauper: that is, not only a pauper in fact but also in hope.[14]

---

then picks up with the words, "quoniam in eo eventu . . ." ["For in that event . . ."].

12. Collet, *Praelectionum theologicarum Honorati Tournely continuatio*, cap. 2 a. 6 sect. 3 concl. 3.

13. See *ST* 2-2.78.4c.

14. In book III, §520, "Quaeritur 5°," Alphonsus asks whether a person who, faced

But here I maintain, employing the same distinction as above, that, if the participant helps the thief to inflict the harm because of fear of similarly grave harm to his own goods, in this case he is obliged to make restitution, for no one can cooperate in harm to another in order to avoid personal harm to one's goods. — The situation is different, I believe, if he helps the thief, coerced by the fear of death or of grave infamy.[15] The reason is that then this person is not obliged to make restitution: not by reason of a thing accepted, nor by reason of an unjust accepting. Not by reason of a thing accepted, because he is made richer in nothing; not by reason of an unjust accepting, because he has not sinned, as we have already shown. But you will say: Why, when he is not absolutely a pauper, is he who in extreme necessity uses something belonging to another, obliged to make restitution? I respond: the reason he is obliged is that he can provide for himself from that which is his own. In accepting things

with extreme necessity, has secretly taken something belonging to another, once the necessity is no longer present, is obliged to make restitution. He begins his answer by saying that the answer to this question depends upon the answer to another question: i.e., whether a rich man satisfies his obligation to help the poor if, when he comes across a person in extreme need, he does give but with the stipulation that, if the poor man's fortunes change for the better, he (the rich man) will be paid back. Also a factor here is Thomas Aquinas's teaching (*ST* 2-2.66.7 ad 2) that one who is in dire need licitly appropriates goods not belonging to him, in effect then becoming their owner. (Restitution is not owed, of course, with respect to one's own property.) Alphonsus's answer to this complex question is that, if the "pauper" at the time of his need, is *absolutely* a pauper, the rich man is "obliged to come to his aid entirely gratis" ["si pauper tempore necessitatis est absolute pauper, tunc dives tenetur omnino gratis ei succurrere"]; if, on the other hand, the person at the time of his need has goods in another location or has a reasonable hope of attaining such goods, the rich man can simply make him a loan, for the other "is not absolutely a pauper, nor can he absolutely seize the thing of another and make it his own" ["quia tunc ille non est absolute pauper nee posset rem alterius absolute arripere, et suam facere"]. In the present passage, therefore, it is presumed in all the cases under consideration that the cooperator (or the "participant"), at the time when he is forced to cooperate, is in need: a pauper "in fact" ["re"]. The question then is whether he is also a pauper "in hope" [spe], that is (as Alphonsus says in book III, §520) whether, at the time of his need, his situation is a temporary one with a good hope of being remedied later. If the latter is the case, then the cooperator (participant) is not a pauper "absolutely" and so is obliged to make restitution.

15. In a note, the Gaudé edition says that the position enunciated here must be tempered, given what Alphonsus says in his *Istruzione e prattica*: see above, note 7.

that belong to another, when he is not able to accept that which is his own, which he has in another place, at that point he ends up more rich – and so he is obliged. But, in our case, the cooperator becomes richer in nothing and therefore he is obliged to make restitution of nothing. Neither is he obliged to offer or substitute his own goods in order to repair the harm done to the other.

Agreeing with me is the learned Father, Master Milante, where he says that he who contributes actions such as help the thief does not sin, nor is he obliged to make restitution. For he writes as follows: *And so whoever cooperates with these out of fear affecting a constant man cooperates without inflicting harm.*[16] *For why is seizing the property of another ... evil, and indeed intrinsically so ... ? Without a doubt, for this reason solely: because the owner or the creditor suffers the evil unwillingly.... But in the aforementioned case, the owner and the creditor would not be unwilling regarding whichever evil that they suffer, the thing indeed having been borne away.... And in this way it is to be presumed ..., since no one can be presumed unwilling in a case in which a neighbor or cooperator in a theft ... is impelled by such a great harm or danger; no one indeed can disregard the life of a neighbor for the sake of a temporal good, as is common sense and a dictate of nature.*[17] At this point he

16. Milante is referring here to the acts he has just introduced: (1) someone's putting instruments useful for break-ins at the disposal of a thief when the thief threatens harm to one who refuses, and (2) a debtor's failure to pay a creditor when his reason for so failing is "fear affecting a constant man." Such acts are introduced as part of an objection to his own arguments in support of Innocent XI's condemnation of proposition 51 (which proposition maintains that a servant who "submits his shoulders so that his master can ascend through windows to ravage a virgin" does not sin mortally if he does this out of fear of probable harm). The objection argues that, given that the aforementioned acts do not require restitution to the owner or to the creditor, why can a servant not help his master ascend through a window? The expression "out of fear affecting a constant man" ["ex metu cadente in virum constantem"] was a standard way of referring to fear that is not the unreasonable fear of the pusillanimous man. This reasonable fear is found midway between the temerity of the rash man and the fearfulness of pusillanimous man. The basic idea comes from Aristotle: see *Nicomachean Ethics* 2.7 1107a33–b4. The particular wording employed by Milante appears in Sánchez's *De sancto matrimonii sacramento*, book 4 ("De consensu coacto"), disputation 5 ("Quae sint mala gravia, & sufficientia metus cadentis in virum constantem?").

17. By his use of ellipses, Alphonsus has rather mangled the sense of the original. Milante's basic point is that, in cases such as that in which burgling tools are supplied,

asserts that the cooperator is well excused both from guilt and from restitution. And the same is found in the position of Laymann, who, along with Pedro de Navarra and Medina, in a similar case says the following: *If someone should throw merchandise belonging to another into the sea lest he perish himself, he is not obliged to make any restitution, for he neither inflicts harm, nor does he take possession of something belonging to another.*

The situation is quite different, I believe, if one should cooperate in a way that confirms or augments the bad will of a thief — for instance, if one should protect the back for the thief (to use the colloquial, *guardasse le spalle*),[18] or if one should inform him of the opportune time for thieving, and such like — for in these cases one brings one's influence into the corrupt will of the thief, rendering him at the least more eager, and in this way one cooperates formally in the sin of the other, which is never licit.

The situation is also different if one should provide acts of cooper-

---

there are two instances of harm: that inflicted by the malefactor and that inflicted (under grave pressure) by the cooperator. One of them, the owner of the stolen property can be said to suffer unwillingly: the harm inflicted by the thief. The other, the harm inflicted by the cooperator, given that it is forced upon the latter, the owner suffers willingly, since presumably he would not want the cooperator to lose his life (for instance) in order to safeguard the property. (As mentioned in the previous note, Milante also mentions a case having to do with a debtor who, out of "fear affecting a constant man," fails to pay a creditor. Alphonsus has attempted — not wholly successfully — to excise this second case from the quotation since it does not correspond precisely to the cases that here interest him.) Here is the passage from Milante without the excisions: "At in casu paritatis opera illa in medium producta nullimode sunt adversa divinae naturali legi, ideoque iis innoxie cooperatur quicumque ex metu cadente in virum constantem ad ea concurrit. Ut quid enim aliena rapere , aut debitum non restituere malum est, & quidem ab intrinseco, & contra legem divinam naturalem? Procul dubio ex eo solum quia dominus vel creditor invitus patitur malum, hinc eiusdem ius laeditur. At in casu praefato dominus & creditor inviti non forent circa utrumque malum, quod paterentur, ablatae nimirum rei, vel debiti non redditi, sicque praesumendum est de utroque: cum nemo possit praesumi invitus in casu in quo proximo, aut cooperanti in furtum, aut non restituenti debitum, tam grave damnum, & periculum immineret. Nemo quippe potest proponere vitam proximi temporali bono, ut est omnium sensus & naturae dictamen" [Milante, *Exercitationes dogmatico-morales in propositiones proscriptas a SS. Innocentio XI*, ex. 28, p. 302a].

18. The Italian expression means (if one should) "watch the shoulders"; the reference is to the activity of a lookout.

ation to one who is about to kill, handing over a sword or keys for the purpose of killing (see book III, §697, at *Probabilissimum*), or offering one's shoulders for the purpose of ascending, or carrying a ladder, etc. — the Salmanticenses, along with Soto, Lessius, Bañez, Tapia, Aragon, Villalobos — also Lacroix, along with Sánchez and Bonacina, say correctly that this is to be understood if the person might deny his cooperation without danger of death or of some equally grave danger, for otherwise he is not obliged to prevent the harm of the other (even if the other stands in extreme peril of suffering harm) with equal injury to himself. — Hence we have said in *de Caritate*, book II, §66, that, when the master wants to ascend in order to debauch a virgin, fear of no harm, except of imminent death, can excuse a servant in helping his master by carrying a ladder, lowering his shoulders, etc. For only the life of the servant prevails over the honor of the virgin.

On this point, however, I am bewildered why Fr. Milante, when he has said that the aforesaid actions, in connection with cooperation with stealing, are not intrinsically evil, in the same place should assert that the same actions are intrinsically evil in connection with cooperation with fornicating, when equally in either case no disparity can be attributed — as the Salmanticenses rightly acknowledge. — But we, having exhaustively considered the matter from its own principles, judge it to have been clearly proved that in neither case are those acts of cooperation, a just and proportionate cause intervening, intrinsically evil.

APPENDIX 3 ALPHONSUS LIGUORI, *THEOLOGIA MORALIS*, BOOK 2, §§43–45 (ON SCANDAL) DUBIUM V: REGARDING SCANDAL

Article 1: What is it? How multiform is it? What sort of sin is it?

43. What sort of thing active scandal is, and what passive. – 44. Busenbaum's resolution of various cases. – 45. When is scandal a special sin. – 46. Whether the circumstance of inducement must be mentioned explicitly in confession. – 47. Whether it is licit sometimes to request of someone who is prepared to sin that which he cannot give without sin.

43. I RESPOND THAT SCANDAL IS SAID TO BE A SIN WHICH IS "OCCASIONED"; IT IS ALSO TWOFOLD: ACTIVE AND PASSIVE.

ACTIVE IS A SOME LESS THAN CORRECT REMARK OR DEED (BY WHICH TERM IS UNDERSTOOD ALSO AN OMISSION) THAT PROVIDES OCCASION FOR ANOTHER'S SPIRITUAL RUIN. THIS IS FROM ST. THOMAS, SÁNCHEZ, AZOR, LAYMANN AND BONACINA. — BY "LESS THAN CORRECT" I MEAN WHAT IS EITHER IN ITSELF BAD (IF, FOR INSTANCE, YOU SHOULD SAY LEWD THINGS BEFORE A YOUNG PERSON) OR HAS THE APPEARANCE OF EVIL (IF, FOR INSTANCE, ON LEGITIMATE GROUNDS, YOU

SHOULD EAT MEAT ON A DAY WHEN IT IS FORBIDDEN BEFORE OTHERS WHO KNOW NOTHING OF THESE GROUNDS).

— ONE TYPE OF ACTIVE SCANDAL IS PER SE; ANOTHER IS PER ACCIDENS. SCANDAL IS CALLED *PER SE* WHEN THE RUIN OF THE OTHER IS DIRECTLY INTENDED, THAT IS, IF SOMEONE DOES SOMETHING PRECISELY IN ORDER THAT SOMEONE MIGHT BE LED INTO SIN: E.G., IF AN ADULTERER SHOULD INDUCE A WOMAN WHO IS NOT HIS WIFE [*ALIENA*] TO COMMIT ADULTERY. SCANDAL IS CALLED *PER ACCIDENS* WHEN THE SIN OF THE OTHER IS ONLY INDIRECTLY AND INTERPRETATIVELY CAUSED: IF, FOR INSTANCE, YOU ARE AWARE THAT THAT WHICH YOU DO IS, HERE AND NOW, INHERENTLY APT TO LEAD THE OTHER INTO SIN BUT YOU DO IT ANYWAY—IF, FOR INSTANCE, YOU SIN IN FRONT OF "LITTLE ONES," OR IF, ON A DAY WHEN IT IS FORBIDDEN, YOU SHOULD EAT MEAT, NOT EXPLAINING THAT YOU ARE PERMITTED TO DO SO; AND, SIMILARLY, IF A CLERIC SHOULD MAINTAIN IN HIS HOUSE A WOMAN HELD SUSPECT BY THE PUBLIC, GIVEN THAT NO SIN OR EVEN DANGER OF SIN IS PRESENT. SEE SÀ, LAYMANN, BONACINA.

PASSIVE SCANDAL IS THE VERY RUIN OR SIN INTO WHICH A NEIGHBOR FALLS ON THE OCCASION OF THE REMARK OR DEED OF ANOTHER; AND THIS IS DIVIDED INTO *GIVEN* SCANDAL OR SCANDAL *OF THE LITTLE ONES*, WHICH COMES ABOUT BECAUSE OF ACTIVE SCANDAL, AND *ACCEPTED* SCANDAL, WHICH DOES NOT COME ABOUT BECAUSE OF ACTIVE SCANDAL BUT BECAUSE OF THE MALICE OF THE ONE WHO TAKES SCANDAL, SUCH AS WAS THE HOSTILITY AND ENVY OF THE PHARISEES WITH REGARD TO CHRIST, THE OCCASION BEING HIS WORDS AND ACTIONS; AND SO THIS IS CALLED SCANDAL *OF THE PHARISEES*.

FROM ALL THIS IT IS CLEAR THAT:

1ST. IT IS NOT REQUIRED FOR ACTIVE SCANDAL THAT IT RESULT IN FACT IN PASSIVE, BUT IT IS SUFFICIENT THAT THE OCCASION BE GIVEN, THE NATURE OF WHICH IS SUCH THAT IT COULD RESULT: IF, FOR INSTANCE, YOU SHOULD WISH TO INDUCE SOMEONE TO A SIN—WHO, HOWEVER, DOES NOT CONSENT, JUST AS, ON THE OTHER HAND, PASSIVE SCANDAL CAN BE GIVEN WITHOUT ACTIVE.[1] LAYMANN.

1. The Latin here reads: "sicut etiam contra, passivum potest dari sine activo." One might avoid difficulties of interpretation by translating this, "just as, on the other hand, passive scandal can be attributed without active"; but, since Busenbaum introduces the term *scandalum datum* in this section, that would seem to be too easy a solution.

2ND. PASSIVE SCANDAL IS NOT THE SPECIAL SIN, NOR DOES IT ADD AN AGGRAVATING CIRCUMSTANCE. FOR EXAMPLE, ONE WHO, HAVING SEEN THE THEFT OF ANOTHER, ENGAGES IN THEFT HIMSELF, DOES NOT FOR THAT REASON SIN MORE GRIEVOUSLY. LAYMANN.

3RD. IT IS NOT ALWAYS SCANDAL IF YOU SIN BEFORE OTHERS BUT ONLY WHEN, TAKING INTO CONSIDERATION CIRCUMSTANCES BOTH OF THE PERSON WHO ACTS AND OF THOSE BEFORE WHOM THE ACT IS PERFORMED, IT IS POSSIBLE THAT IT IS PROBABLY TO BE FEARED THAT BY MEANS OF THAT ACT THOSE MIGHT BE DRAWN INTO SIN WHO OTHERWISE WOULD NOT GO ON TO SIN. — SÁNCHEZ, LAYMANN.

4TH. EVERY ACTIVE SCANDAL, DIRECTLY INTENDING THE RUIN OF A NEIGHBOR, IS A SPECIAL SIN CONTRARY TO CHARITY, THIS BEING MAINTAINED BY ALL. BUT WHETHER THE SAME HOLDS WHEN IT IS INTENDED INDIRECTLY, THIS IS DEBATED BY THE SCHOLASTICS, WITH SCARCE REFERENCE TO PRACTICE. — SÁNCHEZ, AZOR, BONACINA.

ON THE BASIS OF WHICH YOU CAN RESOLVE THE FOLLOWING CASES:

44. — 1ST. HE WHO GIVES OCCASION TO ANOTHER OF MORTAL RUIN SINS MORTALLY, UNLESS LACK OF DELIBERATION EXCUSES HIM. AND IN THIS WAY A WORK THAT IS EITHER INDIFFERENT OR VENIAL OFTEN BECOMES MORTAL, BY REASON OF SCANDAL—FOR EXAMPLE, IF A RELIGIOUS MAKES A REMARK IN JEST BEFORE WOMEN OR BEFORE THOSE WHO MIGHT DRAW FROM IT THE OCCASION OF MORTAL SIN. — LAYMANN.

2ND. HE WHO GIVES TO ANOTHER THE OCCASION ONLY OF VENIAL RUIN SINS VENIALLY BY REASON OF THE SCANDAL. THIS IS TRUE EVEN THOUGH HE INTENDS THE RUIN DIRECTLY AND, INDEED, BY MEANS OF AN ACT THAT IS MORTAL. SÁNCHEZ, DRAWING ON THE COMMON POSITION, AGAINST SUÁREZ. THE REASON IS THAT THE RUIN IS SLIGHT. AND THIS IS CLEAR FROM A PARALLEL CASE—IF, FOR INSTANCE, BY MEANS OF FORNICATION SOMEONE INTENDS TO STEAL SOME TRIFLING THING: THE THEFT ITSELF WILL BE VENIAL.

3RD. ONE WHO SCANDALIZES COMMITS, BESIDES THE SIN OF SCANDAL, ALSO A SIN OF THAT SPECIES TOWARD WHICH HE INDUCES THE OTHER; AND SO HE IS OBLIGED TO CONFESS THE SPECIES OF MORTAL SIN BY MEANS OF WHICH AND TOWARD WHICH HE INDUCES, ALONG WITH THE NUMBER OF THOSE WHO WERE INDUCED OR PROBABLY MIGHT HAVE BEEN INDUCED. SÁNCHEZ, AZOR, LAYMANN,

Bonacina, Cardinal Lugo, Diana. Cardinal Lugo, however, makes an exception if the person gives scandal beside his intention. — Tamburini [along with Lugo][2] says that, regarding those induced, it is sufficient if you say, "I was one time the occasion of sin for many by my bad example."[3]

4th. Although one who has scandalized others is obliged to give in return good example (as says Sà), if, however, one induced others toward theft merely by his example and has not cooperated by any other particular means, such as by exhortation, counsel, ordering, he is not obliged to make restitution, since such inducing is contrary only to charity and not to justice. [Thus also Sánchez, the Salmanticenses, along with Molina, Bonacina, Dicastillo and others in common with Roncaglia – who says correctly that, even if one sins against justice (according to the more probable opinion that we follow in the following number, §45), he is not obliged to make restitution, since he is not the cause but only the occasion of the injury. See the next number, toward the end.] Lessius teaches the same: if, for example, you should drink with Caius, for example, with the precise intention that he, his money depleted, should steal. See Lessius.

5th. Not regarded as giving scandal is one who, although he sins publicly, does so however before those who are so vile or notorious or morally unsound—or, on the other hand, are so morally sound—that none would be moved to sin: if, for example, someone should fornicate before others who are prepared to do the same and are not moved by his example, or if someone should contend or quarrel or strike another before persons who are tenderhearted. — Sánchez.

6th. A particular deed is not a scandal because another begins to suspect or to think ill of such a man, for he does not sin if he suspects on account of sufficient indications. The situation is otherwise if he should begin to think ill of the Catholic Faith, the clergy, a religious

2. The text interjected here is not in Busenbaum. It does not appear in the 1748 Naples edition of the *Theologia moralis*; it appears as early as the 1785 Venice edition. (Alphonsus died in 1787.) The same holds of other text included in the main text of this translation in square brackets.

3. The Gaudé edition refers the reader to [Alphonsus Maria de Ligorio, *Theologia moralis*, v. 2 lb. 5 §46, ad 4.

ORDER, OR TO BE LESS MOVED TOWARD PIETY. THUS IT IS CLEAR THAT SCANDAL IS MORE EASILY GIVEN BY THOSE IN POSITIONS OF GREAT AUTHORITY, OR WHO ARE ESTEEMED PIOUS, THAN BY OTHERS. — CONINCK.

45. — Here it is worth the trouble to reconsider critically three questions, extremely necessary both theoretically and practically.[4]

Question 1: *When is scandal a special sin?* — There are three opinions.

The *first opinion* asserts that scandal is the special sin against charity only when the spiritual ruin of one's neighbor is directly intended. Thus Sánchez, Bonacina, along with, according to the Salmanticenses, Palaus, Azor, Bañez, Trullench, and so on. The reasoning of these learned men is that, in order for some sin to be distinct in a special way it must have a special end contrary to the corresponding virtue. But, when the ruin of one's neighbor is not intended, charity is not harmed in a special way; harmed rather is that virtue which the neighbor is induced to harm. And so such scandal is reduced to that species of sin toward which the neighbor is induced, whether directly by order or by counsel, or indirectly by words or example.

The *second opinion*, which Lugo holds, along with Navarrus, also Tamburini along with other more recent writers, makes a distinction and says that someone can induce another to sin in three ways: 1st, directly and formally, intending the latter's spiritual ruin; 2nd, directly but not formally, when, that is, someone wants another to violate chastity — not now in order that the other might lose his soul but in order that he might give satisfaction to the very person doing the inducing; 3rd, indirectly, namely when the other draws the occasion of sinning from one's example. — On this basis they maintain that, if the scandal occurs in the first or second way, the one scandalizing sins not only against charity but also against the virtue which the neighbor is induced to harm. — When, however, he sins in the third way, that is, foreseeing but not intending the neighbor's sin, in that case he sins only against charity but not against the virtue which is harmed: he is, therefore, not obliged to make explicit

4. Translated here is just the first (more theoretical) question. The other two are (§46) "Whether the circumstances of inducing to fornication are to be made explicit in confession," and (§47) "Whether it is a sin of scandal to ask of someone something which he will not give without sinning, if he is already prepared to sin."

the species of the latter.[5] The reason is that the rest of the virtues do not oblige one – at least not gravely, according to what Lugo has said – to impede in others the opposed vices; they only oblige one to not positively intend to induce a neighbor to offend those virtues.

The *third opinion*, to which I subscribe, holds that one who directly or indirectly induces a neighbor to sin sins *in two ways*: that is, both against charity and against the virtue toward the harming of which he induces the neighbor.

1st. That he sins against charity cannot, it seems to me, be denied; and I am unable to acquiesce to the first opinion put forward. If charity obliges us, when we can, to correct or impede our neighbor lest he fall ruined into sin, how much more does it oblige us not to impel him into sin by counsel or example! Nor does the argument adduced – that in order to harm charity required is a special end of harming it – stand in the way of this position, for speaking generally it suffices to place something destructive of whatever virtue for that virtue to be offended – even though this is not intended. For instance, if someone kills an enemy in a church, even though he might not intend to commit an offense against religion, nonetheless he sins not only against justice but also against religion, since by the very act he harms it. And so hold Lugo, the author who continued the work of Tournély,[6] Roncaglia, Tamburini, the Salmanticenses, along with Soto, de Valentia, Suárez, Tapia, and Prado. Also St. Thomas expressly teaches this, for, although Sánchez cites him for his own opinion regarding *ST* 2-2.43.3, nonetheless the holy teacher speaks in the following way: "... when someone by an evil remark or deed [facto] intends to induce the other to sin or also, if he does not intend this, the very thing he does [factum] is ... an inducement to sin ..., then he gives occasion of ruin, and thus it is called active scandal."[7]

5. That is, in confession.

6. Reference here is to Peter Collet; see above, appendix 1, note 14.

7. Alphonsus is quoting *ST* 2-2.43.1 ad 4; his quotation, with ellipses, is as follows: "... quando aliquis suo malo verbo vel facto intendit alium ad peccandum inducere; vel, etiam si ipse hoc non intendat, ipsum factum est ... inductivum ad peccandum ... tunc ille ... dat occasionem ruinae, unde vocatur scandalum activum." The fuller passage reads as follows: "One person's remark or deed can be the cause of another's sin in two ways: per se and per accidens. It is per se when someone by an evil remark or deed [facto]

2nd. That, however, he sins also *against the virtue* he induced (although indirectly) the neighbor to harm [neither can this be denied]. The reason is that any virtue not only prohibits contrary acts but also prohibits providing occasion that is inductive of others to sin, for then that occasion, although it is not in itself an inflowing cause, is however a moral cause to the effect that the neighbor sins.[8] That is called a *moral cause* which is substantially equivalent to a cause directly inducing to sin since, without it, the neighbor would not sin. Thus: Cajetan, Sánchez, Roncaglia, the author who continued the work of Tournély, and the Salmanticenses, along with Tapia.[9]

One who, however, by his example might induce another to steal, although he sins against justice with a double sin, is not obliged to make restitution, as are agreed in teaching the learned men Molina, Bonacina, Sánchez, Roncaglia, the Salmanticenses, against the author who continued the work of Tournély, together with Antoine. — The reason is that that example is not a directly inflowing cause but only an occasion, which does not provide a positive inflowing to the stealing such as is required for the obligation to make restitution.

---

either intends to induce the other to sin or also, if he does not intend this, the very thing he does [factum] is such that of its own intelligibility [ratione] it is an inducement to sin: for instance, when a person commits a sin publicly or does what has the appearance of sin. And then he who performs such an act does, properly speaking, give occasion of ruin, and so the act is called 'active scandal.'" Thomas goes on then to speak about the per accidens, saying that it is "beside the intention of the agent and beside the condition of the thing done" ["praeter intentionem operantis, et praeter conditionem operis"].

8. The word *influxiva* (translated here "inflowing") is not entirely a neologism on Alphonsus's part. It appears also, for instance, in John of St. Thomas.

9. Alphonsus at this point refers to what he will say two numbers later: "question 3, §47, toward the end."

APPENDIX 4 THOMAS AQUINAS, *QUAESTIONES DISPUTATAE DE MALO*, QUESTION 2, ARTICLE 6

Whether a circumstance might give species to a sin or alter its species and thereby transfer it into a different type of sin

And it seems that not:

Objection 1: For the principle of a species is intrinsic but a circumstance is extrinsic, as its name suggests. Therefore, a circumstance does not give species to a sin.

Objection 2: But it was maintained that that which is a circumstance for an act considered in its natural species gives species to the act in as much as it is moral. On the contrary, however, as the object stands with respect to the act in general, so stands the moral object with respect to the moral act. But the object gives species to the act; therefore, the moral object gives species to the moral act. And so a circumstance does not.

Objection 3: Moreover, one and the same act of sin has many circumstances. If therefore a circumstance gives species to a sin, it follows that one and the same sin is in diverse species—which is impossible.

Objection 4: Moreover, that which is already constituted under a species does not accept a species from something else unless the first species corrupts. Theft, however, is already constituted in a species of sin, but, through this added circumstance of stealing from a sacred place or of a sacred object, the first species is not removed, for it remains a theft. So, the aforesaid circumstance does not give any species to the sin; nor, for the same reason, does any other circumstance.

Objection 5: Moreover, it appears that sins are differentiated one from the other according to excess or deficiency, for in this way stinginess is opposed to extravagance. But excess and deficiency apparently belong to one and the same circumstance, which is quantity. So, other circumstances do not diversify the species of sins.

Objection 6: Moreover, as Augustine says, every sin is voluntary; but the will does not look to a circumstance. For instance, when someone steals a golden cup which is also consecrated, he does not care whether it is consecrated but is interested only in the gold. So, this circumstance does not give species to the sin; nor, for the same reason, do other circumstances.

Objection 7: Moreover, that which does not remain but immediately disappears cannot be altered by the species that it had earlier. But the act of a sin does not remain but immediately disappears. So, a circumstance cannot alter the species of a sin.

Objection 8: Moreover, just as in certain circumstances a defect might occur in moral matters, so the same happens in natural things, for monstrosities occur in nature sometimes because of the narrowness of a place, sometimes because of an abundance of matter or also because of its diminution, and from other such causes. Nonetheless, however, what is born is the same in species. So, neither in moral matters is the species of a sin diversified through the corruption of diverse circumstances.

Objection 9: Moreover, the end gives species in moral matters, since a moral act is judged to be good or bad because of its intention. But the end is not a circumstance. So, a circumstance does not give species to a sin.

◆

Objection 10: Moreover, sin is opposed to virtue. But a circumstance does not alter the species of a virtue, for to benefit a cleric or a layman pertains to the same virtue, that is, to liberality or to mercy. So, a circumstance does not alter the species of a sin.

◆

Objection 11: Moreover, if a circumstance alters the species of a sin, it is necessary that it make the sin worse. But sometimes a circumstance does not make worse, in particular, one which is seen to alter the species – if one, for example, is not aware of the circumstance. For example, if someone has sexual intercourse with a woman who, unknown to him, is married, he commits adultery; the sin, however, does not appear to be made worse since that which is minimally voluntary has minimally the character of sin. So, such a circumstance does not alter the species of the sin.

◆

Objection 12: Moreover, if this circumstance, that the object is sacred, gives species to the sin while the theft remains, it follows that there are present both a sacrilege and a theft and thus that in one act the person commits two sins. And this would seem to be a difficulty.

◆

Objection 13: Moreover, according to the Philosopher in the *Nicomachean Ethics*, an action in moral matters is like a conclusion in theoretical matters. But a circumstance does not alter the species of a conclusion; so, neither does it alter the species of a moral act. And thus it does not give species to a sin.

◆

Objection 14: Moreover, just as there are certain moral acts, so also there are certain acts of a craft. But a circumstance does not alter the species of an act of a craftsman since it makes no difference, with respect to species of the craft, in what place or at what time or for what reason the craftsman makes a knife. So, neither does a circumstance alter the species of a moral act.

◆

Objection 15: Moreover, it is customary to distinguish evil according to genus from evil according to circumstance. But evil according to genus pertains to the very species of sin; therefore, evil according to circumstance does not pertain to the species of sin. So, a circumstance does not give species to a sin.

◆

Objection 16: Moreover, a circumstance in as much as it makes something worse makes it more evil. But more and less do not diversify a species. So, a circumstance that worsens a sin does not alter its species.

But, to the contrary:

Place is one of the circumstances. But place gives species to a sin, for there is said to be a sacrilege if someone steals from a sacred place. So, a circumstance gives species to a sin.

Moreover, if someone sexually knows a married woman, he commits adultery, which is a species of sin. But for a woman to be unmarried or married is a circumstance of the act. So, a circumstance gives species to a sin.

Response:

To determine this question three things must be taken into account: [I] first, from what does a sin have species; [II] secondly, what is a circumstance; and then, [III] thirdly, it will be possible to explain how a circumstance gives species to a sin.

◆

[I] As to the first, it must be taken into account that, since a moral act is a voluntary act proceeding from reason, it is necessary that a moral act have species according to something considered in the object that is related to reason. And so in the preceding question it is said that, if this thing is in accord with reason, the act will be good with respect to its species; if, however, it is discordant with reason, it will be bad with respect to its species.[1] That which is not in accord with reason with respect to the object

1. "Est autem aliquod obiectum quod importat aliquid conveniens rationi, et facit esse bonum ex genere, sicut vestire nudum; aliquod autem obiectum quod importat aliquid discordans a ratione, sicut tollere alienum, et hoc facit malum in genere" [*De malo* 2.5].

considered can diversify the species in two ways: one way is materially, the other is formally.

[Ia] Materially, because of opposition to virtue, for virtues differ in species according as reason finds the mean in various matters; for example, there is justice according as reason establishes the mean in exchanges and distributions and actions of that sort; temperance, according as it does so in objects of desire; fortitude, according as it does so in objects of fear and daring, and so on with respect to other matters.

Nor ought it to be seen as a problem if the species of virtues are differentiated according to diverse matters, on the grounds that usually diversity of matter is the cause not of diversity of species but of individuals, for also in natural things diversity of matter causes diversity of species when the diversity of matter requires diversity of form. And so also in moral matters it is necessary that there be virtues diverse in species regarding diverse matters in which reason finds the mean in different ways. For example, in objects of desire reason finds the mean in restraining, and so virtue established in these matters is nearer to the deficiency than to the excess, as the very name 'temperance' shows; in objects of daring and of fear, however, reason finds the mean not in restraining but rather in impelling, and so virtue established in these matters is nearer to the excess than to the deficiency, as the very name 'fortitude' shows. Similar things are to be seen in the others.

So too, therefore, because of opposition to virtues, sins differ in species according to their diverse matters, for example, homicide, adultery, and theft. Nor ought it to be said that these differ in species according to a difference of precepts but rather the converse: precepts are distinguished according to a difference of virtues and vices, for precepts exist so that we might act according to virtue and avoid sins. If, however, some things should be sins simply because they are prohibited, with respect to these, it would be reasonable for the sins to differ in species according to the difference of the precepts.

[Ib] But because, regarding a single matter, when there is one virtue it happens that there are sins diverse in species, it is necessary secondly to consider the diversity of species in sins formally—that is to say, as one sins either according to excess or according to deficiency, as timidity differs from presumption and stinginess from extravagance, or rather according to diverse circumstances, as the species of gluttony are distinguished according to the things mentioned in this verse: "Precipitously, sumptuously, excessively, rapaciously, fastidiously."

◆

[II] And so, having established how sins differ in species, to be considered is, what is a circumstance? It is said that a circumstance is that which 'stands around' an act, considered as if extrinsically outside of the substance of the act. [IIa] This occurs, however, [IIa.1] in one way, on the part of a cause, either of the final cause, when we consider why someone did something, or of the principal agent, when we consider who did it, or on the part of the instrument, when we consider with what instrument he did it or with what aids. It occurs [IIa.2] in another way, on the part of a measure, for instance, when we consider where or when he did it. It occurs [IIa.3] in a third way, on the part of the act itself, whether we consider the way of acting (whether, for instance, he struck lightly or forcefully, frequently or only once) or whether we consider the object or matter of the act (for instance, whether he struck his father or a foreigner), or also the effect he brought about in acting (for instance, whether striking, he wounded or also killed). All of which are contained in this verse: "Who, what, where, by what means, why, how, when" – in such a way, however, that not only the effect but also the object is included in "what," so that both "what" and "within what" are understood.

[IIb] Having therefore investigated these things, to be considered is the fact that, just as in other things something which is extrinsic to something higher is intrinsic to something lower – as 'rational' is outside the concept of animal but part of the concept of 'man' – in the same way, something is a circumstance with respect to an act considered more generally which cannot be called a circumstance with respect to an act considered more particularly. For example, if we consider this act which is to accept money, it is not part of that concept that the money belongs to another, and so 'belongs to another' stands with respect to the act so considered as a circumstance; but it is part of the concept of the theft that the money does belong to another, and so that is not a circumstance of the theft.

It is not, however, necessary that everything which is outside the concept of something higher be part of the concept of the lower thing, for just as white is not part of the concept 'animal,' so it is not part of the concept 'man.' It is related, therefore, to both accidentally. And similarly it is not necessary that everything which is a circumstance of a more general act constitute a species in acts, but only that which intrinsically per se pertains to an act. It has already been stated that something pertains per se to a moral act according as it is in accordance with or repugnant to reason.[2] If, therefore, the circumstance added brings in no special repugnance with respect to reason, it does not give species to the act: for instance, to use something that is white adds nothing that pertains to reason and thus 'white' does not constitute the species of the moral act. But to use something 'that belongs to another' does add something that pertains to reason and thus it does constitute the species of the moral act.

◆

[III] But to be considered further is that an added circumstance pertaining to reason can constitute a new species, in two ways.

[IIIa] One way is that in which the species constituted by the circumstance is a particular species of that sin which was previously considered in the more general act, whether the species of sin is constituted formally or rather materially. It is constituted materially if, for instance, on top of that which I called 'using something that belongs to another,' is added 'wife,' on account of which is constituted adultery. It is constituted formally if, for instance, I should take something belonging to another 'from a sacred place,' for it becomes sacrilege, which is a species of theft.

[IIIb] Sometimes, however, by virtue of a circumstance an entirely disparate species is constituted, not pertaining to the original genus of sin: for instance, if I steal something that belongs to another so that I might commit murder or simony, the sin is drawn into an entirely disparate species of sin. And we find something similar also in other things, for, if over and above 'colored,' 'white' is considered, it becomes a species of the quality first considered; if, however, over and above 'colored' 'sweet' is understood, it becomes an entirely disparate species of quality. The reason for this diversity is that, when that which is added is per se divisive of that to which it is added, it produces a species of it; when, however, it is related to it per accidens, it has its own species, which however

2. Thomas makes this point in *De malo* 2.6 [I], but also in *De malo* 2.5.

is not a species of that to which it is added, for that which comes in per accidens does not become one per se with that into which it comes.

In this way, therefore, it is apparent how a circumstance can constitute a species of sin.

Particular responses to the objections:

Ad 1 [as to objection 1]: That which is considered a circumstance and extrinsic with respect to an act considered in a particular way, can also be considered intrinsic with respect to the act considered in another way and to give it species.

Ad 2: Just as in general an act receives species from its object, so the moral act receives species from the moral object, although this does not exclude its receiving species from circumstances, since, on account of a circumstance, a new condition can be considered in the object through which the circumstance gives species to the act. For example, if I speak of 'taking something belonging to another that stands in a sacred place,' in this case the condition of the object is considered from the perspective of the circumstance of place, and so, because of the circumstance of place, it becomes the species of theft which is sacrilege – because, however, of the condition of the object.[3] And similarly this happens necessarily whenever a species of sin, which is constituted through a circumstance, is related to a previously understood sin as a species is related to its genus: as, for instance, sacrilege to theft or adultery to fornication. When, however, a species of sin coming from a circumstance is not a species of a previously understood sin but is another, disparate species, then it can be understood that the circumstance gives species, not because from it there results a condition regarding the object, but because that circumstance is considered the object of another act standing nearby [circumstantis]. For instance, if someone commits adultery in order to steal, there is added another species of sin on account of the act of intention tending toward the bad end that is the object of intention; and, similarly, if someone should perform an indecent act during a sacred time, the sacred time, which is considered a circumstance with respect to the indecent act that

3. Reading with the Leonine edition, "et tamen ex conditione obiecti."

comes about in it, can be considered an object with respect to another near lying act, that is, being contemptuous of sacred time. Similar things can be said of other things.

◆

Ad 3: When a circumstance constitutes a species that is related to a previously understood sin as a species to a subalternate genus,[4] it does not follow that the same thing is in different species, for to be under 'man' and under 'animal' is not to be under diverse species, for a man truly is in essence an animal; the same also holds for sacrilege and theft. But if a circumstance should constitute another disparate species of sin, it follows that the same act *is* in diverse species of sin. But neither is this a difficulty because, as stated above,[5] the species of a sin is not a species of act according to its nature but according to its moral being, which is related to the nature of an act as a quality to a substance—or rather as a deformity of a quality to a subject. Just as, therefore, it is not a difficulty that the same body might be white and sweet, which are diverse species of quality, and that the same man might be blind and deaf, which are specifically diverse defects, so also it is not a difficulty that one and the same act might be in diverse species of sin.

◆

Ad 4: And from this the response to the fourth objection is obvious.

◆

Ad 5: Not every difference among sins is according to excess and deficiency; it occurs rather according to diverse matter and according to deficiency or excess in diverse circumstances. Excess and deficiency have

4. The term can be traced back to Aristotle's *Categories* 1b20–24: "Of genera subordinate to one another nothing prevents them from having the same differentiae. For the higher genera are predicated of those below them, so that all differentiae of that which is predicated are differentiae also of the subject." But Thomas probably knows the term from Boethius: see the latter's first commentary on Porphyry's *Isagoge* [Boethius, *In Porphyrium Dialogi a Victorino Translati*, vol. 64, Patrologia Latina (Paris: J.-P. Migne, 1847), col. 40AB]. See also Porphyry's *Isagoge* §2 and Jonathan Barnes's commentary thereupon [Porphyry, *Introduction*, translated with a commentary by Jonathan Barnes, Clarendon Later Ancient Philosophers (Oxford; New York: Oxford University Press, 2003), 107–8].

5. That is, in *De malo* 2.5.

to do, however, not just with quantity but with any circumstances, for whether someone act where he ought not to or when he ought not to (and similarly in other regards), there will be excess; but there will be deficiency if he is deficient in any of the aforesaid.

◆

Ad 6: Although the will of the thief is directed, not toward the sacred thing principally, but rather toward the gold, it is directed upon the sacred thing by consequence: for he would rather take the sacred thing than be without the gold.

◆

Ad 7: When it is said that a circumstance changes the species of a sin or transfers it to another genus, the idea is not that an act existing previously in one species is resumed once again and becomes an act of another species; the idea is rather that an act, which considered without a circumstance would not be in a certain species, has that species of sin when the circumstance supervenes upon it.

◆

Ad 8: A defect of a circumstance in nature does not change the substantial species of nature but it changes the species of the deformity, for what is caused by narrowness of place and by abundance of matter is a different species of monstrosity. And the situation is similar in the present question, as has been stated.[6]

◆

Ad 9: A moral act does not have its species from the remote end but from the proximate end – which is its object. It has been stated,[7] however, that a circumstance gives species in so far as it is the object of an act *or* in so far as from a circumstance there results a certain condition of the object.

◆

Ad 10: Also with the virtues, a circumstance – although not every circumstance – transfers to another species. To make a great expenditure is an act of magnificence, but to make a great expenditure in constructing a place of worship is an act of religion.

6. In the body.

7. In the body.

◆

Ad 11: It is necessary that every circumstance that constitutes some species of sin makes it worse, since, if without this circumstance it would not be a sin, it makes what was not a sin to be a sin; but if it was a sin, it introduces additional deformities of sin. If, however, the circumstance is such that it is wholly unknown, the result of such ignorance as bears no guilt, it does not constitute a species of sin formally speaking but only materially. For instance, if a man has intercourse with a married woman whom he does not believe to be married, he does commit that which is an act of adultery but not as an adulterer, for the form of a moral act is from reason and the will. That of which one is ignorant is not voluntary. And so, if he should have intercourse with the wife of another whom he thinks is his own wife, he would be without sin, as in the case of Leah who was led in to Jacob instead of Rachel.

◆

Ad 12: If a circumstance constitutes a species that is related to a previously understood sin as a species of it, as adultery is related to fornication, there are not two sins but one, just as Socrates is not two substances because he is both man and animal. But if it constitutes a disparate species of sin, there will indeed be one sin because of the one substance of the act but it will be manifold because of the many diverse deformities of sin, just as an apple is one sort of thing because of the unity of the subject but multiple sorts of thing because of the diversity of color and flavor.

◆

Ad 13: The similarity between a conclusion and a moral action consists in the fact that just as one's syllogizing terminates in a conclusion so also the process of reasoning in moral matters terminates in an act. The similarity, however, does not hold in every respect, for moral activities are in singulars, in which the various circumstances are considered, but conclusions in speculative matters abstract from singulars. But it is also the case that conclusions do vary with respect to some circumstances having to do with the nature of the syllogism. Conclusions in necessary matter are different from conclusions in contingent matter, and in different sciences the manner of drawing conclusions varies.

◆

Ad 14: Also the actions of a craft vary according to diverse circumstances pertaining to the nature of the art. A craftsman goes about his work differently depending on whether he constructs a house from stones rather than from clay, in one region rather than another. But it is worthy of note also that some circumstances pertain to the nature of moral action that do not pertain to the nature of a craft, and vice versa.

Ad 15: When evil according to circumstance is distinguished from evil according to genus, at issue is the evil according to circumstance that makes a sin worse but does not transfer it into another genus.

Ad 16: More and less sometimes follow upon diverse forms, and in that case they diversify the species, as when, for instance, we say that something red is more colored than something pale. Sometimes, however, they follow[8] upon a diverse participation in one and the same form, and then they do not diversify the species, as when, for instance, something is said to be more white than another thing.

8. The Leonine edition has *consequitur* here; the Marietti edition has *consequuuntur*. The Leonine edition mentions no variants.

APPENDIX 5 THOMAS AQUINAS, *SUMMA THEOLOGIAE* 2-2.64.7

Whether it is licit for someone to kill someone in self-defense

Objection 1: *It appears that it is licit for no one to kill someone in self-defense*, for Augustine says to Publicola, "Regarding the killing of men lest someone be killed by them, the suggestion does not sit well with me, unless perhaps the person is a soldier or obliged by virtue of a public function, so that he would not do this on his own behalf but for others, having accepted the proper authority, if it accords with his person."[1] But he who kills someone in self-defense kills him lest he be killed. It appears, therefore, that this is illicit.

Objection 2: In *De libero arbitrio*, book 1, it is said: "How in view of divine providence are they free from sin who, for these things which one ought to despise, are defiled by human bloodshed?"[2] But he says that

1. Augustine, *Epistulae*, in *Corpus Scriptorum Ecclesiasticorum Latinorum*, Vol. 34, ed. Alois Goldbacher (Prague / Vienna / Leipzig: Tempsky / Tempsky / Freytag, 1895), 135 (epist. 47).

2. Augustine, *De libero arbitrio*, vol. 74 <6.3>, *Corpus Scriptorum Ecclesiasticorum Latinorum*, ed. William Green (Vienna: Hoelder-Pichler-Tempsky, 1956), 1.5.13.

those things ought to be despised which men "might lose unwillingly," as is clear from what precedes.[3] Among these is life in the body. Therefore, it is licit for no one to kill a man in order to conserve his own life in the body.

Objection 3: Pope Nicolaus says, and it stands written in the *Decretals*, distinction 50: "Regarding the clerics about whom you have asked advice, that is, who defending themselves kill a pagan, if, having done penance, afterwards they can return to their pristine state or rise to a higher one, be it known that We grant no such opportunity, nor do we concede to them any permission in any way whatsoever to kill any man."[4] But clerics and laypersons alike are bound by moral precepts. Therefore, it is not licit also for laypersons to kill someone in self-defense.

Objection 4: Murder is a more grievous sin than simple fornication or adultery. But it is licit for no one to commit simple fornication or adultery or whatever other mortal sin for the preservation of one's life, for the spiritual life is to be preferred to the life in the body. Therefore, it is licit for no man, defending himself, to kill another in order to conserve his own life.

Objection 5: If the tree is bad, so also is the fruit, as is said in Matthew 7.17. But defense of self itself appears to be illicit, according to what is said in Romans 12.19: "Not defending yourselves, beloved ones."[5] Therefore, the killing of a man which issues therefrom is illicit.

But to the contrary is what is said at Exodus 22.2: "If a thief be discovered breaking into or digging beneath a house and, having been wounded, dies, the one who struck him shall not be guilty of blood." But it is much more licit to defend one's own life than one's own house. There-

3. Augustine, *De libero arbitrio*, 1.5.11.

4. Aemilius Ludovicus Richter and Aemilius Friedberg, eds., *Decretum Magistri Gratiani*, vol. 1, *Corpus Iuris Canonici* (Leipzig: B. Tauchnitz, 1879), 1.50.6 (col. 179).

5. The Greek text actually speaks of not avenging oneself: μὴ ἑαυτοὺς ἐκδικοῦντες, ἀγαπητοί.

fore, even if someone kills someone in defense of his own life, he will not be guilty of homicide.

◆

Nothing prohibits there being two effects of a single act, only one of which is intended, the other being beside the intention. Moral acts, however, take their species with respect to what is intended, not from that which is beside the intention, since this is per accidens, as is made clear above.[6] So, from the act of someone who defends himself there can follow a double effect: one, the conservation of one's own life; the other, killing of the aggressor. Such an act, therefore, in so far as what is intended is the conservation of one's own life, does not have the character of the illicit, for it is natural to whatever thing to conserve itself in being as far as possible.

It is possible, however, for some act proceeding from a good intention to be rendered illicit, if it is not proportionate to the end. So, if someone in defending his own life uses more force than is called for, the act will be illicit. If, however, he should repel a force moderately, the defense will be lawful, for, according to law, it is licit "to repel force by force," provided it is "with the moderation of blameless self-protection."[7] Nor is it necessary for salvation that a man omit an act of moderate self-protection so as to avoid the killing of another, since one is obliged to take more care of one's own life than of the life of another.

But because it is illicit to kill a man, unless by public authority for the common good, as was made clear above,[8] it is illicit for a man to intend to kill a man in order to defend himself, except for one who has public authority, who, intending to kill a man in self-defense, refers this to the public good, as is apparent in the case of the soldier fighting against foes

6. Modern editions of the *Summa theologiae* direct readers to *ST* 1-2.72.1 and 2-2.43.3.

7. Richter and Friedberg, *Decretalium Collectiones*, Decretal. Gregor. 9.5.12.18 (coll. 800–801). On the more distant origins of these phrases, see Stephan Kuttner, *Kanonistische Schuldlehre von Gratian bis auf die Dekretalen Gregors IX: systematisch auf Grund der handschriftlichen Quellen dargestellt*, Studi e Testi (64) (Vatican City: Biblioteca Apostolica Vaticana, 1935), 336–43.

8. *ST* 2-2.64.2–3.

and of the minister of a judge fighting against a thief—although even these sin if they are moved by private passion.

Particular responses to the objections:

Ad 1 & 2 [as to objections 1 and 2]: The authority of Augustine is to be understood as applying to that case in which someone intends to kill a man in order to free himself from death. It is with respect to this case also that the authority, introduced from *De libero arbitrio*, is understood. And so significantly it is said, "for these things [pro his rebus]," by which is designated intention.

And, with this, the response to the second objection is obvious.

◆

Ad 3: Irregularity results from the act of killing, even if it involves no sin, as is apparent in the case of a judge who justly condemns someone to death. And for this reason a cleric, even if it is in defending himself that he should kill someone, is irregular—and even though he intends not to kill but to defend himself.

◆

Ad 4: An act of fornication or adultery is not ordered toward the conservation of one's own life from necessity, as is an act from which a killing sometimes follows.

◆

Ad 5: Prohibited there is defense accompanied by vindictiveness. And so the gloss says:

"'Not defending yourselves,' that is, you ought not to be striking adversaries back."[9]

9. Peter Lombard, "In Epistolam ad Romanos," in *Collectanea in omnes D. Pauli Apostoli epistolas*, vol. 191, Patrologia Latina (Paris: J.-P. Migne, 1854), col. 1502.

BIBLIOGRAPHY

Aertnys, Joseph. *Theologia moralis secundum doctrinam S. Alfonsi de Ligorio Doctoris Ecclesiae*. Tornaci [Tournai]: Casterman, 1890.

Aertnys, Joseph, and Cornelius Damen. *Theologia moralis secundum doctrinam S. Alfonsi de Ligorio Doctoris Ecclesiae*. 9th ed. Galopia [Gulpen]: Alberts Filii, 1918–19.

Aertnys, Joseph, Cornelius Damen, and Joannes Visser. *Theologia moralis secundum doctrinam S. Alfonsi de Ligorio Doctoris Ecclesiae*. 18th ed. Turin: Marietti, 1967.

Alphonsus Maria de Ligorio. *Homo Apostolicus instructus in sua vocatione ad audiendas confessiones, sive praxis et instructio confessariorum*. 3 vols. Mechelen: H. Dessain, 1867–68.

———. *Theologia moralis*. 4 vols. Edited by L. Gaudé. Rome: Typographia Vaticana, 1905–12.

Anscombe, G. E. M. "Action, Intention and 'Double Effect'." In *Human Life, Action and Ethics: Essays by G. E. M. Anscombe*, edited by Mary Geach and Luke Gormally, 207–26. St. Andrews Studies in Philosophy and Public Affairs. Exeter, U.K.: Imprint Academic, 2005.

———. *Faith in a Hard Ground: Essays on Religion, Philosophy, and Ethics by G. E. M. Anscombe*. Edited by Mary Geach and Luke Gormally. St. Andrews Studies in Philosophy and Public Affairs. Exeter, U.K.: Imprint Academic, 2008.

———. *Intention*. Cambridge, Mass.: Harvard University Press, 2000.

———. "Murder and the Morality of Euthanasia." In *Human Life, Action and Ethics: Essays by G. E. M. Anscombe*, edited by Mary Geach and Luke Gormally, 261–77. St. Andrews Studies in Philosophy and Public Affairs. Exeter, U.K.: Imprint Academic, 2005.

———. "Sins of Omission? The Non-Treatment of Controls in Clinical Trials." In *Human Life, Action and Ethics: Essays by G. E. M. Anscombe*, edited by Mary Geach and Luke Gormally, 285–91. St. Andrews Studies in Philosophy and Public Affairs. Exeter, U.K.: Imprint Academic, 2005.

———. "War and Murder." In *Ethics, Religion and Politics*, volume 3 of *Collected Philosophical Papers*, 51–61. Minneapolis: University of Minnesota Press, 1981.

Augustine. *The City of God against the Pagans*. Edited and translated by R. W. Dyson. Cambridge Texts in the History of Political Thought. Cambridge: Cambridge University Press, 1998.

———. *De libero arbitrio*. Edited by William Green. Corpus Scriptorum Ecclesiasticorum Latinorum 74. Vienna: Hoelder-Pichler-Tempsky, 1956.

———. *Enchiridion ad Laurentium de fide et spe et caritate*. Edited by E. Evans. Corpus Christianorum, Series Latina 46, 21–114. Turnhout (Belgium): Brepols, 1969.

———. *Epistulae*. Edited by Alois Goldbacher. Corpus Scriptorum Ecclesiasticorum Latinorum 34. Prague: Tempsky, 1895.

Barnes, Jonathan. "Logical Form and Logical Matter." In *Logica, Mente e Persona*, edited by A. Alberti, 7–119. Florence: Leo S. Olschki, 1990.

Berg, Thomas V., and Kevin L. Flannery. "*Amoris Laetitia*, Pastoral Discernment, and Thomas Aquinas." *Nova et Vetera (English)* 16, no. 1 (2018): 81–111.

Boethius. *De topicis differentiis*. Edited and translated by Eleonore Stump. Ithaca, New York: Cornell University Press, 1978.

———. *De topicis differentiis, libri quatuor*. Patrologia Latina 64, coll. 1173–1216. Paris: J.-P. Migne, 1847.

———. *In Porphyrium dialogi a Victorino translati*. Patrologia Latina 64, coll. 9–70. Paris: J.-P. Migne, 1847.

Bonaventure. *Opera omnia*. Quaracchi: Collegium S. Bonaventurae, 1882–1902.

Brock, Stephen L. *Action and Conduct: Thomas Aquinas and the Theory of Action*. Edinburgh: T & T Clark, 1998.

Busenbaum, Hermann [Hermannus Busembaum]. *Medulla theologiae moralis facili ac perspicua methodo resolvens causa conscientiae ex variis probatisque auctoribus concinnata*. Münster [Monasterium Westphaliae]: Bernhardus Raesfeldius, 1650.

Busenbaum, Hermann, and Alphonsus de Ligorio. *Medulla theologiae moralis R.P. Hermanni Busembaum Societatis Jesu theologi, cum adnotationibus per Reverendum Patrem D. Alphonsum de Ligorio*. Naples: Alexius Pellechius, 1748.

Cajetan (Thomas de Vio). "Tractatus 31: Responsiones." In *Opuscula omnia Thomae de Vio Caietani Cardinalis*, 126–37. Lyon: Haeredes Iacobi Iuntae, 1562.

Capps, Charles F. "Formal and Material Cooperation with Evil." *American Catholic Philosophical Quarterly* 89, no. 4 (2015): 681–98.

Cardenas, Juan de. *Crisis theologica, in qua plures selectæ difficultates ex morali theologia ad Lydium veritatis lapidem revocantur ex regula morum posita a SS.D.N. Innocentio XI. P.M. in diplomate damnante sexaginta quinque propositiones*. Seville: Typis Thomæ Lopez de Haro, 1687.

Charles, David. *Aristotle's Philosophy of Action*. London: Duckworth, 1984.

Cicero, Marcus Tullius. *Rhetorici libri duo qui vocantur De inventione*. Edited by Eduard Stroebel. Bibliotheca Scriptorum Graecorum et Romanorum Teubneriana. Leipzig: Teubner, 1915.

[Collet, Peter]. *Praelectionum theologicarum Honorati Tournely continuatio: sive Universae theologiae moralis tractatus: I. de actibus humanis, II. de justitia & jure, III. de contractibus, IV. de virtute religionis, V. de beneficiis & simonia, tomus primus*. Venice: N. Pezzana, 1746.

Congregation for the Doctrine of the Faith. "Some Principles for Collaboration with Non-Catholic Entities in the Provision of Health Care Services." *National Catholic Bioethics Quarterly* 14 (Summer 2014): 337–40.

Coughlin, John J. "Divorce and the Catholic Lawyer." *Jurist* 61, no. 1–2 (2001): 209–310.

Cretoni, Nicola. "Nota I (to v. 1 §249)," in *Compendium theologiae moralis, auctore P. Ioanne Petri Gury, S.I., editio secunda romana, novis adnotationibus et SS. Congregationum resolutionibus locupletata*, edited by Nicola Cretoni, vol. 1, 568-78. Rome: Typographia Polyglotta S. C. de Propaganda Fidei, 1875.

Cummings, Andrew McLean. *The Servant and the Ladder: Cooperation with Evil in the Twenty-First Century*. Leominster, Herefordshire (U.K.): Gracewing, 2014.

Denzinger, Heinrich, Peter Hünermann, Helmut Hoping, Robert Fastiggi, and Anne Englund Nash, eds. *Enchiridion symbolorum definitionum et declarationum de rebus fidei et morum / Compendium of Creeds, Definitions, and Declarations on Matters of Faith and Morals*. San Francisco: Ignatius Press, 2012.

Di Camillo, John A. "Organizational Cooperation with Evil: Conceptual Analysis and Renewed Understanding of the Principles Governing Cooperation with Implications for Catholic Health Care Collaborations in the United States." Rome: Athenaeum Pontificum Regina Apostolorum, 2016.

Donagan, Alan. "Thomas Aquinas on Human Action." In *The Cambridge History of Later Medieval Philosophy*, edited by Norman Kretzmann, Anthony Kenny, Jan Pinborg, and Eleonore Stump, 642–54. Cambridge: Cambridge University Press, 1982.

du Cange, Charles du Fresne. *Glossarium mediae et infimae Latinitatis*. Paris: Librairie des Sciences et des Arts, 1937–38.

Finnis, John. "Absolute Rights: Some Problems Illustrated." *American Journal of Jurisprudence* 61, no. 2 (2016): 195–215.

———. *Intention and Identity: Collected Essays, Volume II*. Oxford: Oxford University Press, 2011.

———. *Moral Absolutes: Tradition, Revision and Truth*. Washington, D.C.: The Catholic University of America Press, 1991.

———. *Natural Law and Natural Rights*. 2nd ed. Oxford: Oxford University Press, 2011.

———. "Object and Intention in Moral Judgments According to St. Thomas Aquinas." In *Finalité et Intentionnalité: Doctrine Thomiste et Perspectives Modernes*, edited by J. Follon and J. McEvoy, 127–48. Paris: Librairie Philosophique J. Vrin, 1992.

Flannery, Kevin L. *Action and Character According to Aristotle: The Logic of the Moral Life*. Washington, D.C.: The Catholic University of America Press, 2013.

———. "Aristotelian Resonances in Aquinas' Conception of Evil." In *Evil in Aristotle*, edited by Pavlos Kontos, 205–21. Cambridge: Cambridge University Press, 2017.

———. "Capital Punishment and the Law." *Ave Maria Law Review* 5, no. 2 (2008): 399–427.

———. *Christian and Moral Action*. Washingon, D.C.: IPS Press, 2012.

———. "The Common Good in Aristotle and Thomas Aquinas." In *Self-Transcendence and Virtue: Perspectives from Philosophy, Psychology, and Theology*, edited by Jennifer A. Frey and Candace Vogler, 154-72. London: Routledge, 2018.

———. "Determinacy in Natural Law." *Nova et Vetera (English)* 9, no. 3 (2011): 763–73.

———. "The Field of Moral Action According to Thomas Aquinas." *The Thomist* 69, no. 1 (2005): 1–30.

———. "The Moral Principles Governing the Immigration Policies of Polities." In *Catholic Social Teaching: A Volume of Scholarly Essays*, edited by Christian Brugger and Gerard V. Bradley. Cambridge: Cambridge University Press, forthcoming.

———. "Moral Taxonomy and Moral Absolutes." In *Wisdom's Apprentice: Thomistic Essays in Honor of Lawrence Dewan, O.P.*, edited by Peter A. Kwasniewski, 237–59. Washington, D.C.: Catholic University of America Press, 2007.

———. "On Counseling the Lesser Evil." *The Thomist* 75, no. 2 (2011): 245–89.

———. "Thomas Aquinas and the New Natural Law Theory on the Object of the Human Act." *National Catholic Bioethics Quarterly* 13, no. 1 (2013): 79–104.

———. "Two Factors in the Analysis of Cooperation in Evil." *National Catholic Bioethics Quarterly* 13, no. 4 (2013): 663–75.

———. "Voting, Intrinsic Evil, and Commensuration." *American Journal of Jurisprudence* 60, no. 2 (2015): 181–97.

———. *Ways into the Logic of Alexander of Aphrodisias*. Philosophia Antiqua, vol. 62. Leiden: Brill, 1995.

Garvey, John H., and Amy V. Coney. "Catholic Judges in Capital Cases." *Marquette Law Review* 81 (Winter 1998): 303–50.

Gauthier, René-Antoine. *La morale d'Aristote*. Paris: Presses universitaires de France, 1958.

Gauthier, René-Antoine, and Jean Yves Jolif. *L'Éthique a Nicomaque: Introduction, traduction et commentaire*. 2nd ed. Louvain-la-Neuve: Éditions Peeters, 2002.

Glendon, Mary Ann. *Rights Talk: The Impoverishment of Political Discourse*. New York: Free Press, 1991.

Grisez, Germain. *Christian Moral Principles*. Vol. 1, *The Way of the Lord Jesus*. Chicago: Franciscan Herald, 1983.

Heath, Thomas L. *Euclid, the Thirteen Books of the Elements: Translated with Introduction and Commentary*. New York: Dover, 1956.

Jensen, Steven J. "Do Circumstances Give Species?" *The Thomist* 70, no. 1 (2006): 1–26.

———. *Good and Evil Actions: A Journey Through Saint Thomas Aquinas*. Washington, D.C.: The Catholic University of America Press, 2010.

Jones, Frederick M. *Alphonsus de Liguori: The Saint of Bourbon Naples, 1696–1787*. Dublin: Gill and Macmillan, 1992.

Kaveny, Cathleen, and Kevin Flannery, S.J. "Response and Rejoinder: On Voting, Intrinsic Evil, and Ranking of Political Issues." *American Journal of Jurisprudence* 61, no. 2 (2016): 259–73.

Kuttner, Stephan. *Kanonistische Schuldlehre von Gratian bis auf die Dekretalen Gregors IX: systematisch auf Grund der handschriftlichen Quellen dargestellt*. Studi e Testi (64). Vatican City: Biblioteca Apostolica Vaticana, 1935.

Laymann, Paul. *Theologia moralis: In V libros distribuita, quibus materiae omnes practicae, cum ad externum ecclesiasticum, tum internum conscientiae forum spectantes, noua methodo explicantur.* Padua: J. Manfrè, 1733.

Lombard, Peter. "In Epistolam ad Romanos." In *Collectanea in omnes D. Pauli*

Apostoli epistolas. Patrologia Latina 191, coll. 1301–1534. Paris: J.-P. Migne, 1854.

MacIntyre, Alasdair. "Social Structures and Their Threats to Moral Agency." In *Ethics and Politics: Selected Essays, Volume* 2, 186–204. Cambridge: Cambridge University Press, 2006.

Milante, Pius-Thomas. *Exercitationes dogmatico-morales in propositiones proscriptas a SS. Innocentio XI*. Naples: Ex typographia Januarii, et Vincentii Mutio, 1739.

Noldin, Hieronymus. "Über die Mitwirkung zur Sünde des Nebenmenschen." *Zeitschrift Für Katholische Theologie* 3 (1879): 494–526.

Noldin, H., A. Schmitt, G. Heinzel, and A. Schönegger. *Summa theologiae moralis*. Innsbruck: Felizian Rauch, 1961–63.

Noldin, H., and A. Schmitt. *Summa theologiae moralis*. Innsbruck, Leipzig: F. Rauch, 1939–40.

"Petrocorensis." *Theologia moralis, ad usum seminarii Petrocorensis, tomus IV: De sacramentis poenitentiae, extremae unctionis, ordinis, & matrimonii, una cum tractatu de beneficiis, & sanctificatione festorum*. Padua: J. Manfrè, 1752.

Pilsner, Joseph. *The Specification of Human Actions in St. Thomas Aquinas*. Oxford University Press, 2006.

Porphyry. *Introduction*. Translated with a commentary by Jonathan Barnes. Clarendon Later Ancient Philosophers. Oxford; New York: Oxford University Press, 2003.

Prümmer, Dominicus M. *Manuale theologiae moralis secundum principia S. Thomae Aquinatis*. Freiburg im Breisgau: Herder, 1961.

Pseudo-Dionysius the Areopagite. *De divinis nominibus*. Edited by Beate Regina Suchla. Vol. 1 of *Corpus Dionysiacum*. Patristische Texte und Studien 33. Berlin: De Gruyter, 1990.

Richter, Aemilius Ludovicus, and Aemilius Friedberg, eds. *Decretalium Collectiones*. Vol. 2 of *Corpus Iuris Canonici*. Leipzig: B. Tauchnitz, 1881.

———. *Decretum Magistri Gratiani*. Vol. 1 of *Corpus Iuris Canonici*. Leipzig: B. Tauchnitz, 1879.

Robertson, D. W., Jr. "A Note on the Classical Origin of 'Circumstances' in the Medieval Confessional." *Studies in Philology* 43, no. 1 (1946): 6–14.

Roy, Roger. "La cooperation selon Saint Alphonse de Liguori." *Studia Moralia* 6 (1968): 377–435.

Salmanticenses (Collegium Salmanticense). *Collegii Salmanticensis cursus theologiae moralis*. Venice: Pezzana, 1715.

———. *Collegii Salmanticensis cursus theologiae moralis*. Venice: N. Pezzana, 1750.

Salmanticenses [Collegium Fratrum Discalceatorum Beatae Mariae de Monte Carmeli Primitivae Observantiae]. *Cursus theologiæ moralis: Tomus tertius, quatuor continens tractatus: I. de legibus; II. de justitia et jure; III. de restitutione; IV. de contractibus*. Venice: N. Pezzana, 1750.

———. *Cursus theologiæ moralis: Tomus quintus, quatuor continens tractatus: I. de principiis moralitatis; II. de primo praecepto decalogi, ubi de fide, spe, charitate et religione, necnon de vitiis his virtutibus oppositis; III. de secundo praecepto decalogi, ubi de adjuratione; IV. de tertio praecepto decalogi, ubi de Ecclesiae praeceptis*. Venice: N. Pezzana, 1750.

Sanchez, Thomas [Tomás Sánchez]. *Opus morale in praecepta decalogi*. Madrid: L. Sanchez & I. Hasreij, 1613.

———. *Tomus secundus disputationum de sancto matrimonii sacramento*. In *De sancto matrimonii sacramento*. Antwerp: M. Nutii [Nuyts], 1620.

Schenk, Richard. "*Perplexus supposito quodam*: Notizen zu einem vergessenen Schlüsselbegriff thomanischer Gewissenslehre." *Recherches de théologie ancienne et médiévale* 57 (1990): 62–95.

Schlitzer, Albert L. "Catholic Lawyer and Divorce Cases." *Notre Dame Law Review* 29, no. 1 (1953): 37–48.

Sommervogel, Carlos. *Bibliothèque de la Compagnie de Jésus*. Brussels/Paris: Schepens/Picard, 1890–1932.

Stephinsky, Eduard. "Über den Begriff der materiellen und formellen Mitwirkung zum Bösen." *Der Katholik* 56, no. 2 (1876 II): 337–51.

Thomas Aquinas. *Commentum in quatuor libros Sententiarum Magistri Petri Lombardi*. Parma: Petrus Fiaccadori, 1856–58.

———. *Expositio super Iob ad litteram*. Vol. 28 of *Opera omnia*. Rome: Commissio Leonina, 1965.

———. *In duodecim libros Metaphysicorum Aristotelis expositio*. Edited by A.M. Pirotta. Turin: Marietti, 1950.

———. "In librum primum Aristotelis De generatione et corruptione expositio." Edited by Raimondo M. Spiazzi. In *In Aristotelis libros De caelo et mundo, De generatione et corruptione, Meteorologicorum expositio*, 313–85. Turin: Marietti, 1952.

———. *In octo libros Physicorum Aristotelis expositio*. Edited by P. M. Maggiòlo. Turin: Marietti, 1965.

———. *Scriptum super libros Sententiarum Magistri Petri Lombardi Episcopi Parisiensis*. Edited by Pierre Mandonnet & Maria Fabianus Moos. Paris: Lethielleux, 1929–47.

———. *Sentencia libri De anima*. Vol. 45.1 of *Opera omnia*. Rome/Paris: Commissio Leonina/Librairie philosophique J Vrin, 1984.

———. *Sententia libri Ethicorum*. Vol. 47 of *Opera omnia*. Rome: Commissio Leonina, 1969.

———. "Super Epistolam ad Ephesios lectura." In *Super epistolas S. Pauli lectura, II*. 8th ed., edited by R. Cai, 1–87. Turin: Marietti, 1953.

Thomas Aquinas and Thomas de Vio (Cajetan). *Summa theologiae, cum commentariis Thomae de Vio Caietani Ordinis Praedicatorum*. Vols. 4–12 of *Opera omnia*. Commissio Leonina. Rome: Ex typographia polyglotta S. C. de Propaganda Fide, 1888–1906.

Tongiorgi, Salvator. *Institutiones philosophiæ moralis Salvatoris Tongiorgi e Societate Iesu ab eodem in compendium redactae*. Rome: B. Morini, 1863.

Torrell, Jean-Pierre, OP. *St. Thomas Aquinas: The Person and His Work*. Washington, D.C.: The Catholic University of America Press, 1996.

United States Conference of Catholic Bishops. *Ethical and Religious Directives for Catholic Health Care Services, Sixth Edition*, 2018. http://www.usccb.org/about/doctrine/ethical-and-religious-directives/.

Verbeke, G., and J. R. Moncho, eds. *Némésius d'Émesè: De natura hominis, traduction de Burgundio de Pise*. Corpus Latinum Commentariorum in Aristotelem Graecorum. Leiden: Brill, 1975.

Waffelaert, G. J. *Dissertations Morales. Première série comprenant une étude sur la cooperation au mal surtout en matière politique et religieuse et une dissertation sur l'espèce morale du scandale*. 2nd rev. ed. Bruges: C. Beyaert, 1892.

———. *Étude de théologie morale sur la coopération surtout en matière politique et religieuse, suivie d'une dissertation sur l'espèce morale du scandale*. Bruges: Vandenberghe-Denaux, 1883.

Weigel, George. Tranquillitas Ordinis: *The Present Failure and Future Promise of American Catholic Thought on War and Peace*. Oxford: Oxford University Press, 1987.

INDEX OF REFERENCES TO THOMAS AQUINAS AND ARISTOTLE

Thomas Aquinas

INDEX OF NAMES

INDEX OF SUBJECTS

Cooperation with Evil: Thomistic Tools of Analysis was designed in Agmena with Mr Eaves Sans display type and composed by Kachergis Book Design of Pittsboro, North Carolina. It was printed on 60-pound House Natural Smooth and bound by Sheridan Books of Chelsea, Michigan.